[英国]罗伯特·琼斯 著　史正永 丁景辉 译

牛津通识读本·

# 品牌学

Branding

A Very Short Introduction

译林出版社

图书在版编目（CIP）数据

品牌学 /（英）罗伯特·琼斯（Robert Jones）著；史正永，丁景辉译. —南京：译林出版社，2023.8
（牛津通识读本）
书名原文：Branding: A Very Short Introduction
ISBN 978-7-5447-9692-7

Ⅰ.①品… Ⅱ.①罗… ②史… ③丁… Ⅲ.①品牌-研究 Ⅳ.①F760.5

中国国家版本馆 CIP 数据核字（2023）第 098841 号

Branding: A Very Short Introduction by Robert Jones.
Copyright © Robert Jones 2017
Branding: A Very Short Introduction, First Edition was originally published in English in 2017. This licensed edition is published by arrangement with Oxford University Press.
Yilin Press, Ltd is solely responsible for this bilingual edition from the original work and Oxford University Press shall have no liability for any errors, omissions or inaccuracies or ambiguities in such bilingual edition or for any losses caused by reliance thereon.
Chinese and English edition copyright © 2023 by Yilin Press, Ltd
All rights reserved.

著作权合同登记号　图字：10-2019-588 号

品牌学　［英国］罗伯特·琼斯 ／ 著　史正永　丁景辉 ／ 译

| 责任编辑 | 陈　锐 |
| --- | --- |
| 特约编辑 | 茅心雨 |
| 装帧设计 | 景秋萍 |
| 校　　对 | 梅　娟 |
| 责任印制 | 董　虎 |

| 原文出版 | Oxford University Press, 2017 |
| --- | --- |
| 出版发行 | 译林出版社 |
| 地　　址 | 南京市湖南路 1 号 A 楼 |
| 邮　　箱 | yilin@yilin.com |
| 网　　址 | www.yilin.com |
| 市场热线 | 025-86633278 |
| 排　　版 | 南京展望文化发展有限公司 |
| 印　　刷 | 江苏凤凰通达印刷有限公司 |
| 开　　本 | 890 毫米 ×1260 毫米 1/32 |
| 印　　张 | 9.25 |
| 插　　页 | 4 |
| 版　　次 | 2023 年 8 月第 1 版 |
| 印　　次 | 2023 年 8 月第 1 次印刷 |
| 书　　号 | ISBN 978-7-5447-9692-7 |
| 定　　价 | 39.00 元 |

版权所有·侵权必究

译林版图书若有印装错误可向出版社调换。质量热线：025-83658316

# 序　言

陈素白

　　五月的一天，我受邀为译林出版社从牛津大学出版社引进的中英双语"牛津通识读本"书系中的《品牌学》一书作序。因为本人从1997年进入广告学专业求学到如今在中国高校从事相关教育工作，长期以来一直对品牌有着深厚的兴趣，所以我毫不犹豫欣然应允，事后想来甚至是有点不知天高地厚地接受了这项工作，因为要知道该书的作者可是赫赫有名的世界著名品牌咨询公司沃尔夫奥林斯（Wolff Olins）的策略师、《品牌管理杂志》编委会成员罗伯特·琼斯。

　　在当下注意力高度碎片化的时代，能在繁忙的工作之余，静下心来认真阅读一本纸质版的书籍，毫无疑问是一件非常奢侈而幸福的事情。在本书中，罗伯特·琼斯讨论了品牌日益普遍的存在，并分析了它们是如何发挥魔力的。他认为品牌的巨大潜力是商业、社会和文化的力量，并研究了许多不同类型的品牌——从产品、服务和艺术财产到公司、慈善机构、体育俱乐部和政党。在定义"品牌"一词的含义时，他深入探讨了品牌的积极性和消极性。他还考虑了品牌业务的发展，就品牌的概念是否开始衰落这一问题作出回应，并展望了它的未来。

　　放眼国内外，关于品牌的著作可谓汗牛充栋，要如何在媒介环境和消费市场飞速剧变的背景下，化繁就简，深入浅出地把品牌最核心的要义向读者们梳理透彻，长期在高校从事品牌教育和研究工作的我深知绝非易事。《品牌学》全书一共八章，逻辑清晰，章章相扣。从第一章"品牌创建的胜利"到第八章"品牌创建的未来"，作者紧紧围绕"品牌是什么？品牌有什么用？品牌将去向何处？"三大核心问题，犹如在回答"我是谁？我从哪里来？我要到哪里去？"这样一个亘古不变的哲学命题，将对品牌的拆解层层推进。在阅读全书的过程中，我更像是在作者的带领下经历了一趟品牌奇幻之旅，整个过程酣畅淋漓，意犹未尽。见字如面，从书中可见作者毫无保留倾囊相授的用心态度和循循善诱的长者风范，或许从第一章到第四章，有一定品牌知识积累的读者会觉得推进节奏略慢，但是从第五章"品牌创建业务"开始，大量丰富的前沿案例贯穿始终，马上会让你目不暇接。

　　全书也展现了一位资深从业者充满智慧和幽默的精彩论断，更多时候我感觉像是沉浸在和罗伯特·琼斯先生的对话中，如在第六章"品牌创建项目"里，作者抛出了诸多引人深思的问题——在全新客户关系管理中，新客与老客孰轻孰重？如何才可以恰到好处地对待产品定位？广告是否会面临消亡？……第七章"品牌创建伦理"是全书中我个人最喜欢的一章，大量的思辨让本书充满了哲学层面的思考。毋庸置疑，品牌是一个与时俱进的概念。品牌发展到今天，有许多的批评家不断在质疑品牌的作用，品牌究竟是减少了焦虑还是增加了不满足？对于个体和国家而言,品牌创建孰优孰劣?很多年前,我自己在论述品牌创建如何促进消费分层从而加速社会阶层裂变的时候,还鲜有学者提及品牌伦理的切入视角,如今该书向我做出了深切的回应,引起了我的共鸣,大有相见恨晚之感。

正如作者自己所言,这本书是根据其二十五年品牌顾问的经历写就,所以如果您和我一样有幸能够打开这本书,一定会产生和我在阅读时一样强烈的感受,那就是被作者信手拈来的精准案例所深深折服。品牌是一个看似简单,阐述起来却相当复杂的概念。如果不是作者有着丰富的一线实战经验和豁达通透的理论积淀,无论如何是无法在一本并不太厚的论著中解释清楚的。所有的案例都有一种点到为止的精辟之感,让你欲罢不能,从而对身边发生的品牌故事产生浓烈的继续探究之情。

译林出版社多年来一直致力于通过牛津通识读本系列为国内读者打开一扇扇通往各个学科领域的大门,截止目前已经出版超过一百三十个品类。牛津通识读本系列的宗旨是"大家小书",我相信罗伯特·琼斯先生的这本《品牌学》又一次做出了最好的回应,小书之"小"在其短小精悍,品牌之"美"在其"美美与共",这应该是品牌创建终将走向共创的终极使命吧。

献给良师益友布莱恩·博伊兰

# 目 录

致　谢　**1**

导　言　**1**

第一章　品牌创建的胜利　**3**

第二章　何谓"品牌创建"？　**17**

第三章　品牌创建的历史　**31**

第四章　品牌创建的作用方式　**51**

第五章　品牌创建业务　**71**

第六章　品牌创建计划　**89**

第七章　品牌创建伦理　**107**

第八章　品牌创建的未来？　**119**

索　引　**135**

英文原文　**147**

# 致　谢

我想感谢玛丽·乔·黑奇,她把我介绍给了本书的杰出编辑安德里亚·基冈,从而启动了这本书的出版。沃尔夫奥林斯品牌咨询公司的伊杰·诺克利和萨拉·阿什曼给了我创作本书的时间和空间。许多人在这一过程中帮助了我,包括瓦尔·阿兰姆、汉斯·阿诺德、黛博拉·卡德伯雷、霍普·库克、安东尼·加尔文、丹·加福肖恩-布拉迪、蒂尔德·赫丁、肯尼·雅各布斯、内森·贾维斯、彼德·麦肯纳、克里斯·米歇尔、克里斯·穆迪、珍妮·纽吉以及简·斯克鲁顿。克雷格·莫兹利给了我一些颇有思想创见的反馈。我的客户们拓宽了我的思想和视域:卢克曼·阿诺德、道恩·奥斯特维克、萨利·考德利、迈克尔·戴伊、史蒂芬·德夏尔、凯茜·费里尔、丹尼·霍曼、安东尼·詹金斯、斯图亚特·利普顿、米歇尔·麦克埃特里克、史蒂夫·莫里斯、西蒙·纳尔逊、史蒂芬·佩奇、法拉·拉姆赞、戈兰特·菲奥纳·雷诺兹、克里斯·索尔、马格纳斯·谢文、尼克·塞罗塔、戴维·苏登以及詹姆斯·提普勒。我在东英吉利大学的同事们让我对品牌创建有了许多新视角：我特别要感谢詹姆斯·康福特、保罗·道博森、尼古拉·约翰逊、罗斯·凯米、肯·勒·莫尼埃-菲茨休、彼得·施密特-汉森和尼克斯·卓卡斯。我的学生们促使我不断地思考。布莱恩·博伊兰，我二十年来的导师，跟往常一样给了我他那尖锐的评论反馈。和过去一样，我的伙伴尼尔·麦肯纳慷慨地给予我温暖的鼓励和明智的建议。

# 导　言

不管喜欢与否，我们每天都会暴露在数以千计的品牌广告词之中。各种品牌的兴起，已非常显著，且势不可挡。现如今，从平凡琐碎之事到深奥的道理，品牌创建在每一个层面都塑造且定义着我们的世界。

品牌创建已被称作一门科学、一门艺术，甚至是一种隐蔽的企业阴谋。经济学家、市场营销人员、设计师、组织机构的专家、心理学家、哲学家、社会理论家和文化评论家均已对其进行了研究。然而，这些专家中鲜有人能够达成一致：何谓品牌创建，以及它是如何起作用的。它很重要且令人兴奋不已，却毫无规则，让人难以捉摸且定义不清。

因此，本书旨在为您带来一次快速导览。它给以下几个重大问题提供了一些简单明了的答案。一个品牌的确切含义是什么？品牌创建如何发展和传播？品牌如何对我们产生作用？那些品牌背后的人是谁？他们做了什么？品牌创建是在引导我们还是在奴役我们？品牌创建的下一步将走向何方？

正如我希望表明的,品牌创建远不只是它可能显现的那样,也不仅仅是市场营销的某个方面:它是一种更加宽泛的活动,影响着某个公司机构所做的大部分事情。由此可推断,其不仅仅对消费者产生影响;它还是一种同样重要的力量,引导并激励着员工。而且,最后一点很重要,品牌创建所具有的不仅仅是商业影响;它同时还是一种强大的社会力、文化力,且在其最宽泛的意义上来看,还是一种政治力。

   本导言不是根据教科书撰写而成,而是根据我二十五年品牌顾问的经历写就。这不是对品牌的终极评价——永远不会有终极评价,不过我希望它让读者看到品牌创建的非凡突出之处,并略微揭示品牌背后的工作如何塑造了我们周围的各种品牌。

第一章

# 品牌创建的胜利

在肯尼亚的马林迪，你会在一面鲜红的围墙上发现一幅海报，其上由油漆喷绘了一个可口可乐的瓶子和一句标语——"相信非洲，十亿个理由"。

标语所说内容并非可口可乐能够给你止渴，而是可口可乐在某种程度上是乐观主义和非洲发展的一部分。它暗示存在"十亿个理由相信非洲"——那大概就是居住在非洲大陆上的十亿人。

这幅非洲海报（参见图1）对"品牌创建"这一奇特现象留下了一张极具吸引力的快照。当然，这也表明品牌创建广告无处不在，在每个大陆、城市和乡村、富人区和贫民窟都有。而且它还表明，在我们这个全球化的世界，品牌创建还常常试图使该品牌隶属于某个特定的地方：这幅海报旨在让人认为"可口可乐"是地道的非洲品牌。

这表明，品牌创建依赖符号——表达意义的图像。品牌就是意义（所指），通过诸如标识语符号（能指）加以辨识。而且，

图1 品牌创建的作用：肯尼亚马林迪的一幅海报，暗示可口可乐不仅仅是一种饮料，还是非洲未来的一部分

尽管这是2012年发起的一项广告运动的一部分，但它却永久性地漆在一面波纹金属围墙上。品牌创建广告并非总是转瞬即逝的。

尽管品牌创建一开始的目的是向消费者售卖产品，但它常常不局限于此。它把产品与更大的思想创意联系在一起：在此情况下，含糖饮料与人类进步有关。当你停下来想一想，会发现这是一个奇特的、近乎神奇的思维过程。可口可乐公司全球品牌总监洛娜·索姆维尔解释道："当一个思想创意触及人类一项根本真理时，它的传播便可以没有边界限制。"有时，品牌触及"许多真理"：更多的时候它也许触及了人们普遍的希望与渴望。

因此，一个品牌不仅仅是一个产品的名称。在世界各地，许多普通商业产品正注入更大的思想创意，让人们对该商品感觉良好，因此多加购买。每一个品牌都希望让你相信某种东西。品牌创建旨在给我们各种"亿万个相信的理由"。

品牌存在已有几个世纪了，不过在20世纪80年代之后这一观点才变成我们生活中重要之事。在过去三十年左右的时间里，品牌广告变得普及，甚至触及地球上最贫穷的地方。实际上，品牌广告已成为现代世界一个主要特征。这是如何形成的？为何会这样？

## 更为宏大的理念

品牌广告把普通事物与一种更为宏大的理念联系起来。这种宏大的理念具有改变人们所作所为的力量：尤其是会多购买，而且愿意多花钱。可口可乐只不过是有滋味的糖水而已。正是这个品牌使得它的售价不菲,并因此给可口可乐公司带来利润。迪士尼更宏大的理念是"家庭娱乐";沃尔沃的理念是"安全"。这就是品牌创建的本质。

这就是品牌拥有者——比如可口可乐公司——所使用的一种手法,创造各种意义,让我们对该产品感觉良好,于是我们就会购买这种产品。可口可乐公司对把产品与进步、乐观与幸福等理念联系起来的传播交流进行投资。一旦这种传播交流起作用了,这些意义就形成了可口可乐的品牌。于是在最后,人们就会更多地购买可口可乐。品牌创建改变人们的思考、感觉和行为方式。

不过,这也是消费者用来理解全世界过量商品的一种方法。面对成千上万种选择,人们赋予它们各种意义,这样便可在头脑里对其进行归档,并巩固其自我身份的意义。比如,我们可能会把可口可乐与能量联系起来,或与儿童时期的各种记忆联系起来,因而我们中的许多人把自己定义为"可口可乐人",与之相对的(比如说)是"百事可乐人"。品牌创建是由大公司启动的一项游戏——不过这是一项几乎每个人都参与的游戏。对公司而言,理想状态就是我们头脑中的思想与他们试图投射的理念相匹配。

可口可乐海报只是过去几十年已变得非常普遍的一种现象个案而已。品牌创建是由像可口可乐这样的产品开始实施的。接着,进入了服务业——比如,像美国富国银行这样的银行,或者像家乐福这样的零售商,以及像阿联酋航空这样的航空公司。随后,它延伸进入思科(Cisco)、联合利华和LG集团这样的公司。最近,品牌创建已把自己的影响力扩大到书籍、电影和电视剧等方面。《哈利·波特》、歌手碧昂斯、《星球大战》以及《权力的游戏》都不仅仅是书籍、歌手、电影或者电视剧了：它们是全球品牌。整个类型流派也能变成一个品牌，比如"宝莱坞"。而且在过去二十年，大量的线上品牌逐渐主导世界，从"阿里巴巴"和"亚马逊"到"照片墙"（Instagram）和"优步"（Uebr）。

尽管品牌创建始于西方，但已传遍全球。如前所述，全球品牌试图在某一地域引起局部反响。本土成长的品牌则模仿全球大品牌的特征，采用闪亮的标识、容易记住的标语以及光泽富丽的包装。

品牌创建还推广到了各种小公司之中。在英格兰北部有一个名叫"贝蒂斯"（Bettys）的连锁茶室，堪称品牌创建的典型：它采用了瑞士/约克郡传统，给日常餐饮生意添加了精确、雅致和温暖的创意。随着城市区域被改造得越来越高档，甚至小店面也要进行复杂的设计并渴望成为品牌。每一家线上企业的开张，其背后都有一种品牌创建因素。而且我们无论走到哪里，我们都会看到品牌创建活动。我在大英图书馆撰写本书时所处的空间不叫"报纸档案馆"，而是有着更为让人兴奋的名字，叫"新闻编辑室"。这也是一种品牌创建。

## 最伟大的商业发明？

当然，品牌创建的好处是让人购买东西。品牌在我们日常的购买决策中扮演了重要的角色——比如购买苹果平板电脑这样的大决策；又或认为我的猫更喜欢一种叫作"托马斯"的猫砂这样的小决策。品牌增加了购物时的兴奋度，降低了焦虑感。

不过，品牌的力量也有限制。实际上，许多产品极少有什么额外意义。当我们买一支铅笔、给车加油或申购某项保险时，我们选择的牌子可能在我们头脑里没有多深的关联。一项研究表明，尽管80%的市场营销总监认为他们的产品是"有差异的"，或者在消费者的头脑里有某种显著意义；但只有10%的消费者认同这一点。就大多数产品而言，大多时候，大多数人都没时间去加以关注。我们每个人的头脑里只有少数几个品牌。对我来说，这些品牌可能是苹果公司、英国广播公司（BBC）以及零售商维特罗斯超市（Waitrose），除此之外几乎没有别的。汉威士传媒的一项研究也强调了这一点，该研究表明，如果74%的品牌消失了，大多数人根本都不会在意。人们买各种品牌，因而买进了品牌创建，不过他们也是满腹狐疑。我们认为异想天开的电视广告很荒谬：实际上，我们可能会快进跳过。我们以看透公司的各种品牌创建活动为豪。

7　　而且品牌还是许多公司价值的主要来源。你若仔细看一个典型公司的价值，便会发现其中一些价值来自公司的楼房建筑、设备和库存——看得见摸得着的有形资产；但许多价值来自无形资产，比如消费者的良好意愿、各种专利或者其品牌。实际上，全球市场研究顾问米尔沃德·布朗估测美国最大公司的股市价值中，品牌价值占比超过30%，我们会在第四章中分析其中的原因。对某一类公司来说，品牌就没有那么重要：比如，对一家办公室清洁公司来说，品牌的意义相对来说就没有那么重要。但是，对其他公司来说，比如奢侈品公司，品牌价值在公司价值的占比可达到90%。总体来说，全球所有公司价值的三分之一来自品牌。不管根据什么标准，这都表明品牌创建始终是最有效的商业发明之一。

## 最有效的文化形式？

就像我们所看到的那样，大多数人都意识到了品牌创建现象。他们讨论、解读、评论品牌创建。作为一种有效的商业技艺，品牌创建也是我们共享文化的一部分。

品牌是一种社交参考点，即我们都拥有的共同点。每年九月份我的学生们第一次相见时，他们在几小时内就结成了纽带，部分原因是他们都拥有共同的品牌——不管是"依云"还是"节拍"（Beats）又或"路易威登"，这些品牌是得到公认的，因此在任何地方都意味着大体相同的事物，人们也根据其所喜欢的品牌来界定自己（和他人）。甚至有一种棋盘游戏，即商标游戏，选手就其所知的品牌知识进行竞赛。

品牌同时也是我们用来记住过去的一种方法。这一点在伦敦的品牌博物馆体现得尤为明显，游客们会在那里穿过一条由1890年以来的包装与广告组成的时光隧道。随着他们走近当代，怀旧之感便会席卷而来：游客中最普遍的反应就是"啊，我记得那个（牌子）"。品牌提供了一种时空捷径。就我而言，"雷鸟"（Thunderbirds）这个牌子让我回想到20世纪60年代；"马汀博士"（Doc Martens）把我带回到70年代；"奥迪"把我带回到80年代，诸如此类。

品牌思维渗透了我们生活的方方面面。品牌有助于我们敏锐认识能指与所指之间的相互影响。能指——事物的称谓，以及它们的外观——确实很重要。政治正确是品牌创建的一个例子：仔细地把事物重新打上标签，为的是改变人们对这些事物的看法与感觉。一方面，自由派的共识是标签不重要；但在另一方面,它们必然很重要。

品牌常常被艺术家和作家使用或利用。实际上,在品牌创建和艺术之间有一种密切关系,就像两种并行不悖的意义创造方法。法国画家艾德华·马奈的最后一幅重要作品是《女神游乐厅的吧台》,这幅创作于1882年的画作描绘了忧郁不满的酒吧女招待,这是一位被盖伊·德·莫泊桑描写为"饮料与爱的兜售者"的人物。在这幅画的右下角是一瓶"巴斯"啤酒,该标识是最早合法注册的商标,注册于创作这幅画五年前的1877年。马奈塑造了一个由观众解读而产生意义的形象——而且他把"巴斯"标识涵盖其中,同样也会产生意义。

许多人把品牌看作文化中的一种负面力量。有一个名为"广告破坏者"的加拿大反消费主义团体,他们自我描述为"艺术家、行动主义者、作家、恶作剧者、学生、教育家和企业家"。"广告破坏者"对品牌广告进行强有力的嘲讽和模仿,他们称之为"广告颠覆"。他们采用广告手法来攻击广告,因此"广告破坏者"凭自身的头衔而成为一种品牌。

或许最有力的批评家一直都是艺术家自己。品牌是表明人们身份或志向抱负的一种快捷方式,因此也是一种讽刺物质社会的简单方式——这是由电影编剧希拉·麦克法登1977年在《穿行》中首创的一种方法,八年后布莱特·伊斯顿·艾利斯在《零下的激情》中也采用了这种方法。最近,诸如查普曼兄弟这样的艺术家利用品牌形象,以一种更为无礼粗鲁的方式批判消费文化;一个中国艺术家将可口可乐商标画到古代花瓶之上:这是一种姿态,既破坏了这个古代花瓶,又美化了这个商标。

不过,与此同时,其他艺术家参与品牌创建,而且并不认为商业广告和更高级的文化之间存在冲突。电影钟情于利用各种品牌作为传达人物和情境信息的快捷方式，自詹姆斯·邦德采用"阿斯顿·马丁"（汽车）以来都是如此。2014年的科幻电影《星际穿越》中女主角的姓氏就是布兰登（Brand），而电影结尾暗示她就是未来，这是否是一种巧合？最有名的或许是安迪·沃霍尔，他在1972年的作品《金宝汤罐头》中采用了品牌形象。沃霍尔被批判为向消费主义屈服，不过他写道，"挣钱是艺术，工作是艺术，而好的生意则是最佳艺术"。

## 最近三十年

因此，品牌创建是一种与产品、服务、组织机构、文化产品、地点、人甚至是概念有关的渗透性符号系统。这些符号有助于赋予上述事物额外的意义——非其固有之意。就像我们在第三章要讨论的那样，品牌创建虽已存在几个世纪，但只是到最近才成为文化的主要部分。

谷歌的"ngram浏览器"是一款智能软件，可计算某个单词在经谷歌数字化的所有书籍中的出现频率。"品牌"这个词的曲线图在1900年之前是水平状，在1940年之前呈缓慢上升趋势，然后是稳定期，之后在1980年之后又呈上升趋势，在千年之末加速上升。聚焦于"品牌资产"概念的品牌创建的学术研究也始于20世纪80年代。为何品牌创建在尤其是最近三十年的时间里变成了一个如此普遍的概念？

市场经济学的胜利创造了一个全球竞争的世界，各公司机构必须采用创建品牌的方式胜过对手一筹。如今市场随处皆是——在过去的三十年里也包括中国。而且这些本地市场都合并到一个全球市场之中。股东们要求公开上市的公司要不断地发展壮大，这意味着要增加市场份额或者开辟新市场。政府需要国有公司占据自己的市场，有时要与外国竞争对手在国内或者出口市场上进行竞争——因此，他们也必然进行品牌竞赛。即使是垄断寡头也在为某些事物竞争——以适当的价格吸引资金，或者吸引最优秀的潜在员工。

而且，开展竞争的不仅仅是公司。国家和城市间开展竞争，以吸引游客、雇主、学生和居民。非营利机构、运动俱乐部、政党甚至宗教都竞相吸引支持者。品牌创建现在是世界上最大的两个行业卫生和教育领域的一个热门话题：医院、大学和学校现在都非常重视他们的牌子。过去大约十年里，在所有这些领域采用品牌创建的语言和方法已成为可接受甚至是时髦的做法。比如，十年前，博物馆工作人员将品牌创建看作迎合大众、降低艺术水准的概念而予以拒绝。但是现今，几乎所有博物馆都乐意谈论其品牌的重要性。由于互联网是一种全球媒介，所有事物都在跨越国界线开展竞争，这就意味着同类的概念和方法很快就会扩展到任何地方。

市场力量的崛起和物质主义的兴起，使得人们无论作为消费者还是员工都越来越需要生活中的意义。人类总是需要意义，这是超越功利主义、超越我们日常必须要做的世俗之事的一个因素。人们需要一种身份感（我是谁？）和归属感（我会安身何处？）。在过去，这些意义来自家庭、村镇、宗教、民族——但所有这些都受到都市化、世俗化和全球化的破坏。物质主义造成了意义的真空，于是品牌创建试图填补这一真空。消费者需要的不仅仅是"物有所值"，而且是"物超所值"。

作为回应，一种特殊类型的品牌创建已成为主流——把品牌不再看作一种产品，而是一种概念。肯尼亚那幅可口可乐的海报（图1）就是一个绝好的例子。许多公司都对以下观点兴奋不已：他们不仅仅是物质产品的制造商，还可以成为思想观念的提供者，甚至是丰富文化、给予人们新的身份感的理想典范。"苹果"、"维珍"和"宜家"都是非常典型的例子——这些品牌都是过去三十年才诞生的或者才腾飞起来的。

## 身份与归属

而且，就在同一时期，消费者也加入这个游戏之中。品牌创建已由公司为我们做事转变成一种我们大多数人都参与的一种游戏。在同一时间段内，学术界人士对品牌创建的态度已由实证主义者向建构主义者转变——换言之，他们把品牌看作我们都在帮助建构的事物。

随着人们变得更加富有，能够获得更多的商品，他们开始部分地通过看似世俗的选择来界定他们自己：所穿的鞋子、购买家具的商店、观看的连续剧套装、所崇拜的公司，甚至最喜欢的含糖饮料。他们采用品牌来帮助构建他们的身份，即他们是谁这一认知。不管好坏，几百万甚或几十亿的人——从一个非洲村庄到上海的一套顶层豪华公寓，再到中西部的一间购物商场——利用品牌来帮助构建他们的自我形象，或者帮助界定他们想属于的"部落"。

当然，品牌并非唯一选择。很显然，许多人用他们所支持的慈善团体、所追随的运动俱乐部、所投票的政党、所参观过的地方或者所崇拜的名人来识别自己的身份。许多人抵制品牌创建,而且少数人对品牌具有免疫力。品牌对他们来说,一点也没有这种充满魅力的力量。在经历了十年的公司丑闻和金融崩溃之后,世界上的反企业精神日益高涨。

不过,对许多人,尤其是年轻人来说,品牌创建已变得如此普遍、如此常规,以至于它已失去了刺激性。他们发现进行品牌创建游戏是很正常的,不再把品牌创建只看作一种商业现象。他们从一系列品牌中进行选择——不仅仅有"阿迪达斯"和"苹果",还有视频网站"维密欧"(Vimeo)和"薇思"(Vice),并将各种品牌思想混合在一起,把它们用作身份感创建的组成要素。他们通过社交媒体来做到这一点,因此这是一项共享活动,在此过程中流行时尚不断变化演进,因此他们的身份也在调整变化。

通过参与这种神奇的品牌创建活动,人们赋予身边的事物以价值,它们已不再是它们自己,而是获得了意义——特别是在周围每个人都这么做的情况下。这种意义常常存在于你我之间。我是英国"第一直销银行"(First Direct)的一名客户,因此,如果我看到在我前面排队结账的人拿着一张"第一直销银行"的银行卡,我就会感到一种莫名的亲近感。我有这种感觉是因为我们都选择了同一家银行,他或者她一定有一些与我相似之处。

在社交媒体时代,于分秒之间分享事物已成本能行为,因此毫不奇怪:品牌——一种易于分享意义的标志,已成为我们生活和想象力中非常重要的事物。分享"内容"已几乎成为普遍的习惯。现在,把刚发生的甚或正在发生的事情发布到"脸书"上,是很正常的事。在这种新的分享文化中,很容易使品牌繁荣发展。这种现象还在进一步发展:每当有人在"脸书"、"推特"或

"照片墙"上发布内容时，他们都在培育自己是何许人的身份思想。不管是否故意而为，他们都在构建他们自己的个人品牌。从这个意义上讲，这个世界现在几乎包含了二十亿个品牌营销商。

## 商业与文化

现代世界是由一系列的现象整体界定的，从社交媒体到气候变化，从都市化到肥胖症，从群体迁移到对名流的崇拜。但其中的一种现象如此普遍，以至于我们视为当然之物——这就是品牌创建。

由于市场逻辑现在是非常普遍的存在，对共享身份感的需求是如此迫切，所以品牌创建已成为现代世界的一个规定性特征。

通过品牌创建，就像清洁剂这种令人厌烦的事物，像软饮料这种日常用品，以及像网址这样无形的事物已获得了个性和意义，于是人们推荐它们，感受不同派别之争，原谅它们的缺点过失——全是因为公司需要竞争，而人则需要感知和分享意义。

品牌创建现在已是世界上最有效的一种商业和文化力量。但是，它的确切之义又是什么？（参见方框1）

> **方框1 安卓：无属的与大家的**
>
> "安卓"可能是世界上最大的品牌，有十亿用户以及90%的市场份额。但它并非一家公司：它是一个由四百家公司共享的品牌。而且这也是它成功的秘诀。谷歌公司在2008年发布了安卓，作为移动设备上一种可定制、易理解，

以及最重要的是开放的操作系统,它现在已用在手机、平板电脑、手表、汽车等装置上。从法律上讲,该品牌属于谷歌公司,而制造商则购买了一种生产许可。但从情感上讲,这个品牌属于所有人,但又不属于任何一个人。而且,它并不强迫所有使用它的制造商必须保持一致,而是鼓励变化、变异。它的标语"群而不同"抓住了当前品牌创建潮流的主旨。

第二章

# 何谓"品牌创建"?

为了给"品牌创建"定义,我们首先需要给"品牌"定义。当我们谈论"网飞"流媒体品牌、时尚快销品牌"H&M"或者"阿里巴巴"品牌时,我们真正要表达的是什么意思?

或许一个品牌仅仅是一个名字:"网飞"或"H&M",或者"阿里巴巴"。但并非每一个商标名都是一个品牌。比如,想一想你们当地偏僻街巷的汽车修理公司。它有一个名字——"韦伯斯特汽车(修理厂)"或者类似的名字,而且可能在当地很受尊敬。就像人们讲的那样,它可能"有一个好名字",但我们不会自然地称之为一个品牌。我们倾向于认为,一个品牌是以一种比采用当地广告牌画家作品更复杂的方式精心设计出的。

那么,是设计造成了差异吗?品牌是否就是一个商标、一种特别的颜色或一句标语,比如耐克公司的飞驰状商标、曼联足球俱乐部的红色、本田公司的标语"梦想的力量"?以下是维基百科对"品牌"的定义:"一个能够区分某个销售者的产品不同于其他销售者产品的名字、词语、设计、符号或其他特征。"不过这个定义并未解释品牌的力量——如果它们仅仅是我们身边所看到的装饰物,那么它们就不再那么有趣了。

因此,或许一个品牌更多的是关于产品本身?实际上,我们常常很难在脑海里区分"品牌"和"产品"。人们所喜爱的是什么,苹果公司的产品还是"苹果"这个牌子?——或者它们是否是相同事物?半岛电视台新闻服务与半岛电视台这个品牌联系甚密。但它们并不完全相同。人们很有可能喜欢一个牌子,但不喜欢某个产品,反之亦然。我最喜爱的汽车品牌是"奥迪",但我实际上决定购买一辆"宝马"。

## 比产品更重要

实际上,一个品牌在某种程度上比一个产品更加重要。我们有时把它看作某个产品之上的光环,或者某种产品之外的精神气质,抑或产品背后的原产地。人们有时使用"牌子"(make)来指代"品牌"(brand)——如"'将军'(Aga)是一个很好的灶具牌子",这不仅意味着它是一种好的灶具,而且生产它的公司也是广受赞誉的。"苹果"的粉丝们会告诉你,他们敬佩其产品,不过同时也赞颂其产品背后的观点——而且有些人担心,在史蒂夫·乔布斯死后,这种观点就会慢慢地消失。一位参加英国版电视真人秀节目《学徒》的竞赛者自称是"斯图尔特·巴格斯品牌",意思是指他不仅仅是一个人,在某种程度上还是一组更大的创意。很显然,这就是"可口可乐"在肯尼亚的海报中所要表达的意思(参见图1)。

所以对产品来说品牌是某种额外的东西。品牌创建专家马丁·科恩伯格说过,一个品牌就是"功能性+意义":也就是说,产品加一种思想。在他看来,品牌是完整的体系——"三角巧克力"(Toblerone)这个牌子是指巧克力块,再加上与瑞士、阿尔卑斯山等事物有关的意义。

相反地,市场营销师菲尔·巴登则认为,"品牌是框架体系:它们通过架构设计暗中影响着人们对产品以及产品体验的价值期望"。根据该观点,产品就像一幅图画,而品牌就是画作之外的画框,让它有了背景和力量。巧克力块就是这幅画,而瑞士特色就是让巧克力块更有趣、让人更加难忘、更有价值的一个画框。16

这种额外的意义对品牌的力量至关重要。品牌让我们做事情,它们改变了行为,创造了价值,这是因为它们不是纸上静态的图像,而是我们头脑中动态的思想。可以这样简单地描述:一个产品的品牌就是它所代表的东西。"韦伯斯特汽车(修理厂)",除了表达一个汽车修理场所之外,并不代表任何意义,因此,它不是一个品牌。耐克公司的飞驰状商标并非"耐克"所代表的意义,因此它也不是一个品牌,它只不过是表示更大的意义——挑战和成就——的标识语符号(能指)而已。"科罗娜"是一个很好的产品,但它的品牌代表的不仅仅是啤酒,还与墨西哥、夏天和沙滩有关。这个产品本身并非是一个品牌。

## 代表某种东西

重要的是,"代表某种东西"可能根据你的视角不同而有两种不同的含义。

从组织机构内部来看,它可能意味着你们内部的精神气质,你们的身份:你们想代表的思想观点。"宜家"想代表"为多数人创造更加美好的日常生活"这一理念。这是其官方用任性奇特的英语所做的观点声明（参见图2）。我们会在第五章看到，大多数公司机构都会精心界定他们的品牌，并积极加以管理。

可是，从外部来看，这可能表示你的各种联想、意义和形象：你在人们心中实际上所代表的理念。如果你问人们在想到宜家时头脑中会出现什么，他们会说出诸如"家具""厨具""扁平包装""商店"等显而易见的东西；但他们也会说出购物体验，诸如"肉丸"、"当日往返的短途旅行"或"排队"；以及更重要的思想，比如"设计"、"生活"甚或是"爱"。这是一个品牌令人兴奋的真实情况：人们头脑中一系列强有力的想法会影响他们去哪儿，以及买什么。

有两个截然不同的"品牌"视角。

从业者——即那些管理品牌的人以及那些提供建议的人，

图2　在宜家购物：顾客形成他们对宜家品牌印象的一种体验，不仅包括质量和价格，而且还包括设计和生活方式

自然会有一种内部观点。一些经营者对待他们的品牌非常认真。通用电气公司想代表"梦想启动未来"这个理念，而且它的首席行政官杰夫·伊梅尔特曾说过，"对通用电气来说，'梦想启动未来'不仅仅是一句标语或一个时髦口头禅。它是一种存在的理由"。广告机构常常把品牌看作大创意，这是他们所有信息交流工作的源泉。广告大师大卫·奥格威说过，"除非你的广告包含了一个大创意，否则它就像夜晚漂流而过的一艘船一样悄无声息"。品牌创建专业顾问们把一个品牌看作一组思想，不仅会影响沟通交流，而且会影响一个公司机构所做的每一件事。品牌专家丽塔·克利夫顿支持品牌是"成功公司重要的组织原则"。根据这个观点，一个品牌就是公司机构内的一组思想。

不过，学术界在将品牌作为一种现象进行分析时，往往采取一种局外人的视角。商业学校的学者常常把一个品牌看作消费者头脑中影响其购买行为的一些联想。当然，在这方面存在不同的版本：实际上，存在多少学者就可能有多少种理论。在校园里，另一类专注文化研究的学者往往强调把品牌看作是符号标记，在消费者文化中起着一种重要的作用——不过，他们还是采取一种局外人的视角，而且常常充满批判。

马丁·科恩伯格的书《品牌社会》清晰地将以下两种观点联系了起来：把品牌看作改造管理（内部观点）和生活方式（外部观点）的某种东西——以及把品牌看作将生产（局内人）与消费（局外人）联系起来的某种东西。

## 界定"品牌"

因此，一个品牌就是内部所代表的意义及外部所代表的意义。品牌创建学者大卫·艾克把这种内部视角观点看作"身份",将外部视角观点看作"形象"。"品牌"既表示身份,又表示形象。但是,我们应把哪一种观点看作基本定义呢?哪一种观点能最佳地反映品牌的力量呢?哪一个是"真正的"品牌——公司所要获得的身份,还是我们其他人所看到的形象?谁的观点更加清晰明了——从业者的观点,还是学者的观点?

尽管我的工作背景是一名从业者,但品牌创建学者凯文·莱恩·凯勒的话却深深打动了我:"一个品牌的力量存在于顾客头脑中。"因此,我们在本书中采用了这种外部视角观点:一个品牌主要指"一个商业的、有组织的或文化性的实体在人们头脑中所代表的思想和情感"。

"全食超市"(Whole Foods Market)这个有机食品品牌就是人们头脑中的一组联想:质量、健康、有机以及质优价高。"瑞安航空"(Ryanair)这个品牌给人们带来的印象就是低价、简单直接的态度以及基本的航空服务。"三星"这个品牌的概念就是更加智能的新科技、闪亮的设计以及中等价位。诸如此类。

亚马逊公司的杰夫·贝索斯似乎强化了这一观点,他把一种品牌描述为"你不在房间的时候人们对你的评价"。这是一个简洁的定义——但对从业者来说,这也是一个让人感到恐怖的定义。不过,这也许是因为他的表述与其说是"品牌"的定义,不如说是"声誉"的定义。这两个概念彼此意义非常相近,但声誉往往是一种理性的、口语性的东西,是对你所做之事的描述,而品牌往往更感性、更直观,而且是一种信念:我将来要从你那儿获得什么。实际上,一家公司很有可能在名声不好的同时拥有一个好品牌。消费者对其评价不好,却不断地从它那儿买东西。具有讽刺意味的是，亚马逊公司自身就是这种现象的一个典型。

品牌专家马蒂·纽梅尔站队支持更加情绪化的观点。他把品牌定义为"一个人内心对某种产品、服务或公司机构产生的直觉"。这就引发了一个问题：他头脑中想的是哪一个人？因此，最好把品牌想象成每个人直觉感受的综合体。或者，更完整地说，因为品牌不只是情感上的，更是每个人思维和感受的组合：简言之，是他们所有想法的总和。

## 不只是思想

不过，一个品牌不仅仅是想法。各种品牌都建立在具体事物之上。"全食超市"、"瑞安航空"和"三星"这些品牌并非没有出处：它们都是由这些公司机构的所言所行塑造出来的。我们关于雀巢咖啡的印象部分程度上是由几十年来的广告塑造形成的——由雀巢咖啡的广告宣传塑造而成。我们关于"声田"（Spotify）的想法依赖于用户日复一日所体验到的质量——由"声田"所提供的服务质量决定。可口可乐不仅仅是一种关于非洲进步的抽象概念——它还是一种甜美的、泡沫腾涌的饮料。在这些想法背后，都存在物质。

品牌的迷人之处在于，它们似乎都有一种符号、标记或标签即一种有特色的方式。再回到维基百科的定义，品牌的确有非常有趣的名字、词语、设计、符号以及其他特征。每个品牌都有一个品牌名称，而且几乎每个品牌都有一个标识语。"英国石油"（BP）有其绿色和黄色的标识；"博柏利"的格子图案标识；"米其林"的轮胎人图案；"伦敦地铁"的打字机字体。"耐克"的标语"想做就做",以及《经济学人》独特的书写风格。新加坡航空公司甚至有其特殊的味道。让人迷惑的是,这常常被称作"品牌身份":在品牌创建方面,"身份"既可指"我们想代表的东西",又可指"我们所使用的符号"。这些符号常常吸引我们头脑中更为直观或者更为感情化的区域——吸引着纽梅尔所说的"直觉感受"。

因此,为了本书的写作目的,(我们认为)一个品牌是指:

- 有关某个产品或其他存在物的一组想法和感受
- 由该产品所言所为塑造
- 并通过一种独特的风格得到认可

比如,"麦当劳"这个品牌就是有关汉堡、儿童、方便快捷食物、"开心乐园餐"以及其他许多东西的一组想法。这是由我们多年来对其餐厅和广告的体验而塑造出来的。金色拱门以及麦当劳叔叔的形象都是它的象征。

再举一个例子,宝马公司的"迷你"(MINI)这个品牌是一组关于个性、灵巧的设计、城市驾驶以及冒险体验的想法。这个品牌是由多年的广告以及非常有特色的车身四角各一个车轮的设计——以及许多电影(比如《偷天换日》)中对该汽车的特写塑造而成。而且它的符号表征就是"MINI"这个标识以及"MINI"散热器格栅的特殊形状。

因此,这就是我们的工作定义——用来解释我们头脑中品牌的力量以及这些思想如何留在我们的头脑之中。但是,不管我们决定如何定义"品牌",人们在使用这个词时实际上是很随意的。

它常常用于表示"一个创立品牌的产品或公司",比如,

"'英国航空'这个品牌正努力与成本更低的竞争对手进行斗争"。有时，它用于表示标识本身：市场营销总监常常要求他们的广告机构"在这个广告上把我们的品牌凸显得更加重要"。而且，有时"品牌"用于表示品牌创建活动。从事市场营销的人会说这样的话，"'现代'（Hyundai）品牌的目标是增加市场份额"。

事实是，这个词很复杂，又因为它的意义非常模糊而十分实用。实际上，这个概念弥合了各种差距。一个品牌就是处在具体与抽象的结合部：位于一个产品与一种思想之间。它连接着内部与外部：一个公司想要代表的"身份"和它实际代表的"形象"。它联结了员工的生产世界和顾客的消费世界。它将形式和功能——标识与产品——结合在一起。而且，它既包含了商业又涵盖了文化。

## 品牌与品牌创建

"品牌"与"品牌创建"之间的差异是什么？简单地说，品牌创建就是一个品牌拥有者所做的一系列事情，以确立一个品牌。如果一个品牌就是"你所代表的东西"，那么品牌创建就是一种方法技巧，公司借此让数百万人头脑里都认为其产品代表着某种东西。"品牌创建"是活动，"品牌"是结果："品牌创建"是因，"品牌"是果。

当人们谈论品牌创建或"重新创建"某个品牌时，他们通常表示要把一组有关该事物的新思想植入人们的头脑之中。或许他们还表示，作为加快这种思想变化的一种方法，赋予该事物一种新的风格（名称、标识、颜色或其他任何东西）。当英国零售商"合作社"重塑品牌时，它是想改变人们对其业务的看法——

于是它就采用了一个新标识来表明这种改变。

在做这类事情的过程中，品牌经理们试图缩小"形象"和"身份"之间的差距：让他们的产品实际上所代表的意义尽可能地接近他们希望它所代表的意义。对于那些像"苹果"这样的大品牌来说，这种差距很小；对于小品牌来说，这种差距要大得多。有时，这意味着又回到过去："合作社"选择不去设计新的标识，而是回到之前用过的标识，旨在重燃顾客心中的旧思想：本土便利性、道德交易以及物有所值。

当然，所做的这些都是为了提高公司的商业成绩。品牌创建的目的不仅是让人们改变他们的思想，还要改变他们的行为——最明显的就是多购买——我们会在第四章详细讨论。亿贝网的品牌营销旨在让越来越多的人去亿贝网购买新产品——把它看作一个零售商，而不仅仅是拍卖网站。对于非营利机构来说，品牌创建更多是瞄准社会目标，而不是商业目标。比如，改革网（change.org）就采用品牌创建来鼓励人们加入改变政府政策的运动中去。而且，越来越多的商业机构也瞄准了社会目标——联合利华公司就是一个非常好的例子。事实上，他们把社会影响和商业影响看作一种良性循环——你若是更好的市民，消费者在你那儿购买东西就会更开心。

因此，我们可以这样界定品牌创建：塑造产品或公司机构的所言所为，目的是以一种创造商业价值（有时也有社会价值）的方式改变人们的思考、感觉和行为方法。

## 相同与差异

因此，品牌创建始于改变人们的思考与感觉方式：这关乎意义的创造或者改变，而这是一项精细的任务。

为了创造意义，你得在一开始遵守习俗惯例——要与其他人行为类似——否则人们根本无法理解你。

语言和符号通过约定俗成的意义发挥作用。一家航空公司需要看起来有点像其他航空公司。像英国时尚零售巨头"新面貌"（New Look）、爱尔兰服装零售商"普利马克"（PRIMARK）以及英国快时尚店铺"顶尚店"（Top Shop）这些时尚零售商都有着极其相似的标识。在开始创建品牌时——无论对象是果汁饮料还是一所大学，你的所为、所言以及外观都需要在某种程度上遵照果汁饮料或大学的常规表达。否则，人们不会理解你是什么样的人，也不会信任你。

但是你也得显现出不同之处，甚至要打破常规，否则你无法表达任何新东西，人们也不会注意到你。因此，品牌创建往往追求差异性，力求突显于人群，偏离一致性。就像凯文·莱恩·凯勒说的那样，"品牌创建就是创造不同"。越是不同，风险就越大，但同时潜在的回报也越高。1999年，泰特美术馆的新品牌广告设计在呈交给托管人时受到了抵制，"那不是一个传统艺术展览馆的样子"。但是这个设计确实被采用了，引起众人关注，帮助泰特美术馆实现游客数量翻倍，而且现在看来显得很正常，成为一种新传统。一些品牌创建专家追求他们所称的"MAYA"，即"最先进超前但仍可接受的（most advanced yet acceptable）"。

因此，品牌在某些方面与其竞争对手相同，而在其他方面则不同。即使在不同的国家，情况也基本是这样。一致性很重要：否则，我们每次旅行时的预期都会被打乱，信任也会被打破。但是，即使像星巴克和麦当劳这样的连锁店，似乎到处看起来都是一个样，实际上为了迎合当地口味也有所不同。连锁酒店追求全球一致性，但大多数酒店连锁公司鼓励地方性差异。一个优质的全球品牌，部分意义上是与熟悉程度、可预测性以及让人放心有关，部分意义在于它的变化差别、惊喜之处和地方色彩。

就像品牌从一地到另一地都相同类似，大多数品牌也会年复一年保持不变。我们依赖连续性：大多数品牌从熟悉感中获得力量，追忆童年时代，比如"迪士尼"、"亨氏"、"玛氏"或者"强生"这些品牌。不过同等重要的是，没有什么品牌可以一成不变。消费者在变，态度在变，技术在变，因此品牌创建也必须进行细微的调整变化。变化的速度不一：一个时尚品牌可能变化迅速，而一个基础设施品牌的变化则会慢得多。但是所有的品牌创建都在创造意义，部分程度上与持久性、传承性和成熟感有关，部分程度上与活力、未来感和年轻态有关。

因此，品牌创建任务与下列决定有很大关联：与你的竞争者保持多大程度的相同之处，在不同国家之间保持多少相同之处，与去年的状态保持多少相同之处——以及要保持多大的差异。

## 创造意义，创造价值

因此，品牌创建有助于一个产品或公司机构去代表某种东西，因而突显出来，引人注目。比如，宜家精心设计的广告表明一种特殊的生活方式。其设计的产品和门店都让每个人都买得起设计方案。它细心地管理它的象征符号，比如蓝与黄的颜色、它的标识语以及它离奇古怪的产品名称。而所有这些都帮助它代表"为多数人创造更加美好的日常生活"这一理念。这是当代全球品牌创建的顶点。

品牌创建所做的这一切都出于一个原因：以创造价值的方式改变我们的行为方式。品牌创建创造了各种品牌——我们头脑中的意义、思想，为的是影响我们的所作所为。它让消费者去购买，让员工努力工作，从而实现盈利和发展的商业目标——有时也会实现诸如社会福祉和可持续性这样的社会目标。宜家的品牌创建吸引着顾客，鼓励他们常来光顾并购买更多的商品，因而支持宜家发展壮大，到世界上越来越多的国家开店。不过，它也缓步推动消费者采取更绿色的生活方式，途径是把低能耗灯泡变成标准，推动它所谓的"循环经济"，即顾客不仅可以购买新家具，同时也可把旧家具卖给其他人再次使用。

因此，品牌创建改变人们的观念，是为了创造不同类型的价值（参见方框2）。不过，就像宜家案例分析所表明的那样，品牌创建获得当前这样的范围和力量乃近期之事。几个世纪以来，品牌创建在变化、发展并急剧拓展。

方框2 "易集"（Etsy）：一个生产商的平台

"易集"是一个帮助手工艺者在世界范围内售卖其产品的平台，他们因此建立了自己的品牌。它由罗伯特·卡林于2005年在纽约的布鲁克林建立，作为"一个在线社区，手工艺者、艺术家和生产商能够售卖他们手工制作的、有特色的商品，以及手工艺品储备"。更为重要的是，"易集"认为其任务是"以建立一个更有成就、更持久的世界的方式重新设想商业贸易"。"易集"现在将一百六十万名交易频繁的卖家与两千六百万名买家联系了起来，每年售卖二十四亿美元的东西。就像亿贝网一样,这是一个非常好的平台品牌案例,让卖家有了一个从未可能有过的市场规模。但与亿贝网不同的是,它向着我们时代的另一个方向发展:不仅有消费东西的欲望,而且还有制作东西的欲望。

第三章

# 品牌创建的历史

1865年,乔治·吉百利正在荷兰考察一个生产可可饮料的新机器。他的家族自1824年就在伯明翰售卖茶、咖啡和巧克力饮料。依照宗教派别划分,他是贵格会教徒,一个想给人们提供健康、无酒精饮料的理想主义者。他同时也是一个需要挣钱的商人,因为破产的贵格会教徒需要离开这一教派。后来,在这个世纪之末,他还为他的工人带来了各种进步的创新——通风的工厂、各种假日、学校,甚至一个被称作伯恩维尔的市镇。

不过,再回到1865年,他被这个荷兰新机器吸引住了,因为它解决了可可饮料的一大问题。可可饮料中满是油脂,使得它饮用起来口感不佳。传统上,这些脂肪采用添加剂去除,包括使用有害的锯末。但是这个机器利用液压压榨可可豆,将大部分油脂挤压去除。吉百利第一次能够给英国人提供一种真正的纯巧克力饮料(参见图3)。

而且在随后的许多年里,吉百利不仅生产了一种产品,还创建了一个品牌。早在1867年,他就开始打广告(生活朴素的贵

图3 品牌先驱：一幅1888年的吉百利海报，通过纯真意象售卖可可饮料

格会教徒不会自然而然地想到这一点)。他使用了一个大胆的口号:"绝对纯正,因此最好。"他把这个口号投放到伦敦的马拉公共汽车上,这是一种不容忽视的宣传活动。

吉百利不仅促销了可可饮料,而且提倡了"纯真"这一概念。他委托以儿童为形象做广告——儿童正是纯真的象征。他甚至发起了一个追求纯真食物产品的商业活动。吉百利是天生的品牌创建者,领先了所处的时代几十年。很快,他的公司在1905年推出了"牛奶巧克力",它的第一个大型产品品牌——而且这是有创造力、富有品牌创建特征的另一次飞跃,它把巧克力与乳制品的意象联系了起来。在整个20世纪,"吉百利"成为糖果大品牌之一,不过在21世纪,它被一个名为"亿滋国际"的企业集团收购。

乔治·吉百利帮助品牌创建成为现今的模样。通过巨大的商业想象力,他发现了一个新方法来做品牌创建所做的非凡之事——把一个普通的产品与一个更大的概念联系起来,部分通过产品的表现,部分通过产品广告中的话语,部分则通过它的包装和海报这样显著的视觉方式。

不过,尽管他是现代品牌创建的奠基人,但品牌创建的历史可追溯到他之前许多年,实际上是好几个世纪之前。吉百利辉煌的策略只是一系列非凡的、富有创造力的各种飞跃中的一个,因为人们已发现了新的、更大规模且更大胆的方式来运用品牌创建。实际上,多年来,存在五种不同版本的品牌创建方法。第一种可追溯到文明之初。

## 标记所有权

在大英博物馆的展厅中,有一件非常精巧的青铜制品,发现于埃及,或许来自底比斯附近。它不比一支钢笔大多少,但它没有笔尖,取而代之的是一个扁平的圆盘,上有复杂的抽象图案。它已有三千五百年的历史。

古代埃及人把这样的物体在火中加热,直到它们变得通红,然后用它们在他们的牲畜身上烙上一个标记。每头牲畜都有其自己的标记,于是烙印符号就表明了所有权。这个特殊的铁块有一个母狮子符号,表明这些奶牛属于赛赫美特女神庙。

品牌创建始于火——而且英语中"brand"这个词来自维京语"brandr",意思是"烙印"。"品牌"与"火"之间的联系很有趣。就像火一样,品牌创建总是包含着一种兴奋感,甚至一种危险感,同时又有一种温暖和舒适感。你可以把现代品牌创建之力想象成把思想烙印到我们头脑之中的方式。而且我们依然谈论着"崭新"(brand new),意为直接从火上拿下来,这个短语我们非常熟悉,故而我们对"品牌"的认知与新颖和新奇密切相关。因此,各种品牌,尤其是最新的品牌,被描述成"热门的"(hot)——不过与此同时,说来也奇怪,它们也被描述成"酷炫的"(cool)。

再回到古埃及,在牲畜身上打烙印正是我们现在所看到的品牌创建的典型案例:使用符号赋予一个物体(一头奶牛)更深层的意义(它的拥有关系),为的是改变人们的行为(不要偷它),从而创造价值。这一做法的出现伴随了一个非常了不起的发明——以一个小小的标记,传递一个重大的意义——尽管这种做法现在感觉再自然不过了。这是品牌创建最早期的形式,也是第一个版本。

几千年来,人们烧制烙印、蚀刻、印刻和雕刻各种标记,把意义附加到无生命的物体之上——这是现代品牌创建的先驱。建筑工总是把他们的标记蚀刻到石头之上,制陶工人把标记刻在陶器之上,画家则把标记雕刻在岩洞的洞壁上。这些标记表明"这是我的"或者"这是我制作的"。罗马帝国曾有一个标语——"SPQR",意为元老院与罗马人民——你会在硬币上看到它,而且在整个帝国范围内的罗马遗迹的石头上都有这种印刻。在此情况下,标记就更具有一种社会意义:"这是我们的。"

在中世纪,纹章术的复杂技巧传遍欧洲——包含一个标识(盾形纹章)和一个标语(常常是座右铭)。每个贵族都有其标记:一种血统家系的标记,一种家族成员的标记,以及一种与该家族有着密切经济关系的标记。而且在中世纪,现代公司开始出现,使用一种商标名称,同时还常使用某种意象。不少品牌名称可追溯到这个时期——比如,时代啤酒(Stella Artois)可追溯到1366年。黑狮牌啤酒的狮子符号可追溯到1383年。

打烙印的实践也曾有过黑暗的一面:在奴隶的身上烙上标记,也是表明所有权;或者在罪犯身上打上烙印,表明他们犯了罪。尽管我们不再把标记烙在彼此身上,但这种"打烙印"的负面感觉依然非常普遍,尤其是报纸的标题中。政府的政策被"打上一种失败的标签";政客的诺言被"打上各种欺诈伎俩的标签";医院被"打上数量不够的标签"。

当然,如果一位农民给其动物打上烙印,那么很快所有农民都必须这样做:于是打烙印很快传播开来,因而成了规范。不过,得克萨斯州一位农场主在19世纪50年代因为拒绝在其牲畜上打烙印而出了名。他的名字叫塞缪尔·马弗里克,而英语单词"maverick"就来自他的名字,表示某人特立独行。马弗里克解释说，他不想让他的牲畜受到痛苦折磨；其他人指出他可以宣称任何没有烙印标记的动物都是他的。因此，就像现在一样，试图逃避标记体系是没有用的。不打烙印标记只不过是另外一种标记形式。

在动物身上做烙印标记当今依然存在，不过常常采用冷冻法而不是烙印法。我最近在罗马尼亚特兰西瓦尼亚的一个利皮扎纳马场看到了打了烙印的马，但这种复杂的标记系统不再表示所有权，而是血统遗传。

让人感到欣慰的是，极少有人被打上烙印，但纹身的做法正在兴起：这是一种给自己打上标记、表明自己的热爱的方式，奇怪的是，有时人们会纹上一些商业标识，比如哈雷·戴维森摩托的标识。

而且公司机构依然在其财产上打上标记：罗斯柴尔德家族就在其不动产上打上了家族标识；而每个公司都在其办公室、工厂和仓库展示其标识。

## 保证质量

再回到18世纪，给财产打上烙印标记的做法已得到确立。而且对于手工艺者来说，把制作者的标记贴到作品之上已有悠久的传统。手工艺者行会采用标记，就是想消灭赝品伪造；而且法律要求金匠和银匠的作品要由一个独立的"检验办公室"打上标记。但是随着工业革命和大规模生产的到来，出现了新的观点：如果你是一家工厂的拥有者，你可能不会把标记贴在你的财产上，而是贴在你的产品上。你可以把一个产地标识变成一个明确的质量标识。你可以把标识的意义由"这是我的"以及

"我生产了这个产品"调整为"这是一个你可以信赖的产品"。在一个可以大规模生产假冒产品以及常常生产掺假食品的时代,这些标记能够赢得消费者的信任——并获得更高的价格。这是品牌创建的第二个版本。

做标识的方法开始发生变化。烙印标记演变为在产品上印上标识,比如在陶器上印标识;接着又变为在包装上印标识。伟大的陶器生产商乔西亚·韦奇伍德就是这一思想的先锋,自1759年起就在其产品上印制"韦奇伍德"。十年之后,他开始加上"伊特鲁里亚"(Etruria)这个词(这是他给他的工厂起的富有灵感的经典名称)。他知道这类品牌创建可以向迅速扩大的中产阶级说明,他们正把辛苦挣来的钱明智地花在耐用的产品上,让他们放心。

到了19世纪20年代,"品牌"这个词就明确地采用了这个新义。品牌的名称以及品牌的声誉成为重点,于是出现了一种新的专业知识:设计商标和包装。这种工作大部分都是由商业艺术家完成,现在早已被人遗忘了;不过,公司偶尔也会采用著名画家的作品。梨牌香皂多年使用一幅名为《肥皂泡》的油画,其原名为《一个孩子的世界》,由约翰·艾弗里特·米莱斯所画。

品牌创建在19世纪70年代获得了巨大的新力量,因为你能够以"注册商标"的方式来保护这些新资产。设计与法律进行了有效的结合,因而许多早期注册的商标现在依然是有效的价值创造者,比如"巴斯"、"金宝"和"家乐氏"。(当然,"巴斯"商标正是马奈在1882年的画作《女神游乐厅的吧台》中所描绘的。)

"可口可乐"于1886年开始注册商标(在早期,每一份配方中含9毫克可卡因),"金宝"是在1898年注册商标的,而"家乐氏"注册于1906年。当然,上述品牌现在依然都是大品牌:品牌创建可以拥有非凡的寿命。这些品牌都使用了红色——一种能够突出的颜色,一种能够表达温暖和能量的颜色,同时也是火的颜色。并且,所有这些商标都用了一种看起来像手写的印刷体。它们看起来就像签名,就像对质量的个人保证。

到如今,制造商通常使用广告来促销其产品,通常提供简单、实用的好处,比如可口可乐公司的广告强调"美味"和"提神"。这类品牌创建的设计是为了在人们头脑中培养出相当简单的概念,主要是关于质量和实用性。而且这种方法现在依然盛行:一个非常有名的例子就是木材着色料品牌"朗秀",它的广告标语自1994年以来一直都是"桶上所见,正如所得"。

实际上,大多数品牌创建依然按照这种方式进行:把一个名称印刻到我们的头脑中,让我们记住那个名字,并把名字与有限的几个主要功能联系在一起。比如,大多数家用产品的品牌创建都是这个套路。一个零售商品牌,比如说"约翰-路易斯"(参见方框3)或"目标",其表达的主要意义就是它所生产或售卖产品的质量。

---

**方框3 "约翰-路易斯":快乐的员工**

"约翰-路易斯"不仅仅是一家几乎人人羡慕的零售商,而且还是英国一项几乎人人羡慕的制度。它打破了所有市场营销的规则,其首要目标不是为了顾客的幸福,而是为了员工的幸福。但是它一直被投票选为英国最受喜爱的零售商。它是由约翰·斯皮丹·路易斯在1920年按照现在的公司形式建立的，公司采取一种合作形式，由代表公司工人的托拉斯所拥有。89 000名"合伙人"共同经营着40个百货商店和350多个"韦特罗斯超市"，提供非常好的顾客服务。这些合伙人所获得的年度奖金，几年后可达到工资薪水的五分之一。"约翰-路易斯"品牌的主题是由其奠基者于1925年所写："从不刻意抛售"——这句出人意料的英语表达意在安抚中产阶级购物主体：他们在其他任何地方都不会找到比这更有价值的产品。公司的秘诀很简单：快乐的员工产生快乐的顾客。或者，换一种略微不同的表述：品牌创建始于内部。

## 充满希望的快乐

不过，故事并未到此为止。大约在20世纪初，大规模生产伴随着大众媒体的到来得到了加强。工厂所有者意识到，他们必须联合媒体拥有者，以赋予他们的商标更大的力量。他们发现，通过报纸以及后来的电影院和电台来做广告，能够做的远远不只是保证质量。他们能够把他们的产品与某种有影响力的概念联系起来——就像吉百利公司所提出的"纯真"概念。

这类品牌创建正如我们在本书一开始看到的可口可乐公司在肯尼亚的海报广告（参见图1），尽管现在看起来是普通之举，但它在当时是又一次的大胆飞跃。品牌创建能够做的不止是保证质量。它可以带来更大的理念、更大胆的隐喻和诗意的联想：不仅仅是功能质量，还有更深层次的快乐愉悦。以此方式，你可以激起人们的欲望，去购买他们本来不想要的东西，这会促进销售额；而且会让人们感觉与你的品牌有一种情感联系，并且在理想情况下，忠于你的品牌。这是品牌创建的第三个版本。

比如，可口可乐公司在1932年把广告标语由平实的表述"美味提神"改为让人惊讶不已的诗意表述"冰爽阳光"。威蒂斯麦片（Wheaties）的广告语在1934年变成了"冠军的早餐"。戴比尔斯公司在1947年提出"钻石恒久远，一颗永流传"。

品牌创建方法再一次转变成广告和公共关系的新艺术。像心理分析这样的文化力量在这方面发挥了作用。西格蒙德·弗洛伊德的外甥爱德华·伯奈斯是公共关系的奠基者，而且他发现了利用潜意识来操控人们行为的方法。（他认为操控是一件好事。）

像伯奈斯这样的人认为，可以把产品与抽象概念联系起来，抽象概念要胜过产品的实用性好处。他说服妇女抽烟的方式是拍摄女影星独自在纽约大街上抽烟，把香烟与某种私下娱乐，甚至更重要的是与独立性的思想联系了起来。此刻，一根香烟可能就会让你独立不受约束。一个普通的产品可能也会让你在别人面前显得更好，而且自我感觉也更好。

## 品牌创建大师

广告商开始展现这种诀窍，利用一种主张和一种个性来界定品牌，以产生非常有说服力的交流沟通。这种主张清楚表明该产品给消费者提供的各种好处。其巅峰就是"独特的销售主张"理念（缩写为USP），由泰德·贝茨在20世纪40年代创造：你的广告应向顾客传递一种你的产品（尽可能）独有的优点。

接着,《哈佛商业评论》1955年的一篇文章介绍了"品牌个性"这一概念,使其更具情感或潜意识上的吸引力。现在的品牌创建可能对情感和理智都有吸引力,刻意去改变人们的思考与感觉方式。

大型消费品生产商——如可口可乐公司、宝洁公司、福特公司以及许多其他大生产商,变成了品牌创建大师,并把这种实践看作一项长期的战略投资。广告大师大卫·奥格威的信条是"每个广告都是对品牌个性长期投资的一部分"。广告不仅仅是关于短期销售的,更是长期的品牌建设,广告机构成了他们客户品牌的拥护者、守护者,甚至是牧师。

20世纪60年代,伴随着电视机进入家家户户以及广告业的"创意革命",品牌创建的版本改变了方向并逐渐壮大,产生了更加复杂的品牌信息,通常使用电视机为媒介。可口可乐公司不再宣传它解渴的功能如何强大,而是通过像"好品位的标识"这样的标语使得你在朋友面前看起来很优秀。后来,它通过著名的"我想给世界买瓶可乐"宣传运动,让你觉得自己是一位乐观的世界公民。

比尔·伯恩巴克在其广告机构恒美广告公司中逐步提出精致微妙的反转讽刺性广告,以迎合受众对自身判断力的感知。一个著名的案例就是1959年大众汽车公司"甲壳虫"汽车所做的广告,纯黑白的图像配有一行大字标题,将美国汽车业中普遍认可的智慧逆转成这样的表述"想想还是小的好"。广告牌几乎都是空白。大字标题后面用了句号,显得像一句断言陈述,而非销售标语。文本诙谐新颖、机敏而有智慧,清楚地说明了小即好的方方面面(油耗、停车空间、价格),并暗示你若想显得与众不同,更时髦雅致,那么当然要选择一台大众汽车。

除了产品品牌,还开始出现各种服务业品牌,如"美国运通""希尔顿""泛美航空"等品牌。自然,广告常常要展示那些提供这类服务的人。为某种服务创建品牌本身就成了一门艺术,要比产品品牌创建更为复杂。"泛美航空"聚焦其服务的有形部分:服务卡本身。其他的广告将乘客(理想的)体验编写成剧本展现出来。一份泛美航空公司的广告这样说道:"飞往欧洲途中,鸡尾酒与咖啡相伴。"

因此,一家航空公司、一家酒店或一家银行的品牌创建要依赖公司员工去做正确的事情,以兑现广告中所做的诺言。品牌创建首次不再是市场营销部门一个部门的工作:品牌创建现在涉及整个公司。按照这种方式,品牌创建开始涉及的不仅仅是产品,还有产品背后的人:公司企业。

## 带来归属感

在20世纪中期,社会上出现了一种新生力量:后工业时代的股份有限公司。公司成为巨大的、超国家的力量中心。大型股份有限公司以及他们的机构投资者认为,他们能够将品牌的影响力从个人产品扩大到公司本身。这又是一次大胆的飞跃,因此品牌创建超越消费者,开始对新的受众——员工、投资人和舆论创造者,产生作用。公司现在可以是"股份有限品牌",而这种品牌创建能够做到的不仅仅是许诺快乐。它能够给各种股份持有者带来一种归属感。有了归属感,员工就会更加勤奋地工作,而消费者就会更持久地忠于(这个品牌)。这就是品牌创建的第四版。

品牌创建实践发生了变化，变成对一个公司机构的目标（或者说是"愿景"又或者说是"中心思想"）进行界定，通过视觉设计予以表达——即标语以及辅助设备，并且通过股份有限公司用于建设内部工作文化的各种机制进行分享。于是一种新的专家登上了舞台中央：以设计为基础的品牌顾问。

这个概念最初被称作"企业认同感"，早期的先锋包括第一次世界大战前德国家电公司AEG的品牌顾问彼得·贝伦斯，接着是20世纪20年代的伦敦公交公司，20世纪50年代的美国国际商用机器公司（IBM）。不过，这在20世纪80年代才开始受到普遍欢迎。里根主义和撒切尔主义又进一步美化了股份有限公司，并造就了一大批新的私有化公司——比如像英国航空公司和英国服装品牌"博柏利"这样的公司。这是股份有限公司的黄金时代。

有趣的是，个人电脑与此同时给了个体一种新的力量感，在苹果麦金塔电脑上达到了顶点，于是20世纪60年代出生的一代人开始认同表面上反大企业的新公司，比如苹果公司、维珍集团或西南航空公司。这种新现象感觉起来就像消费者品牌，于是"企业认同感"这样的旧术语就转变成了"企业品牌"——不过，在某些方面，"非企业品牌"可能更为恰当。

## 公司与公司的对抗

苹果公司是这类艺术的大师。它用一个著名的广告发布"苹果麦金塔"个人电脑，广告由里得雷·斯科特执导，展示的是一名女运动员（代表麦金塔电脑）跑进一个体育馆，接着把一把长柄大锤扔到屏幕中"老大哥"的脸上（代表商业计算的旧世界）。这个广告戏剧化地呈现了一种新的时髦企业品牌，取代了以IBM为典型代表的旧的企业身份模式。它邀请消费者加入一项帮助打败"老大哥"的运动之中。

这些新一代企业品牌甚至能够从一个产业扩展到其他产业，利用他们的品牌将客户带到新产业中。"维珍"从唱片起家，又发展到航空业，接着又参与了金融服务、火车、移动电话等产业。

像"维珍"这样的企业品牌对消费者有吸引力，但品牌创建也成为公司间买卖的一个有力工具。除了B2C（商业公司到消费者）品牌之外，出现了一种新的B2B（企业到企业）品牌，许多品牌都是信息技术领域的，如"埃森哲"、"思科"、"甲骨文"、"SAP"、"高盛"、"3M"以及"路透社"。

而且就是在这个时间节点，品牌创建方法开始传播到企业之外的领域，包括非营利组织、体育俱乐部、政党、城市、国家和名流界。越来越多的人讨论"品牌"，并著书立说。

## 行动的激活赋能

20世纪末，消费者行为模式随着互联网的到来而发生了改变。消费者也能够破天荒地成为生产者。像阿尔文·托夫勒这样的作家早在20世纪80年代就讨论过产消合一者，但是互联网让产消合一者成了主流。突然间，人们比以前具有更多的知识和力量，并获得巨大的新机会去生产和售卖东西，同时还购买这些东西。

全新的行业改变着一个又一个产业："亚马逊"、"亿贝"、"谷歌"、"优兔"（俗称油管）、"讯佳普"（Skype）、"脸书"、"维基百科"、"爱彼迎"和"优步"。这些产业都没有许诺快乐或者（在任何深层情感意义上）带来归属感，但它们都给人们提供了一个平台做新奇之事。它们为行动激活赋能。有了"亿贝"，你能够把你的东西向全世界售卖；有了"优兔"，你可以浏览海量视频剪辑的同时上传你自己的电影；有了"爱彼迎"，你可以"列出你的共享空间"，把你的家租给来自全球的游客。这是品牌创建的第五版。

这些新行业并非利用品牌创建来售卖东西，而是鼓励使用网络影响：使用这些产品的人越多，它们就变得越有用。因此，品牌创建的方法再次发生了改变。新的平台根据它们在人们生活中的作用以及支持用户体验的原则来思考问题——而且它们的成功依赖于那种体验的效果。以前的广告和标识设计艺术在这个（新）世界里不再那么重要了——而且事实上，这些新品牌大多数都没有经过专业标识设计或者进行广告宣传活动。相反地，其中的专业知识就在于技术公司自身，在于服务设计者这样的专业人员。

这些平台导致一种新品牌的诞生，即对等品牌（或缩写为P2P）："亿贝"上的个体销售者品牌，或"优兔"上的视频博主品牌，或"爱彼迎"上房产的"主人"品牌。

## 我们现在身在何处

所有五个版本的品牌创建都依然存在着。动物们依然在被打上烙印。许多最普通的产品依然利用广告宣传其质量和功能。或许，占主导地位的品牌创建依然是这些方法：赋予产品更深层次的情感联想、许诺快乐或维护自尊心——因此从事这项工作的广告机构依然是品牌界最强大的力量。与此同时，大多数大公司都非常认真地对待其公司品牌,因而品牌顾问(公司)的影响力依然巨大。

最新的品牌创建类型,即第五版本,还很年轻。我们无法预测它如何逐步发展,而且也不清楚这种新类型的品牌创建专家会是谁。而且,历史的发展并非一条直线。

几个最大的网络品牌背后的创业公司,现在都变成了全球大公司,开始做品牌广告,并且重新设计了他们的标识,使之看起来更像传统公司,这一点我们会在第八章中看到。他们徘徊在征募参与者的新型品牌创建方法和为公司促销的老品牌创建方法之间。

## 控制程度

有了这些不同类型的品牌创建方法,几乎任何东西现在都可以进行品牌创建。不同之处就是所涉及的控制和复杂程度不同。

产品、服务和内容的商业品牌创建(比如《蜘蛛侠》《小马宝莉》)受到所有者及其律师的严格控制,不过相对简单:它帮助一个公司向消费者销售某种东西,以便从该产品中获取最大价值。

公司、非营利机构、体育俱乐部、政党等机构品牌创建更为复杂。其目的就是鼓励人们对该机构给予最大支持,但这也意味着要涉及更多类型的人(经理、员工、所有者、投资者、支持者、会员),于是常常出于必要,控制和管理就没有那么紧。

关于区域地方、种族、各种运动和概念的文化创建最为复杂,因此可能无法按照任何公司的方式予以控制。其中的目的是传播某种理念,这种理念常常不属于某一个人。

而事实情况是,许多品牌横跨不止一个领域。"IBM"是一个产品品牌,一个服务品牌,同时也是一个企业品牌。"杰米·奥利弗"(Jamie Oliver)既是一个产品品牌,又是一个具有特定个性的人的品牌。"英特尔"是一个企业品牌,也是一个产品品牌。品牌创建是一个动态的、充满机会的活动,不断打破学者和顾问们试图构建的概念类别。

# 企业到企业模式

"英特尔"实际上就是"企业到企业"品牌模式的一个典型案例,它通过"内置英特尔芯片"活动也进入了"企业到消费者"领域。英特尔生产先进的计算机芯片并卖给计算机公司,不过,他们在20世纪80年代后期发现很难与价廉的竞争对手竞争。因此,它开始支付其客户,即计算机生产商,让他们在其产品上贴上"内置英特尔芯片"标签,以表明其附加值。这些计算机的销量飙升。消费者感觉"内置英特尔芯片"代表了质量(以及某种神秘元素),于是英特尔通过一家"企业到企业"公司在消费者之间迅速成名。

许多"企业到企业"品牌现在正采取一些"企业到消费者"的品牌创建方法,以赢得客户头脑的方式吸引他们客户的消费者。"空客"和"波音"卖它们的产品给航空公司,但它们的品牌也为乘客所熟知:最新款的波音飞机能够吸引消费者去一家使用该款飞机的航空公司。

传统上,品牌创建在"企业到企业"领域所起作用很小:客户购买你的产品、服务或者你的专业知识,并非你的品牌。但是这一切正发生变化。即使像"普华永道"和"安永"这样理性的大审计公司现在也重资投入品牌创建,尤其想要吸引最聪明的毕业生。在许多方面,"埃森哲"一直是先锋,它自成立那天起就重视在品牌创建上进行投资,一直使用"追求卓越"这个标语。

## 豪华奢侈悖论

在天平的另一端——能让消费者快乐地支付大量额外费用的,则是奢侈品品牌。一件"拉夫·劳伦"衬衫、一支"万宝龙"笔、一个"卡地亚"包、一双"路铂廷"(Christian Louboutin)高跟鞋或者一辆"法拉利"小汽车,其价值的大部分都在品牌之上,而不是产品之中。不过,奢侈品品牌创建也在发展前进。这些公司不再仅仅面向西方少量的富人,相反地,现在正向中国数量庞大的新中产阶级开展售卖。(曾经的)稀缺已变成了丰富。许多奢侈品公司正拓宽其吸引力范围,比如通过与大众市场的零售商们合作:法国高级时装品牌"浪凡"、意大利知名品牌"范思哲"、美国华裔设计师亚历山大·王(王大仁)就与时尚快销品牌"H&M"合作;法国高级服装品牌"勒梅尔"与日本的"优衣库"合作。"博柏利"生产了一款被其称作"入门级"的香水,比它生产的衣服还便宜。

实际上,在时装行业,品牌传统上对那些喜爱标签、想让别人看到自己穿着品牌标签并想在朋友面前显得受尊敬的那些人具有吸引力。但最近,它开始以一种不同的方式对那些厌倦标签、避免炫耀卖弄、想要自我感觉良好的人产生作用。因此,除了标签外,还有反标签:最新的品牌创建形式就是一种非常有自我意识的匿名低调。"梅森·马吉拉"的衣服常常带有空白的标签——尽管衣服的外面仍可见它缝制的痕迹，因此，这些衣服依然可向那些懂行的人宣示自己。像"唯特萌"（Vetements）这样的新入局者，其服装并不携带设计者的名字或者一个显著的标识，目标消费者是那些不想成为行走的品牌广告的人——"唯特萌"的创始人丹姆纳·瓦萨利亚这样说道："对我来说，终极设计者就是穿上它的女士。"

## 只要有市场

于是，我们身边所看到的就是一个品牌创建的世界。五种不同版本的品牌创建全都在起作用。商业的、机构组织的和文化的品牌创建，每一种都涉及不同程度的控制。在企业对企业模式的品牌创建中，你可能认为品牌作用最小；而涉及奢侈品品牌创建，品牌所起的作用或许最大。

品牌创建在劳动力市场也有很大的影响力。对于最优秀的新员工存在残酷的竞争，而最有说服力的第四版品牌创建吸引着最好的新人才。公司机构也在引资上存在竞争，因而一个强大的品牌会让你在投资者面前更有价值，甚至会从银行那里获得更好的优惠。公司机构不断加强合作，而这种趋势又创造了另外一种市场：一个强大的品牌可能帮助你吸引到最佳的合作伙伴。只要存在市场，就存在品牌创建。

有没有无法创建品牌的东西？有没有什么人类活动如此非公司化，没有设计、粗陋简朴或这样不被别人注意，以至于品牌创建从不起作用？水？空气？幸福？甚至像毒品这样的非法产品常常都有品牌。

## 一种不断变化的力量

我们对品牌思想如此熟悉，因此对我们来说一切都显得很自然。可是，品牌创建其实是经过一系列大胆无畏的飞跃成长起来的：这种飞跃从财产到产品、从产品特性到更广泛的情感联想，从产品到组织机构，而且还从消费到参与。品牌创建也从商业领域扩展到更广阔的组织机构世界，接着又扩展到宽阔的文化空间。而且，它不仅仅在你能预想到的充满魅力的部门（比如奢侈品）发挥影响力，同时也能在更加灰色的"企业到企业"市场发挥影响力。多年来，品牌创建总是不断地发现更多的方法，去改变人们思考、感受和行动的方式。

第四章

# 品牌创建的作用方式

回想一下,你今天是如何开始一天的生活的?作为消费者,你自早晨醒来后就一直进行消费。你还会做出许多被动的选择,尤其是要在你使用的东西和你根据习惯或疏忽而做的事情之间做出选择——你的广播电台、咖啡、沐浴露、电话、社交软件、浏览器,甚至你要去工作的公司——尽管在过去某个时间点,你对所有这一切都做过有意识的选择。其他的事情则是更为积极主动的选择:你要买的东西、要去的咖啡店、午餐地点。当然,有一些事情你无法改变:你要乘坐的公交车所属的公司,你办公用的电脑。

对我们大多数人来说,这些选择在某些阶段大都受到品牌影响。我们选择的麦片口感要好,或者要有营养,价格也要低廉——但也可能是因为这种麦片让我们回想起了童年。我们选择的广播电台要最适合我们的情绪,或者能给我们提供最正确无误的新闻——但它也要能体现出我们乐于让自己成为什么样的人。我们可能选择我们最先遇到的取款机取现——或者是我们认为最符合商业道德的那家银行的取款机。

　　换句话说,我们选择事物时不仅仅考虑其功能,也关乎它们让我们对自己以及与他人的关系感受如何。我们做决定时不仅仅是基于产品考虑,还基于产品所代表的意义(即品牌)进行考虑。

　　各种品牌——从"纯果乐"到"高露洁"、从意大利咖啡品牌"意利"到日本化妆品品牌"资生堂"、从日本娱乐厂商品牌"任天堂"到幻灯片演示文稿软件PPT、从《纽约时报》到美国新闻聚合网站"热报"(Buzzfeed)——所有这些都不是一种被动存在的现象,坐在那里袖手旁观。它们深入我们的内心。它们是一组让我们行动做事的概念、感受、回忆和意象。

　　品牌创建对我们理性的大脑产生作用——同时在更深层次上影响我们的直觉、前意识推理和情感。通过改变我们的思考方式,并且更加深入地改变我们的感受方式,品牌创建最终改变了我们的行为方式。而且它不仅仅影响到消费者,同时还影响到员工。

## 品牌创建改变我们思考与感受方式

　　通过我们使用某种产品的体验以及通过该产品广告所表达的广告词,我们能够建立一套有关该产品的观念。这就是品牌创建理性的一面。古希腊哲学家亚里士多德在其《修辞学》一书中预见了品牌创建方法,并使用"逻各斯"(logos)对之进行了讨论:一个词,也可成为一种理性的论据。("逻各斯"也是标识"logo"的词源,我们用它来表示"品牌标志符号"。)

　　比如,我听说过索尼,我知道这是家日本公司。我知道它生产游戏机、电视机、移动电话(手机)——而且还知道它制作电影和其他形式的娱乐活动。我认为它的技术很棒，尽管也许没有（比如说）LG先进。我认为索尼的产品制造精良、设计精致：它性能可靠，因而价有所值。按照这种方法，品牌创建吸引着我们清醒的、理性的头脑。它提供了一种"品牌建议"，因而有助于我们考虑购买（比如）一件索尼产品的各种好处（参见图4）。这就是第二版品牌创建（即保证质量）起作用的方式。

不过，更加现代的品牌创建的真正影响力在于它发展得更加深入。它还吸引着我们的直觉以及无意识、非理性和情绪化的自我。通过一件产品给我们提供的快乐、通过该产品引起的回忆、通过我们从朋友那里看到的态度、通过其广告里的故事讲述、通过其标识的颜色，我们建立起一系列感受。按照这些方式，品牌创建创造了一种"品牌特性"，有助于我们意识到某个特定决策是正确的。亚里士多德或许会把品牌创建的这个方面

图4　让人们购买：索尼公司的品牌创建改变了人们对其产品的思考和感受方式——同时让他们购买，并持续购买

分析为"气质"（说话者的性格和可信程度）和"感染力"（听众的情感）。这就是第三版的品牌创建。

比如，我已使用"索尼"电视机看了几千小时的电视娱乐节目。实际上，这是我购买的第一台电视机，因此在某种程度上，我是一个索尼支持者。我信任索尼。专家朋友告诉我它的画面质量非常好。我在无数的电影里（其中的一些，毫无疑问是由索尼影业拍摄的）看到索尼的产品看起来很好。我喜欢它的交互风格，甚至喜欢那些有点笨拙的小标识：它们朴素不惹眼，却让人安心、觉得可靠。这些都只是个人感受，写在此处似有误导之意，只因为它们已以预设和下意识的形式存在于我的脑海中。

## 快速思考

实际上，诺贝尔奖获得者、科学家丹尼尔·卡内曼所说的"系统1"思维，就受到品牌创建的强力吸引。他在《思考，快与慢》一书中描写了直觉的"系统1"和有意识的"系统2"思维模式的差异。我们在生活中不断地使用系统1进行思考。比如，在我们开车时，我们不用考虑每次的换挡或方向盘：我们大部分时间都是自动驾驶。品牌创建常常直接吸引着我们自动驾驶状态的大脑，让我们无需有意识地思考就选择超市货架上的某个产品。品牌创建使用标识、符号、颜色、意象、音乐、气味、味道对我们的直觉直接产生作用。通过在人们头脑中产生一种品牌个性，并通过该品牌风格来表达这种个性，品牌创建的目标就瞄准了系统1。

品牌创建常常通过非理性现象——比如"习惯性"和"感染影响"，发挥作用。举个例子，《唐顿庄园》这个电视剧品牌从这两个方面对我产生影响,每年我看这部电视剧是因为我曾经一直看(习惯性),并且因为其他人很多也在看(感染影响)。我们人类易受一系列诸如此类的认知偏见的影响,而品牌创建则常常依赖这些偏见。甚至存在一种受到社会心理学家认可的认知偏见,叫作"宜家效应"——我们仅仅是因为自己动手组装了某种东西,于是就喜欢上它。

习惯性是品牌忠诚目标(第三版和第四版品牌创建的目标之一)的一个重要贡献因素。而感染影响则在第五版品牌创建中至关重要。许多在线商业公司都依赖网络效应:某种服务(比如"爱彼迎"和"优步")的用户越多,它就变得越有用。在这里,功能和情感的相互作用就很关键。"感染影响"变成一件复杂的事情,比如,我选择"爱彼迎",不仅仅是因为其他人也这么选择,而且还因为它有利于我的举止表现能像他们一样。

实际上,大多数品牌创建都是通过将直觉和理性融合到一起而获得影响力。有时,品牌创建首先会产生一种自动、直觉的效果(系统1思维),接着我们会在事后将其合理化(系统2)。我可能会在超市里不假思索地抓起一条英国有机巧克力"绿与黑",因为我下意识地被这种复杂的黑色包装吸引。接着我会告诉自己,我选择它是因为它是健康有机的(食品)。

在其他时候,品牌创建一开始利用一种纯粹的功能性吸引力,但当我们习惯了这个品牌产品时,我们就会向人们说起它,我们对它感到更加亲切,因此它获得了各种情感因素。举个例子,折扣超市"奥乐齐"(Aldi)与"历德"(Lidl)受到欢迎仅仅因为物价便宜,但他们现在变成英国中产阶级自以为豪的身份品牌。给你的宴会客人提供一瓶"奥乐齐"超市买来的红酒,恰恰表明你是一位多么有见识的购物者。

## 大脑内部

一些专家采用脑科学来分析理性和非理性的相互作用。他们认为决定一开始是由我们大脑中那些从爬行动物祖先那里继承下来的原始部位做出的。接着我们大脑中的边缘系统（处理我们社会情感的区域）、或者说我们的脑皮层（我们进行理性思考的区域）将去证明这些决定是正确的。因此，举个例子来说吧，我也许购买了一辆十分耗油的SUV运动型多用途汽车——比如"保时捷卡宴"。我告诉自己，选择"保时捷"是因为开着它走泥泞小路到我乡下小屋很实用：这就是脑皮层在起作用，即事后的合理化。我告诉朋友们，我购买它是因为其驾驶位高，对路上其他人来说更安全些：这就是大脑边缘系统在起作用，让我成为一名好公民。但是，真正的原因依旧是个谜，埋藏在我大脑中从爬行动物继承下来的区域：我选择它是因为它给了我一种原始的力量感。

更精确地说，"消费者脑科学"新领域研究开始揭示品牌如何在大脑内部发挥作用。采用功能磁共振成像设备观察大脑如何对刺激做出反应。科学家们希望看到品牌刺激的效果（比如，呈现一个商标或者给予某个品牌的苏打饮料）。有证据表明，品牌在大脑正中前额叶皮层会产生反应，该皮层位于前额后面，与奖赏感有关。盲测时，可口可乐与百事可乐品尝起来产生的反应相同；但当人们（受试者）能够看到饮料罐时，可口可乐似乎比百事可乐引起了更多的反应。

品牌同时也会在大脑更深部位海马状突起以及前额叶皮层

背外侧区域产生反应。这两个区域均与记忆有关。因此，品牌似乎能通过刺激引发与奖赏和记忆有关的活动。这一切都很有趣，但并不令人惊讶：它告诉我们大脑内产生反应的区域，但没有告诉我们为何会产生反应。而且这是基于核磁共振实验室这种高度模拟环境下人们的反应。我们要理解品牌创建在大脑细胞层面的反应，还有很长的路要走。

## 品牌改变我们的行为方式

那么，这一切是如何影响人们行为的呢？很显然，品牌创建让我们作为消费者购买东西。比如，"优衣库"这个品牌让我们认为，它的产品设计精致，价格却低廉得惊人。这个品牌也让我们同时感受到许多东西：或许我们喜欢优衣库略显奇特，但又非常整洁干净的日本气质。于是我们行动起来：我们购买这种T恤衫（或许在我们逛商店时，还会心血来潮购买其他东西）。

不过，还不止这些。品牌创建吸引来更多的顾客，让他们购买更多的东西。品牌创建还会让他们以新的方式，更频繁地从你这里购买东西。比如，在音乐领域，"苹果"这个品牌让我们从CD转向了下载音乐，接着"声田"又让人们从下载音乐转向了在线流量。而且在很多情况下，还是拿"苹果"来说，这是一个很好的案例：它让人们付更多的钱，支付一种"品牌溢价"。

如果你是一个慈善机构，比如说"牛津饥荒救济委员会"，品牌创建会让人们给你捐款。如果你创设一档像《傲骨贤妻》这样的电视节目，品牌创建会让人们收看这个节目。即使你的服务（表面上）是免费的，比如"推特"，品牌创建也会让人们开始使用它。而且好的品牌创建可以让零售商售卖你的产品，让比价网推荐你的产品,让代理商和经纪人更喜欢你的产品——所有这些都促进销售。

因此,品牌创建让人们购买,这意味着好的品牌无论如何都会增加公司的收益。

但是品牌创建真正的深层影响力在于它让我们继续做某些事情,一直到未来。品牌已把自己烙印到我们头脑之中。它们创造的不是一种单一行为,而是习惯性行为。品牌创建让人们不仅仅从你那购买东西,而且还认同、接受你:不仅仅是支付钱,而且还进行情感投资。因此,用品牌创建专家蒂姆·安姆伯勒的话来说,"一个品牌就是未来现金流的一个上游水库"。良好的品牌创建让你的未来更有预见性。

举个具体的例子,最近几年丰田汽车有大量的质量问题,已迫使其召回维修。但"丰田"的品牌帮助其生存了下来。顾客认为,尽管最近有各种瑕疵,这些都是好汽车。人们喜欢"丰田"相当认真的品牌个性。于是,他们还购买"丰田"汽车。实际上,即使在几次重大产品召回之后,"丰田"汽车依然每年销量九百万台。

这种忠诚行为是有意识的、深思熟虑的,但品牌创建还造就了一种不那么谨慎的忠诚行为:比如说,我们常常仅仅出于习惯去购买某品牌的调味番茄酱。

因此,品牌创建会让整个公司机构以外的人持续购买,而且常常向朋友们推荐该产品。它能够把顾客转变成非正式的销售员。在一些情况下,甚至能够鼓励他们聚集起来成立"品牌社团"——粉丝团。围绕成人或儿童玩具而建立的品牌社团尤为引人注目。"哈雷·戴维森"、"吉普"、"芭比娃娃"和"乐高"都有各种粉丝团,无论是正式的还是非正式的。

良好的品牌能让媒体赞扬你,让政策制定者支持你,甚至可能让监管机构为你铺平道路。而且它会让投资者与你一起共渡难关,而不仅仅是共享繁荣。

用金融术语来说,所有这一切也意味着你的"风险"下降了:你的未来更有保障。在2008年金融危机之后的低迷期间,美国大公司的市值大幅度下跌。但是,相反地,如果你只看那些拥有最富价值品牌的公司,其市值下跌的幅度就很小。他们在2009年夏天就又恢复了增长——几乎比没有品牌的对手早了三年。如果你有一个大品牌,你恢复得更快,因此你的风险就更低。

## 唯狗忠诚

这种消费者的忠诚常被称作"品牌忠诚"。不过,当你对其进行分析时,便会发现忠诚是一件复杂的事情。它可能是一种态度或者一种行为问题,或者两者都有。有时,人们不仅在态度上,而且在行为上都是忠诚的:我必须承认,我不仅喜爱"苹果"产品,还在进行持续购买。在这种情况下,品牌专家常常讨论"品牌之爱",甚至是"至爱品牌"——而且这类消费者是真正的"品牌粉丝"。不过,也存在各种限制。尽管我们中的一些人可能会对一两个品牌有近似于爱的感觉,但极少有人会在心中爱上一两种以上的品牌。品牌之爱总是特例,而非惯常。

随着消费者拥有越来越多的选择,并且对市场情况有了更好的资讯,他们就变得不那么忠诚了。现在,许多人在高档超市进行一些采购,而在折扣店进行另外一些采购:他们非常精明,不会忠于某一种品牌。在超市，购物者常常选择该店自有品牌的产品，而不是传统品牌产品。我们大部分人都携带一大叠各种商店和酒店的"积分卡"。我们并非真正忠于其中的任何一家，我们仅仅做出多重的、不完全的承诺。就像有人曾经悔恨地说道，"唯狗忠诚"。一份由安永会计师事务所管理顾问在2012年所做的研究表明，全世界只有40%的顾客是出于品牌忠诚而购买东西的，而在美国，这一比例只有25%。

"维特罗斯"是我最喜爱的超市，而且我总是向人们推荐它，但在实践中，我在所有的大型超市内购物。我在态度上忠诚，但在行为上并不忠诚。品牌专家拜伦·夏普认为，市场现状由像我这样的心态随意的消费者主导着。比如说，这些人可能觉得忠于"戴尔"，但实际上购买了"联想"或者"华硕"电脑。他称他们为"忠诚转换者"。

在一些其他情况下，人们尽管不喜欢某种产品但却坚持用它。比如，开户后很难变更银行，因此，大多数顾客在行为上忠诚，但在态度上并非如此。我们使用相同的宽带，相同的浏览器，相同的搜索引擎，或许日复一日地使用相同的网上零售商，却并不喜欢他们。在这种情况下，顾客是"习惯性用户"。

因此，现今的品牌创建，理想目标是创造品牌粉丝，但要知道在大多数情况下，最好的结果就是忠诚转换者或者习惯性用户。不过这种不完全的忠诚依然是对品牌的复杂忠诚——而品牌创建仍然有助于降低丧失顾客的风险。

## 品牌创建的回报

20世纪80年代，大卫·艾克和凯文·莱恩·凯勒两位广告撰写人想更精确地描述品牌创建的强大效果。他们提出了"品牌资产价值"这个概念,指一个品牌对公司的价值——人们头脑中那些思想的价值。确切地说,一个产品的品牌资产价值就是它所创造的额外价值,这是相较于某个在人们头脑中不会产生联想或者联想极少的类似产品而言的。凯勒把它描述为"某种产品因过去投资该品牌的市场营销活动而积累的附加值"。因此,品牌创建的目标就是将品牌资产价值最大化。

比如,我可能会去一家药店购买一家名为"重视健康"的公司所生产的布洛芬,花去我35便士。"重视健康"对我来说没有什么意义:它是一个无名的生产商,并非一个品牌。货架上紧挨着它的是一种名叫"诺洛芬"的药品。它有同样的活性成分,但它同时还是"利杰时"公司所拥有的一个品牌。"诺洛芬"是通过多年的时间,花费几百万英镑才建立起来的品牌。而"诺洛芬"的售价是2英镑。这种价格差意味着"诺洛芬"的品牌资产价值——该品牌如此强大,以至于零售商能够每包多收费1.65英镑。

这是一个简单的案例,不过品牌资产价值常常更为复杂。对于廉价航空公司或者折扣超市来说,价格实际上更低:"靛蓝航空"和"历德"的品牌资产价值并非价格溢价,而是更大的销售量或者更快速的增长。而且,资产价值并非总是可以用钱衡量的。一个品牌的资产价值或者说其相对优势可能会以寿命长度、发展速度,甚至社会影响力来衡量。

大卫·艾克将品牌资产价值分三个部分进行了分析:品牌意识、品牌联想和品牌忠诚。品牌意识是最基本的方面,即人们对该产品或公司机构的熟悉程度。品牌联想是指其他一切概念和感受——比如,能让人们联想到"宜家"的概念——正是这些能够让人们选择购买或者不购买,其中人们公认的产品质量也很重要。而品牌忠诚则是最高级的:人们忠于某种特定产品或某个公司机构的情感——忠诚度越高,公司花在市场营销上的钱就越少。

凯勒把这个思想又往前推进了一步,并把他的版本标注为"以顾客为基础的品牌资产价值"。凯勒一开始阐述了"卓越突出"。比如,对于"飒拉"(Zara)来说,这可能意味着"我听说过'飒拉',而且当我想起时尚时,'飒拉'就在我脑中的置顶位置"。接着他(凯勒)又谈论产品的意义,将其分为性能("'飒拉'的衣服制作优良而且定价低")和意象("'飒拉'是西班牙品牌,正流行,快时尚,而且适合像我这样的人群")。

再上升一个层次就是顾客的反应,分为判断("它质量好,我更喜欢爱尔兰服装零售商店'普里马克',我总是顺道去逛逛")和情感("'飒拉'让我感到兴奋,它让我看起来很好,让我自我感觉良好")。并且在顶端位置的是共鸣反响("我感觉自己忠于'飒拉',我总是在那儿购物,我是一个'飒拉'拥趸"),这非常像艾克所说的品牌忠诚。

凯勒把这一切形象化地比喻成一个金字塔,"卓越突出"位于塔基,而"共鸣反响"则位于塔顶尖。这或许是品牌学者们最常用的图解,而且也常常被品牌拥有公司改编后使用。

品牌资产价值可能很坚挺,抑或很疲软。实际上,你还可能会拥有负面品牌资产价值。当某个品牌产品的售价低于没有品牌商标的产品或者低于那些采用自有商标的产品,或者根本就没有人购买它时,这种情况就会出现。1991年,杰拉德·拉特纳作为家族珠宝公司的首席执行官曾开玩笑说道,他商店里的耳环"比玛莎百货商店的对虾三明治还要便宜,不过保质期说不定还要更短",但他的评论立即让拉特纳品牌陷入了负资产价值。

## 从内部打上品牌烙印

因此,品牌创建能创造品牌资产正价值(我们如此希望)。从短期和长期来看它对消费者都有吸引力。这非常明显。而且许多研究品牌创建的广告撰写人写到这里就停止不前了。他们探讨如何沿着一个"梯子"或者顺着一个"漏斗",从品牌意识到偏爱再至忠诚,依次抓住消费者。

但是,品牌创建所产生的内部作用就不那么显眼了:它也对品牌背后的人(即员工)产生作用。在一个品牌公司,人们通常对他们为之努力工作的品牌有着强烈的意识。在一个像通用电气公司这样的场所,如前所述,该品牌正式广告标语是"梦想启动未来",员工可能会思考要把他们的创造力带到工作中,他们可能认为他们喜欢这种创造精神,这种精神可追溯到通用公司的奠基人——托马斯·爱迪生。于是他们勤奋工作,以求发明创造。至少在理论上是如此。

品牌创建让优秀的新员工申请并加入到公司机构中来。品牌的魅力带来新员工,而且,尽管现实情况通常更为平庸和不完美,但品牌却支撑着他们继续干下去。一旦进入了内部,品牌就能够聚焦人们的努力,因此,他们工作更加勤奋。它能帮助人们感觉到更加团结,因而与同事合作,而不是与他们争斗。品牌创建能让人们感到更加积极,用管理学术语来说,更加"投入"——因此,实际上存在一套完整的品牌创建子集,叫作"雇主品牌创建"。带来的结果是,雇人无需那么费力,雇用过程中所犯错误更少，工人的生产率更高，无用的努力变少，内部冲突或者重复性工作减少。

而且品牌创建不仅能对员工产生作用，还会对那些帮助公司生产的其他人产生影响：例如银行和供应商。举例来说，一个强大的品牌会让你对银行更有吸引力，而且能够帮助你谈判获得更低的利率。而且它还可以让你从供应商那里获得尽可能优惠的价格，因为他们渴望与你的品牌联系在一起。

通过这些方法，品牌创建可以让公司机构更加高效——这意味着成本下降。

对于内部员工来说，品牌也具有一直延续到未来的各种影响。在一个像谷歌这样的公司，品牌鼓励人们不仅仅要做当前的工作，还要帮助创造明天的成功。它是你必须要做到的事。谷歌的品牌与组织世界信息有关，因此，它的观点，用埃里克·施密特的话来说，就是"大问题就是信息问题"。万事万物——教育、卫生健康、运输交通、金融、犯罪——都可以用数据来解决，因此，作为一个谷歌用户，你不断遇到挑战，要使用数据去解决一个新的大问题（因此也创造了一个大的新行业）。品牌创建也鼓励公司机构内部人员以许多不同的方式成长发展：至少可以与公司共存，学习新技能，开发新方法，创造新产品，扩展新市场。

所有这些都表明，良好的品牌创建有助员工最大化地利用公司的未来机会。

## 一种公司资产

因此，品牌创建在理性层面对我们的作用就是改变我们的思考方式；而更深层次的作用是在直觉和情感层面，改变我们的感受方式。它影响我们对产品的认识和判断；但它同时还影响我们的感受，知觉和记忆。它还以这些方式改变我们的行为方式——既包括我们有意识的购买决定，又包含我们在超市里自动驾驶般的本能反应。

品牌创建不仅影响消费者的行为，也会影响员工的行为。而且这种影响结果不只是短暂现象，还是持续到未来的长期模式。

从短期来看，良好的品牌创建增加了收入且降低了成本，这就产生了利润。从长期来看，它将风险最小化、机会最大化，这就会带来长期的发展前景。利润与发展相结合，你便获得了商业价值。因此，品牌具有惊人的商业力量，所以，就像我们在第一章所看到的那样，对许多公司机构而言，他们的品牌就是他们最大的资产。

不过，还存在另外一个方面。非营利机构的目标总是瞄准另外一种不同的价值——社会价值，而非商业价值。许多公司现在将这两种价值都视为目标。按照商业价值的方式分析社会价值是可行的，从消费者和员工的角度出发，探求短期和长期的效果。我们将在第七章里探讨社会价值的概念。

## 成功的秘诀

因此，在最好的情况下，品牌创建会创造巨大的价值。不过，成功的品牌创建具体是什么样子的？一些如"强生"这样的品牌具有一种道德伦理影响力，让公司达到普遍很高的标准。一些品牌通过制造工艺占据领先，比如"戴森"或者"华为"（参见方框4）；其他的通过顾客服务，比如"诺德斯特龙"

（Nordstrom）或"约翰-路易斯"。一些则通过认可度加分：比如，"万事达卡"到处可见，且很显著。其他的，像"时代啤酒"——已有几乎700年的历史，只要更长久地维持下去即可。"帝怡咖啡"（Douwe Egberts）可追溯到1753年，"西雅衣家"（C&A）可追溯到1841年；而"李维斯"（Levi's）则可追溯到1850年。

当然，品牌也存在失败的案例。像安达信会计师事务所和《世界新闻报》这样的公司被指控行为不端，因此他们的品牌在人们的头脑中产生了污点，于是他们不再吸引客户。其他的品牌，如"黑莓"、"边界"（Borders）或者"伍尔沃斯"（Woolworth）让人感觉过时或者不再重要。一些像"百视达"（Blockbuster）、"柯达"和"宝丽来"这样的品牌在技术上已被超越。拥有好品牌的公司能够在犯下巨大错误后幸存下来。"泰诺"在1982年遭遇一场危机，当时芝加哥有七个人服用了后来证明含有氰化物的胶囊而死亡。但这个品牌如此强大，以至于仅过了六个月，销售额就恢复到正常水平。"胡佛"（Hoover）在1992年发起了一场灾难性的促销竞争，迫使其赠出价值五千万英镑的免费航班。公司被卖掉了，但这个品牌继续存在。而且，失败的品牌能够起死回生。时尚品牌"博柏利"用现代的方式彻底改造原先的设计原则，开创性地利用数字技术和社会媒体而恢复了其财富——而且，以这种巧妙的方式重塑了它的品牌。"诺基亚"这个品牌已经历了好几轮沉浮兴衰。"魔力斯奇那"（Moleskine）和"宝丽来"这两个品牌都在新业主手中复活再生。实际上，要借用另外一个持久品牌的名称，你可以认为品牌本身就像"特氟龙"：坏消息似乎不会缠着它们很久。

**方框4　华为：枕头大战**

　　华为可能是下一个全球大品牌，下一个"苹果"或者"三星"。这家庞大的中国电信制造商拥有十七万名员工，而且世界上三分之一的人口都在使用其产品（尽管美国有些人还对它持怀疑态度，把它看作一种安全风险）。华为那红色的标识现在已出现在品牌联盟世界前100家最有价值的品牌表上。但它不是一家巨型国有企业：创始人任正非与八万名员工共同拥有它，而且华为每六个月交替轮换其首席执行官。它并非一家在短期挣钱的公司：它规划未来十年的发展，而且公司一半的人都从事研发。公司非常重视其员工，即"华为人"：他们工作极其勤奋，但处于一种温和的自我批评的文化之中，任正非将之比喻为用枕头来击打同事。这种来自东方的新型大品牌，结果可能与西方的老品牌有着微妙的差异。

　　那么，成功的秘诀是什么呢？令人悲伤的是，不存在一道简明的公式，也没有一个打包票的方法。不过，基本常识以及我自己在品牌创建上的经验表明，有三个中心思想可循。

　　首先，成功的品牌创建会脱颖而出。大品牌与众不同。品牌背后的公司在做自己的事情，而不是去抄袭、复制他人。西南航空公司开创了廉价点对点航空旅行的先河。"乐高"玩具与其他玩具截然不同。没有其他制鞋公司能完全像汤姆斯（TOMS）公司那样，每卖掉一双鞋就捐出一双鞋给贫困儿童。在线眼镜零售商"沃比帕克"（Warby Parker）也有类似的项目。相比仅满足现在的消费者需求，大的品牌创建趋向于引领市场："乔巴尼"（Chobani）酸奶、"特斯拉"电动车和"腾讯"都给人们带来了新东西。最佳的品牌创建是激进的，因而其思想也是宏大的。不过这些最伟大的品牌背后的公司未必就是新技术的发明者。就像"苹果"或者天空电视台（他们的诸多方式截然不同），他们是（新技术的）普及者。

　　这就引向了第二个中心思想：大品牌属于我们所有人。它要足够简单，这样才能得到广泛理解和分享，因而才能成为日常文化的一部分。实际上，它有时可能有助于引领和塑造这种文化。大品牌自然会落入那些如此行事的公司：它真实，富有人性，而不是企业化的或机械化的。它易于理解、分享，甚至加入。对于英国中产阶级来说，"约翰-路易斯"就是品牌创建的一个很好的案例，它易于让人喜爱，易于传播扩散。最好的品牌创建是社会性的，因此，其思想也是简单的。

　　而且要成为这样的社会财产，赢得世人信赖，成功的品牌创建还要言出必行。印度的"靛蓝航空"承诺准时，于是就做到了准时。相反，英国石油公司曾承诺要"超越石油"，却未能做到，这破坏了它的品牌。成功的公司知道如何动员其员工日复一日地履行其品牌承诺——这常常意味着要尽可能简单地履行承诺。最好的品牌创建是看得见摸得着的，而且其思想观点也是正确的。

　　对于上述三种理由来说，成功的品牌创建都要依赖坚强的领导。这要通过信念而不是共识来实现——这是一条通向简单的唯一途径。这有赖于实质内容：不仅仅是一个精致的标识，还要对整体顾客体验有一种深思熟虑的设计。而且，就像生活中其他任何事情一样，这也要看运气：在正确的地方、正确的时间使用正确的产品。

## 通过数字创建品牌

因此，品牌创建旨在创立品牌资产价值，并更广泛地创造商业和社会价值。如何衡量这一切呢？ 宽泛地说，你可以对以下三个方面进行衡量：人们的思考与感受方式，他们的行为方式，以及所创造的价值。

对人们头脑中思想和感情的衡量，传统上是通过调查和小组访谈方式进行的。大品牌拥有者自己进行市场研究，或者购买诸如扬罗必凯（Y&R）广告公司的"品牌资产标量"这样的数据库——该公司对数千名消费者和数千种品牌进行持续调查。许多研究使用一种非常简单的衡量方法，叫作"净推荐值"——询问人们打算推荐你的品牌的可能性有多大。最大分值为正100，最小分值为负100。像"苹果"这样拥有非常忠诚客户的品牌，通常会获得60分的分值。

对行为的衡量意味着要追溯诸如顾客数量、购买频次、重复购买率、总体销售额和市场份额等数据。最近，许多公司已开始衡量在线行为，如"脸书"的点赞和"推特"的转发。这些衡量方法要比品牌感知更为客观，但是更难解释：比如，要认定这个月有多少销量增长实际上是由品牌创建活动带来的，常常很难。

一些公司更进一步，试图衡量这些行为所创造的价值。他们的目的是根据品牌能够产生未来收益的能力，给他们的品牌赋予美元价值。每年，四大机构——英图博略（Interbrand）、

"布朗兹"（BrandZ）全球品牌排行榜、英国品牌金融咨询公司和"福布斯"都会制定出各种品牌估价排名表。目前，最有价值的品牌毫无疑问就是那些技术品牌，比如"苹果"、"谷歌"、"微软"和"IBM"。这些品牌的价值出奇地高。比如，2016年，"布朗兹"全球品牌排行榜就把"谷歌"品牌估价为2 290亿美元，这已略等于葡萄牙的国民生产总值。不过，这并非一种精确的科学——四家不同的公司给出的估值差异也很大——因此你只有把品牌卖掉，才会真正准确地得知你的品牌价值（就像你房子的价值一样）。

## 品牌影响力的诸多方面

这些衡量措施集中品牌创建的外部和商业影响力。但就像我们已讨论过的那样，许多公司越来越多地关注品牌创建对员工的影响，以及对社会利益获取潜能的影响。因此，新的、更宽泛的衡量方法正在显现，比如哈瓦斯广告传媒集团开发的"有意义的品牌"指标索引。

正是这种多维度影响力能够解释当今世界为什么对品牌创建这么着迷。品牌创建改变我们思考、感受和行为的方式——既有短期的，又有长期的；既有机构内部的，又有机构外部的。而且它还创造商业和社会价值。

这是一项大工程，要产生这些效果须依赖整个人民大军。这支大军中的步兵就是被称作"品牌经理"的人。

第五章

# 品牌创建业务

　　1931年5月13日,在一家大型消费品公司——宝洁公司内部,一位名叫尼尔·麦克罗伊的年轻市场营销经理写了一份备忘录,开创了整体品牌创建业务。麦克罗伊负责"佳美"香皂的广告营销,它的销售业绩没有宝洁公司其他品牌的香皂好,比如"象牙"香皂。因此,麦克罗伊建议每一个宝洁公司的品牌都应有一个他所说的"品牌负责人"。品牌负责人由一个专家团队辅助,采用市场研究、广告推销和包装设计等方式增加该产品的销售额。按照这种方式,每一个品牌都会得到它应有的关注。麦克罗伊的建议得到了采纳,于是诞生了"品牌经理制"。接着,麦克罗伊在宝洁公司的职务得到不断提高,而且最后令人感到奇怪的是,他变成了美国的国防部长。或者,这也没有什么好奇怪的。也许品牌经理的作用在本质上就是在商业大战中保卫他们的品牌。

　　麦克罗伊的备忘录创造出了一个全新的工作:品牌经理。而品牌经理在品牌创建业务中成了关键角色。他们几乎一直在公司市场营销部门内工作。在他们手下或者与他们一道工作的是负责其他所有市场营销活动的人：市场研究与分析、市场战略、市场营销沟通联络（包括广告、公关、社交媒体、出资赞助、媒体规划），以及产品开发。不过，现今的品牌创建远远不止是市场营销部门的事情，还要依赖市场营销团队以外的许多人，因此品牌经理能影响、协调并训练指导整个公司的其他同事。

有时，这些人企图通过尽可能多地收集数据，探知是什么触发了人们的行为，试验替代方式，以及运用各种有效的方法来科学地创建品牌。但是人类行为几乎无法准确地说明白。很难把品牌创建转换成一道公式，因此品牌创建也取决于创造性：依靠想象力、直觉、超越证据并创造新的东西出来。品牌创建业务部分是科学，部分是艺术——但最终来看，艺术成分更多一些。

## 并非总如看起来那般

在我们所了解以及所爱（或所恨）的品牌背后，是几百万家拥有这些品牌的公司：制造商、服务公司、媒体公司等，也就是这些品牌经理工作的地方。而且不仅仅是商业公司，还有其他类型的机构组织：非营利机构、学校、政府机构、博物馆、政党、城市、国家、名流界。

但在这些熟悉的名字之下，一切都与显现出来的不同。在各种消费品——品牌创建的发源地中，大多数品牌实际上都为更大的公司所拥有，比如雀巢公司、百事可乐公司和宝洁公司这样的大公司。例如，"德芙"和"本杰里"（Ben&Jerry's）属于联合利华公司。"品客"属于家乐氏公司。"伟嘉"属于玛氏公司。"吉百利"和"肯可"（Kenco）属于亿滋国际。"博朗"和"碧浪"

属于宝洁公司。"挚纯饮料"（Innocent Drinks）90%的股权属于可口可乐公司。这些以及其他许多著名品牌的名称看起来就像掌握自身权利的公司，但它们实际上只不过是少数大企业的资产而已。

从另一个角度来看，一些品牌看起来像是属于单个大型公司，实际上却由几十个小公司在经营。他们在一个大品牌的保护伞下，通过特许权和许可证经营。就全世界的麦当劳餐厅来说，85%的餐厅实际上都由一家小公司进行特许经销。大多数大型连锁酒店都是由当地资产公司所拥有，它是根据许可证使用这个品牌名称。维珍集团似乎是一家公司，实际上是400个单独的公司。像维珍银河这样的少数公司完全为维珍集团所拥有。大多数都是维珍集团持有部分股权的公司。一些像维珍媒体这样的公司则是单独的公司，根据许可使用"维珍"这个名称。在会计师事务所巨头普华永道公司，159个全国性伙伴每一个都是一个单独的法律实体，通过一种法律安排获得许可使用"普华永道"这个品牌。

因此，我们日常所见的各种品牌的背后，都存在着一种不太明显但更为复杂的股份拥有模式。换言之，品牌本身就是能够买卖、租借的产品。

## 经营管理还是引领潮流

品牌经理的工作范畴和权力在不同公司有着很大的不同。在一家"企业对企业"的公司，或者一家非营利机构中，品牌创建或许是一种相对不重要的战术工具，因而，品牌经理通常位于公司层级的下端，只有一个小团队，权力很小。他们的作用仅限于联络交流管理或者对设计进行管控。

但在消费品公司、零售商，特别是奢侈品公司中，品牌创建对公司的成功至关重要。品牌创建被视为一种战略行动，涵盖了公司影响其客户的方方面面。品牌小组通常很庞大也很有权势，而且公司高层常就品牌进行讨论。

许多公司现在意识到，品牌创建不能再被仅仅看作市场营销部的一个子部门：实际上，应该反过来，市场营销是品牌创建的一个子部门。一些公司，比如美泰公司、麦当劳公司和宝洁公司都已创设了一个新岗位——首席品牌官，其职能涵盖传统的品牌创建以及其他一些职能，比如对品牌创建至关重要的创新和客服。

因而在一些公司，能处理所有这些工作唯一岗位就是首席执行官。尤其是在那些认为品牌创建不仅影响外部消费者，在内部也有影响力的公司，许多首席执行官现在都把自己看作他们公司品牌（或各种品牌）的管家——在某种意义上说，自视为最大的品牌经理。

广告撰写人大卫·艾克区分了策略上的"品牌管理"和更为宽泛、更富战略性的概念"品牌领导力"。在他看来，品牌管理具有一种短期视角，着手在消费者心中创立可能最好的品牌形象。它的影响力可以（如果可以的话）用销售额和市场份额来衡量。品牌领导力具有一种更具战略性的视角，旨在将品牌资产价值最大化，同时协调保持一整套产品的发展，还要重视员工，并受驱于一个非常明确的宣言——公司想让其品牌代表的意义。你可以更进一步地认为，品牌管理就是维持世界原有的样子：这是一个自上而下、程序繁复的控制机制。相比而言，品牌领导力努力按照可能有的样子来塑造世界；这更是一种横向的、试验性、创造性工具。品牌管理聚焦单个产品；品牌领导力旨在采用品牌理念指导整个公司工作。

## 品牌引领与否

有多少公司按照这种方式进行品牌引领，采用一种学术界称之为"品牌定位"的方法？首席执行官们在这个问题上观点不同。"挚纯饮料"的创始人理查德·里德宣称，"品牌就是公司，公司就是品牌"。有时，就像"挚纯"一样，开启品牌引领的价值体系，是因为首席执行官具有市场营销背景；不过，就像许多欧洲大陆的公司那样，大多数公司在精神上常常更加理智。首席执行官们常常将品牌概念拔高，变成更加崇高的"目标企划"概念。

但是，其他人则把品牌看作其商业生涯中众多因素之一，并不把它看作驱动因素，而当作好的决策带来的结果。一些商业公司对品牌创建概念保持一定的距离。"戴森"喜欢说，这是一种制造工艺业务，而非市场营销行动。"瑞安航空"认为，这是对不切实际的创意太过积极。其他人则认为品牌创建的兴奋期已经过去。一直到最近，品牌对许多公司来说都还是最大的无形价值来源，但是现在有了其他竞争者，比如他们所持有的客户数据。

真实情况表明，实践中各不相同，各个公司持有不同的观点，且都已根深蒂固，甚至称得上是"信仰"。一些公司采用了品牌领导力——品牌身份被看作一种战略资产，不断地用于决策和塑造创新。其他公司则受商业目标或者实用目标驱动。一些公司则旗帜鲜明地管理其品牌，其他公司则依赖创造一种含蓄不明显的气氛。一些公司高层从上到下控制一切，其他公司则允许更多的自由。一些公司不留情面地强迫要一致统一；其他公司则欢迎变化和创新。

## 哲学家与教练

因此，公司机构可能由品牌引领，抑或由品牌辅助。品牌经理因而可能会是一个低职务人员，或者是一个高级市场营销人员，或者是一名新型的"首席品牌官"，甚至有时会是首席执行官。但是，不管他们的身份如何，他们的职责，即负责品牌管理，正在发生变化。

这种职责过去相对容易界定：撰写品牌战略，在品牌创建工作上取得一致，对每一个设计作品进行监督校正，并对品牌的绩效进行跟踪。但在许多公司，品牌创建的范围已不如二十年前那么泾渭分明。在某一阶段，长期的重大意义与目标企划对首席执行官来说至关重要，而在下一个阶段，这种压力就转变成短期成效，于是品牌创建只不过是一种销售工具而已。品牌经理因此要不断地占领高地，去提醒他们的首席执行官注意到投资品牌会获得的长期价值。他们要论证消费者以及员工头脑中价值、意义和理念的重要性。常常是品牌负责人要提醒公司领导们，在员工中树立目标、信心、信念和团结是多么至关重要。他们当前的关键词是"目标"，这个词对许多首席执行官来说比"品牌"更通用些。作为意义和目标的支持者以及很多关于"为什么"的问题的提出者，品牌经理几乎成了他们所在公司的哲学家。

与此同时，品牌经理的影响范围也在扩大。当品牌创建本质上是关于传递信息时,这项工作能够在品牌部门内完成。但是,顾客越来越多地相信行动而非口号;即整体客户体验,而非近期的广告活动。这就意味着要涉及其他许多部门的同事,包括产品设计、制作工艺和客户服务。正如我们已讨论的,许多公司热衷于在员工头脑中树立正确品牌意识,就像他们在员工的头脑中树立正确品牌意识那样。他们利用品牌创建改变员工的思考、感受和行为方式。他们常常制定出一整套员工的行为指导方针——即使关于在消费者看不到的会议上如何举止表现。

因此,品牌经理的任务变成了一种教育指导。在一些情况下,这意味着教授指导整个公司一起给客户提供尽可能最好的体验,为的是在消费者中树立起良好的品牌。在其他一些情况下,甚至更进一步,意味着还要在员工中树立起良好的品牌,让他们"践行品牌"。为了控制外联交流,品牌经理过去常常使用品牌手册和指导方针。现在他们更有可能讨论各种实用工具和在线学习。实际上,品牌经理已变成公司的教练——公司的老师和培训者,使用一系列教育媒介和实用的工具包。

## 科学家与创意总监

现今的品牌经理还要学会科学家的做法。这是因为首席执行官不断要求他们的市场营销人员提供"科学"数据来证明他们的预算是合理的——不再凭印象和直觉,而是凭证据和量化分析。品牌经理因此越来越关注一系列新科学。就像我们在第四章讨论过的那样,消费者脑科学现在还不太成熟,没有多少实用价值。有一种叫做计算美学的新兴学科,旨在仅通过衡量特征(线宽、曲线角度、色彩、亮度等)便能预测哪种设计最有效——不过要达到与人眼相同的效果还有很长的路要走。

但是，另外一种数据——常被描述为"大数据"——目前在品牌创建上起着一种重要作用。一家公司在市场中的大部分表现——沟通联络、销售以及产品或服务的交付，现在都通过网络进行，这就意味着表现可以追踪，而意味着会有数据产生。大数据能够告诉品牌经理哪一种线上活动获得最多的点击量，哪些推特转发最多，哪些折扣最有效，哪些销售渠道最高效，客户是哪些人，在什么地方，他们还喜欢其他什么东西，他们使用你的产品的情况如何，以及他们在"脸书"上如何谈论你的产品。

利用这样的数据，品牌经理的目标就是建立一个领先于人们不断变化的需求的品牌。比如，福特公司在"硅谷"的研发中心可以监控它的客户驾驶习惯。比如，通过分析人们在"谷歌"上的搜索内容，大数据能够帮助你识别新趋势和新需求。大数据能够帮助你获得定价权，帮助你试验新产品。当然，它还能够帮助你将联络目标锁定在适当的人群——比如，根据他们在邮件中所写的内容向他们展示广告。现在，这种个性化的品牌创建很普遍，而且易于做到，以至于品牌拥有者担心"惊怵因素"，即消费者逐渐感觉受到侵犯，这些品牌对他们的生活知道得太多——因此倾向于抵制这样做的公司。

因此，品牌创建人员正不断地成为数据科学家。实际上，在许多公司，市场营销部现在是最大的信息技术（IT）购买者。大数据的唯一问题是它很庞大——要想让它快速发挥作用，其量还远不够大。一份2013年IBM的研究表明，40%的公司依然还没有工具去理解所有这些数据。

而且实际上，品牌创建永远都依赖创造性。品牌创建现在前所未有地依靠创新：不断地提供下一种风味、最新的商店设计、最新的科技。那些不进行改变的品牌会消亡——换言之，公司必须不断更新人们头脑中对他们的看法。史蒂夫·乔布斯过去常常引用他最喜欢的鲍勃·迪伦的话："不忙于新生，必忙于死亡。"许多品牌经理因此重视激励公司不断地自我更新。他们推动快速试验，并且常常试图加快公司的生物钟。实际上，推动更新常常是品牌经理的职责——于是他们成了公司的创意总监。

因此，如今的品牌经理是集哲学家、教练、科学家和创意总监于一体的迷人集合。

## 引进专家

在少数公司中——"博柏利"就是个很好的例子，品牌经理在内部完成所有这些品牌创建的工作。而且有许多迹象表明，其他公司也正向这个方向发展：比如在像IBM这样的公司，设计也正被引入到公司内部。不过，为了增加成功的机会，大多数品牌经理倚重外部机构——广告机构、设计顾问公司、公关公司等。一个机构为一家公司工作的时间常常会比任何一个品牌经理或者营销部主任的任职时间还长：这个机构变成了知识的源泉、品牌的管理者。

最初，品牌经理雇用广告机构和公关机构推广产品信息。广告业务可向前追溯到19世纪（比如，J.沃尔特·汤姆森广告公司成立日期可追溯到1864年），而公共关系业务则发端于20世纪初，我们在第三章介绍过，爱德华·伯奈斯是奠基者之一。

这些先驱们，工作在科学管理时代，常常把自己看作科学家。J.沃尔特·汤姆森建立了自己的"广告大学"，并与心理学家、行为学派奠基人约翰·B.沃森密切合作。曾经存在这样一个观点，无论人类的行为多么不理性，你都能够研究、理解然后控制人的行为。

根据这种科学精神，品牌经理感觉有必要更深入地了解他们的客户，于是市场研究业务就发展起来，以满足这种需求。其中的一位奠基人就是乔治·盖洛普，他在1935年开始了他的业务。多年来，他们开发了一系列方法——"定量分析"（调查）和"定性分析"（小组访谈）。最近，市场研究的重点是消费者所做之事，而不是他们声称要做的事，采取"民族志"方法（观察人们的行为）并分析他们购买行为的"大数据"。还有一些人既不讨论也不观察消费者：相反地，他们采用符号学方法分析消费者身边塑造他们生活的各种人为的文化现象——电影、音乐、设计。

## 购买创造性

与此同时，品牌经理引进了设计和品牌公司，以创造或更新他们的"品牌识别"或"界面外观"。最初，他们使用包装设计公司，接着，随着品牌创建由产品品牌创建扩展到公司品牌创建，他们与企业身份识别公司合作——成立于1941年的朗涛设计顾问公司，就是早期的公司之一。

到了20世纪60年代，这些设计公司与广告界新的"创造革命"的倡导者一道，使得天平由科学向艺术倾斜。品牌经理不再试图控制消费者的行为，而是通过图片设计、照片、图例、电影制作以及广告文案撰写方面的想象力来刺激消费者的行为。

这些广告、公关、市场研究和设计机构在21世纪前主导了市场，而21世纪的数字革命改变了一切。品牌经理不得不迅速掌握数字世界，于是许多不同种类的"数字机构"出现了，从专注在线广告的广告机构——如雅酷（AKQA）广告公司、理查德/格林伯格广告代理公司（R/GA）以及麒灵广告公司，到各种"搜索引擎市场营销"公司——帮助确保人们在"谷歌"上搜索时能找到你。

与此同时，品牌经理需要设计的不仅仅是他们的品牌身份识别。为了塑造好客户对他们品牌的看法，他们不得不切切实实地了解整体客户体验，尤其是在线体验。产品设计公司"艾迪欧"进入了这一领域，像"现场工作"（Livework）和"万无一失"（Foolproof）这样的专业服务设计公司加盟其中。"体验设计"在品牌创建业界已成为最热门的流行语。

与此同时，越来越持怀疑态度的消费者对销售辞令不再那么感兴趣了，而是通过企业博客、社交媒体和杂志来关注更宽泛的"内容"，于是出现了创作此类材料的"内容营销"机构——比如说红杉（Redwood）公司和雪松公司（Cedar）（奇怪的是，两者都以树木命名）。

曾经非常简单的媒体（电视、广播、报纸新闻、海报）在数字世界都变得非常复杂，于是"媒体机构"（从前广告公司内最不令人激动兴奋的部门）已变得与其身份相符，庞大而有权势。像"传立"媒体和"浩腾"媒体这样的专业媒体公司完全知道把你的内容在恰当的时间通过恰当的渠道，以可能最佳的价格推送给恰当的人。科学家们又回来了。

## 四大广告传媒公司

这种力量让广告传媒机构的数量倍增，但与此同时，各种机构也进行了合并。就像世界上的大型消费者品牌已合并成像宝洁和联合利华这样的大公司,传媒公司也开始合并成足够大的公司,以适合其发展。四大传媒集团——埃培智集团、奥姆尼康、阳狮集团以及WPP传媒集团,现在主导着广告传媒领域。

其中最大也最有名的就是WPP集团,是由英国企业家马丁·索罗从零开始建立的。WPP代表"电线和塑料产品":其最初业务是生产购物车。索罗在1985年购买了该公司,把它作为建立一个市场营销公司帝国的一个平台。在短短几年内,他收购了两大广告巨头J.沃尔特-汤姆森公司和奥美公司,该集团目前拥有十二万名员工。它旗下有像"J.沃尔特-汤姆森"和"奥美"这样的广告公司,还有像"扬特品牌联盟"和"朗涛"这样的品牌公司,以及市场研究公司"凯度"、数字公司"雅酷"以及媒体公司"群邑媒介集团"。

正当索罗在伦敦塑造发展WPP的时候,三家美国广告公司合并组成了另外一个叫作"奥姆尼康"的巨头,现在是WPP的最大竞争对手。奥姆尼康旗下有三家大型广告公司,全部以平淡无奇的首字母缩写作为公司名:恒美广告公司(DDB)、天联广告公司(BBDO)以及腾迈广告公司(TBWA)。多年来,该集团还收购了几家品牌公司(比如英图博略和沃尔夫·奥林斯品牌咨询管理公司)、市场研究专业公司"火烈鸟"、内容公司"红杉"、媒体公司"浩腾"以及许多其他公司:现在约有七万人为奥姆尼康公司工作。

WPP公司和奥姆尼康有两个稍微小一点的竞争者。法国的阳狮集团大约有六万名员工,旗下有百比赫广告公司和萨奇广告公司。埃培智集团也是美国的公司,拥有五万名员工:它旗下最有名的公司为麦肯世界集团和未来品牌公司。

一般来说，客户与这些集团内的单个公司互动，而不是与集团总公司互动。这些集团需要保持其成员公司的独立个性，以吸引富有创造性的人，同时将客户冲突最小化。不过，WPP常常把子公司召集起来，联合给像沃达丰公司这样的大客户服务。奥姆尼康公司有一个叫作"尼桑车队"的联合体，给其最大的一个客户服务。行业的趋势可能是走向更加密切的合作。

除了大集团外，还有成千上万的独立公司，每年都有许多新成立的公司。同时也伴随着许多公司的联合与解体。

## 公司内的芸芸众生

在大多数这样的公司内，最显眼的人就是客户经理，有时也被称作"客服"。他们的职责就是在客户和公司之间建立尽可能最好的工作关系，满足客户的需求，并让客户满意。除此之外，他们还得让公司自己的团队满意，并且要确保他们的工作及时完成且符合预算。设计公司和品牌公司可能不是那么重视这种关系，而是更加注重工作，这些人可能被称为项目经理（参见图5）。

除了客户经理还有顾问，有时又被称作战略师或策划师。他们的工作就是确保公司品牌创建建议能够达成客户的商业目标。他们要使用商业语言（至少在一定程度上是如此），还要使用幻灯片软件和Excel表格处理软件。一些人会聚焦客户的公司，推动举办各种研讨会，让公司内部员工塑造其品牌。其他人可能对客户更感兴趣，他们可能委托进行市场研究，或者亲自进行小组访谈。还有一些人可能是数字人员，数据分析专家或者

图5　在品牌公司内部：广告创意是客户和顾问在创造性会议中联合提出来的，就像沃尔夫·奥林斯品牌顾问公司召开的这种研讨会

品牌估值专家，我们已在第四章讨论过了。他们会把项目期间涌现的所有想法组织起来，理解其中意义，并企图发现新思想、新观点和新机会。

任何创造性公司的核心就是这些"展现创新精神的人"或者说设计师们：他们制作广告、创造出包装方案、设计商标，甚至详细说明整体用户体验。大多数人具有艺术学校或设计学校教育背景。许多人会专攻设计的视觉方面；其他人则专攻文字方面，因而可能会以广告撰写人的身份而闻名。对所有这些人来说，目标就是从概念到形式、从理性到情感、从逻辑系统2思维到直觉系统1思维实现创造性飞跃，以便让他们客户的品牌得到突出，受到注意，被记住，并能改变人们的思考、感受和行为方式。

许多公司现在还有第四类人：技术专家。在一个社会中，若对一个品牌的主要体验（有时是唯一的体验）是通过一部手机或计算机来实现时，技术专家就有一种双重职责。他们要帮助人们创设互动体验（使用轻敲、滑动、注音或者点击）。而且他们还负责帮助同事和客户理解技术如何不断改变那些可能事项。他们是技术能够带来各种可能性的倡导者。

在一些公司，工作从一个部门到另外一个部门依次进行，但更多情况下，人们把工作混合在一起，每一件事情都以一种尽量交叉进行的方式完成。公司倾向于以一种非正式、没有层级关系的方式运作（至少表面上如此），但总有一个人负责。在一些公司，客户经理指导安排一切事务；在另一些公司，创造性最重要，因此，运行项目的恰恰是设计师；在少数其他公司，起引领作用的则是商业思维（因此由战略师引领）。

尽管大多数公司提供很多服务，但他们都有一种特定的传统，一个自己擅长的主场。比如，一些公司来源于产品品牌，包装是他们的原始技能，因而可能鲜明的商业重点放在产品销售上。其他公司则来源于企业和服务品牌，因而他们最初的工艺是商标设计。因此，这些公司有时并不那么在意短期销售额，更加关注长期的事物，如身份识别、精神气质和目标追求。

当然，品牌创建是一个时尚行业。要让客户持续感兴趣，要有实质意义，要促进新行业发展，要吸引最优秀的新员工，要让自己不断保持警惕，大多数公司要频繁地改变所讲述的故事或者所提出的命题主张。也有些例外情况，比如，"思睿高"品牌战略咨询公司一直谈论"简明"——但矛盾的是，许多公司善于管理客户品牌，却不擅长自己的品牌管理。

## 超越市场营销

四大广告传媒公司基本上都是市场营销服务公司，但就像我们已讨论的那样,品牌创建现在涉及的不止是市场营销。因此,像麦肯锡公司或波士顿咨询公司这样的全球管理咨询公司,也给客户提供品牌创建建议。他们已超越自己传统上以数字引领的硬方法,转入更加柔和的品牌创建艺术领域。

比如,波士顿咨询公司收购了一家叫作"灯塔"的专业咨询公司,以增强其为客户界定企业"目标追求"的建议能力。又比如安永咨询公司收购了服务设计公司"塞伦",因为它知道成功的品牌创建越来越多地依靠客户体验的各种细节。

与此同时,品牌创建咨询正转向战略领域,为客户提供各种与分析相对的创造性方法,以塑造他们未来的成功。

## 新期望

因此,品牌创建要靠公司和广告机构有效合作。当双方对项目有共同的抱负,对问题有着深刻理解并相互信任时,才能出现最佳效果。

但是也可能存在许多裂隙——尤其是当新期望无法匹配旧的设想时。最近的研究表明,客户现在希望与广告机构按照完全不同于20世纪的方法进行合作。

现今的品牌创建很复杂,因而许多公司喜欢把这个问题拆解成几块,每个部分都由一个专业机构来解决。不过,传统广告公司想处于引领位置,居于首位,成为"代理商",在某种程度上控制其他公司的工作。相反地,他们不得不适应这种情况:他们只是诸多代理商中的一个。"谷歌"新品牌标识在2015年由公司内部设计,不过"谷歌"旗下的许多子公司可能都间接地提出了观点建议。越来越多的咨询公司需要把自己看作是贡献者,而不是创造者。

正如我们已讨论的那样,品牌创建现在既依靠创造力,又依赖数据。广告公司过去常常重视创造力高于一切;品牌经理现在不再这样做了。这就是为何媒体公司近年来变得更加强大的原因之一。品牌公司需要拥有定性分析的想象力,也要能够非常出色地获得定量分析证据。

因此,品牌创建不再仅仅是外联沟通的问题。消费者不相信你所说的话,而相信你所做的事。因此,重要的是整体客户体验的质量——而且现在这是品牌创建的重中之重。在2015年的一份调查中,一位品牌客户表示:"许多公司机构在很大程度上落后了。现在全都是把客户放在第一位,并在技术和创新驱动下设计无缝体验。"

## 市场营销及其他

在许多方面,品牌创建是一个奇特的行业。它起源于充满创造力的市场营销和设计领域,但已发展超越这两个领域,而且现在要处理战略问题和数据。它过去强调一种销售"主张",但现在执着于更深层次的企业"目标"。这是想象力与商业贸易、哲学思想与实用主义、直觉和证据之间的碰撞,是艺术与科学之间持续不断的拉力赛。

进行品牌创建工作的人要不断应对各种压力。我们要努力改变整个公司,还是把重点先放在市场营销上?我们追求实现公司内部的抱负,还是满足外部客户的需求?我们遵循我们的信念(鼓励我们大胆前行)还是调查研究(这常常迫使我们变得保守)?我们要追求长远,还是相信现在无法预测几周后的事情？对于我们所做的工作，我们只创立一种组织思想，还是平行地推出许多小一点的概念？这些是你在每个品牌创建项目上都会发现的一些难题（参见方框5）。

> **方框5　"无印良品"：无品牌**
>
> 　　"无印良品"是一个全球零售商品牌，但它的字面意思意为"无品牌"。1980年由日本零售商"西友"创建的"无印良品"，现在在全球拥有650家商店，每年销售大约20亿英镑的家用品和衣物。用它自己的话说，"作为现今消费社会的一个对立面"而成立的"无印良品"，目标是用自然原料制作简单、实用的产品，以"在生活和那些让生活成为可能的事物之间保持一种理想的、恰当的平衡"。尽管理念崇高，"无印良品"在其产品、商店设计和外联沟通上却都十分朴实低调，而公司的重要人物田中一光就是以谦卑著称。"无印良品"是一种让人着迷而又自相矛盾的品牌创建法则的一个先行者：对许多消费者来说，你表现得越不像彰显自我的传统品牌，并且越显得抵制品牌创建本身，你的品牌就越具有吸引力。无品牌即大品牌。

第六章

# 品牌创建计划

2014年2月,一位名叫肯尼·雅各布斯的爱尔兰市场营销专家加入了廉价航空瑞安航空公司,担任公司首席市场营销官。在三十年里,瑞安航空以低票价、最低限度的服务和一种积极进取的态度成为欧洲最大的航空公司,每年运送八千万名旅客。"瑞安"并没有进行传统的品牌创建——它似乎都不关心客户体验,也不介意其形象和设计,但它已成为一个巨大的品牌。"瑞安"几乎全球闻名,但几乎全球人都不喜欢它,这带来一种可能会毁掉许多其他品牌的严重压力(参见图6)。

雅各布斯的任务是改变现状。他承诺要更多地倾听客户,推出了一项名为"一直向好"的计划。瑞安航空的票价会保持低廉,但网址和应用程序的用户界面会变得更友好,服务水平会提升,并且会在每天更好的时间段飞往交通更便利的机场。这家航空公司会启用一个新的标语,承诺价格优惠之外的东西:"低票价。简单化。"雅各布斯说,这个计划"令人难以置信地带来了快速变化",给瑞安航空公司的"客座率"(飞机满员程度)带

图6 有效的品牌重塑：用这句标语来总结的话，瑞安航空的计划就是在顾客服务方面取得许多重大改进——因而带来航空公司利润的提高

来了6%的显著增长，并且获评为"我一生中最好的一次飞行"。

这曾是一种快速有效的品牌重塑计划。雅各布斯重塑了瑞安航空公司的所做、所言，以及（一点点的）外在形象，为的是改变人们头脑中的观点。而且他是按照典型的瑞安公司方式完成了这一点。"我们只不过是继续之前的工作，"他汇报道，"没有废话，也没有咨询顾问。我们的确有一项品牌战略，但是我们并不过于自我沉溺。我只是把品牌写到一页纸上，然后递交给首席执行官而已。"品牌重建目标在某种程度上非常适度："我并没有'品牌热爱'的自负。我们拥有一个功能性品牌，提供功能性产品——我们不是一个像'维珍'那样的高端品牌公司。"而且他更感兴趣的是估量现实上的变化而非形象上的变化："我们跟踪的是对'瑞安'的体验,而非'瑞安'这个牌子。"

对于一家拥有雄心壮志的航空公司来说,这种品牌创建计划再务实不过了。这就是瑞安航空自己真实的品牌创建方式。因此,最好而最持久的品牌创建活动是诚实坦率的。它一开始是关于一个产品或一种服务,或一家公司的内部忠诚,然后把它变成外部的忠诚。它滋长着消费者头脑中这种观点。就像所有的滋长一样,这是一种持续不断的日常性工作,并不是一件一劳永逸的事情——因此,品牌创建要不断更新这些观点,而且有时要鼓励进行更加深刻的反思。对于一些公司来说,品牌创建是一种重要的哲学,一种存在方式。对其他公司来说,它只不过是众多工具中的一种。但对所有的公司来说,赝品总是昙花一现,而正品则持久不衰。

## 继续之前的工作即可

瑞安航空的例子很好地说明了当前的品牌实践。品牌经理越来越多地把目标放在倾听客户上,甚至让他们参与品牌创建项目中。似乎每家公司都追求"以客户为中心"。品牌创建现在依然受企业自己的日程驱动,但这些优先事项需根据客户所说的想法而进行调整。

品牌创建计划的发展趋势是快捷,意图在几周内而不是几年后产生结果。有时,目标非常远大豪迈——要改变这个行业,或者甚至要改变世界——不过他们的精神更为谦虚和务实。就像雅各布斯所说的那样,"我们只不过是继续之前的工作而已"。在许多行业,一线人员感觉品牌创建一直在不断变化,因此品牌经理们不得不动作迅速:可能没有时间在每一件事情上取得完美。尽管一个项目可能快速完结，但品牌创建任务永无止境，因此，每一个品牌创建计划都只不过是一项伟大征程的一部分而已。

现在的品牌创建计划很少是线性的。曾经，各种计划都是按照一种逻辑方式经过一系列步骤进行的：先研究，然后制定战略，接着设计，然后执行。现今，商业时间期限要求在制定战略的同时执行计划。在任何情况下，品牌创建都是一项创造性工作，而创造性很少与线性计划完全一致。最佳的工作常常是通过快速原型技术开始的——不断地开发、测试和改进概念，而不是传统的分阶段进行的方式。

二十年前，如果公司使用外部顾问，他们会在这些阶段工作，每一步都要展示其工作成果，让客户签字认可。现在，这项工作有更多的互动，因此公司和他们的顾问们一起合作研究提出各种思想观念。广告公司在研讨会上而非介绍会上与客户会面。部分程度上是因为，这是把客户的一手知识带进计划之中的最好方式；部分原因是它有助于公司接受新思想。广告公司激发、唤起、概括思想，并把它形象化，而不是成为思想的创作者。

## 一直向好

非常重要的是，现在的品牌创建计划更加重视公司所为，而不是它的外在形象或者它所说的话。瑞安航空在这个计划中并没有改变其标语或者颜色，而是改变了它的航线、时刻表以及网上订票系统。品牌是通过顾客线上线下体验的最细微的细节建立的。雅各布斯对此进行持续而精确的估量："我们跟踪瑞安航空的体验。"

为了获得这些改变,雅各布斯创造了"一直向好"这个标语。这个标语并非针对瑞安公司的客户,而是它的员工。品牌创建计划现在几乎都是从公司内部开始的,因为要让客户体验实际得到改善,你必须鼓励同事们改变他们做事的方式。现今的品牌创建计划首要的目标就是改变员工的思考、感受和行为方式。

因此,品牌创建计划现在越来越多以客户为导向,快捷、务实并且聚焦员工。它们关乎行为而非言辞,关乎行动表现而非哲学理念。不过它们依然依赖于有影响力的概念。几乎所有品牌创建计划都是从创造一些概念开始的,这些概念将成为其他一切事情的标准。"我只不过是在一页纸上写下这个品牌而已,"雅各布斯这样汇报道。不过,尽管他很谦虚,这对瑞安航空来说却是非常重要的一页纸:这是对公司想要代表的意义所做的一个定义。

因此,如果这是品牌创建计划的整体风格,他们的具体目标是什么?他们如何着手开展呢?

## 有意而为

正如我们所讨论的,品牌创建常常从内部开始,因而许多品牌创建计划并不旨在吸引客户,而是意图激励公司的员工。如果一个公司的行动表现慢了下来,或者说其竞争对手加速发展,那么公司就可用品牌创建方法来激励自己的人。一次改组或一次公司收购(或者一系列公司收购)可能让公司分裂,从而让人们惊讶于这个问题——"我们是谁?"一个品牌创建计划能够帮助创造一种新的身份感。

许多公司过去多在谈论他们的"愿景"（他们工作想达到的未来状态）或者他们的"使命"（他们的企业目标），但在当今来看，这些思想似乎都是自我服务型的。亚马逊公司的"愿景"就是要成为"世界上最能以客户为中心的公司"。日本挖土设备公司小松集团有着非常有名的使命，就是"打败美国卡特彼勒公司"。不过现今的工人们一般想给更大的世界带来不同，而不仅仅是在一场企业竞争中获胜，因此，目标陈述就要试图回答更有价值的问题——"我们为何存在？"

这是最本质的问题，像这样的计划通常由首席执行官启动——但是计划常常由公司资历最高的品牌专家来运作。在这一点上，品牌创建很明显超越了市场营销的范围，而且实际上，像这样的计划通常渗透到战略领域：若不同时思考我们在做什么、处于什么位置，就很难明白我们为什么存在。

瑞安航空极少去担心这样的哲学问题，但许多公司认为一个明确的答案会带来一系列的好处。除了激励现有的员工外，一个让人兴奋不已的目标能够吸引最优秀的新人才。它能够指导并加快整个公司的决策过程。而且对一些公司来说，它还可以吸引外部投资。

大多数公司认为这种价值不仅仅体现在计划的结果里，而且还体现在过程之中。他们常常让他们的高层经理甚至整个公司参与拟定一个（企业）目标。这可能复杂而耗时，但它可以让人们感到自己有价值、受到信任和有影响力。而且"群众的智慧"常常要胜过首席执行官一个人的智慧。

这些计划复杂棘手。涉及很多人就会导致一种折中，而不是决断：打了折扣的目标不会冒犯任何人，但也不会让任何人兴奋。另一个极端是，你最终可能提出一个过于宏大的目标，很难付诸实践。最好的目标陈述既要激进（它们意在改变世界），又要可行（它们是可信的、实用的）和有用（它们足够具体，能够指导日常决策）。"乐购"超市（Tesco）最近改变了其目标，由"一起来把重要的事情变得更好"（说教、唠叨而又含糊不清）变为更为实际的陈述"服务英国购物者，每天进步一点点"。

## 代表何物

肯尼·雅各布斯在一页纸上迅速写下了瑞安航空的品牌（理念），但许多公司在"品牌战略"上投入大量的时间和精力。像这样的品牌创建计划旨在界定产品或公司想在人们头脑中所代表的意义，以及如何实现这一点。有时这也被称作品牌"定位"。

定位常常可以通过广告界的两个概念明确下来：主张和个性。主张阐述了客户花钱所得到的东西——比如，"宜家"的主张是"提升生活品质的实惠解决方案"。这是品牌创建更为理性的一面。另一方面，个性则更富有感情：它详细说明了产品或公司应给人们的感觉如何。当手机品牌"橘子"（Orange）首次发布时，它把其个性描述为"一个七岁儿童眼中的世界"，充满好奇和乐观，不带任何焦虑和愤世嫉俗。

品牌战略计划几乎总是受市场调查研究指导，研究客户——他们的生活、需求和欲望。就像肯尼·雅各布斯所说的那样，聆听非常重要。而且品牌经理越来越不把消费者看作一个团体或者许多"部分"，而是众多个体的集合，他们的世界观不容易统一，这就使得提出一个单一的主张更加困难。

## 一个或多个

品牌战略计划常常要研究另外一个复杂的问题，也是以英文字母P开头的：组合（portfolio）。大多数大公司都运营着一个以上的品牌。为追求发展，他们购买或者创立新品牌以吸引新市场，因此他们最后就有了一组品牌——常常很复杂且难以管理。

这种战略选择的吸引力很快就体现出来了。我们要简化我们的品牌组合，减少品牌数量吗？这一选择能够帮助公司把精力集中在高度发展的活动上。我们要不要更进一步，把我们的各种品牌联系起来，就像维珍公司通过"维珍"这个牌子而把各品牌联系起来？或者我们是否要像"宜家"那样把一切东西都统一到一个牌子下面？这会鼓励员工更多地合作，而不是为了各自的品牌而争斗。而且它可以让市场营销更为有效：创建一个品牌要比创建一百个便宜得多。这种方法有时也被称作"单一品牌"：一家公司拥有一个品牌。

不过，同时保有很多品牌也有好处，每一个品牌在客户看来就像一个独立的公司。如果一个品牌遇到了问题，其他的品牌不会受到影响。而且如果你的客户生活在许多不同的文化之中，生活中的目标有诸多不同，那么你通过扩大品牌赌注便可获得更多客户。这就是"多品牌组合"模式，宝洁公司就是很好的例证。

当今的商业交易很复杂，因此要求简单化的渴望常常驱使公司采用"单一品牌"模式。但同样重要的是，现在的消费者并非标准一致，因此他们不断变化的需求就很难预测：这些需求迫使公司趋向于采取"多品牌组合"模式。这或许毫不奇怪：公司很少满足于一个极端或者另一个极端。许多公司处于动态之中，进行统一或分化。其他的公司则采取混合方式。比如，可口可乐公司有像"芬达"这样显然是独立的品牌，也有像"达萨尼"（Dasani）这样获得可口可乐商标的附属品牌。而且它的四款主要产品——"可口可乐"、"健怡可口可乐"、"零度可口可乐"和"生命可口可乐"——看起来更像一个牌子的不同口味。

除了亚品牌和产品名称外，一些公司还采用特殊类型的品牌。这些品牌以成分要素为名称，传递了一种特别的技能或技术。比如，松下公司使用"莱美"（Lumix）这个品牌名来体现出色的摄影效果。英国广播公司拥有一系列频道品牌，从"BBC-1套"到"BBC广播4套"。许多零售商有"自有商标"或"专用商标"品牌，用于那些专门为其生产的产品。其他零售商则创立了似乎独立的品牌，经过精心设计，看起来就像大家熟悉的大品牌或者甚至就像小的工艺品牌，比如像"大洋"（Ocean Sea）或"花楸山烘焙"（Rowan Hill Bakery）这样的品牌名称。折扣超市"奥乐齐"和"历德"在这方面都很有名气。

品牌团队还把目光转向公司之外——我们还想与其他哪些品牌建立联系？公司采用"代言"的方式给他们的品牌增值——比如，一些"欧莱雅"产品由歌手谢丽尔·科尔为其代言。他们采用赞助的方式影响新的顾客：阿联酋航空通过赞助阿森纳球队而在英国消费者中非常出名。他们采用联盟的方式扩大影响力。泰国航空通过加盟"星空联盟"，能够执飞更多航线，提供更多候机室。而且他们常常通过与竞争对手合资的方式开辟新市场：英国保险公司"英杰华"通过与当地保险公司"萨班哲"合作组成"英杰华-萨班哲"而进入土耳其保险业市场。

## 恰到好处地对待产品地位

　　这些界定目标、主张、个性或者组合的品牌创建项目主要产出的是各种文本、战略、计划。但曾如我们前文所言，重点越来越多地放在行为上。像瑞安航空这样的品牌创建计划一开始就"提供某种东西"——顾客得到的产品或服务。这是收入或利润获得快速增加的最佳方式。亚马逊公司的创始人杰夫·贝索斯这样说道，"在以前的世界，你投入30%的时间创建一项了不起的服务，70%的时间用来宣传。在新世界，这正好颠倒了过来。"

　　在改善已存在的事物与引进新事物之间始终存在一个平衡问题。改善你的品牌最快捷的方式——提升消费者头脑中的观念，常常就是要找出他们对你当前提供的产品最不喜欢的地方，然后解决这些问题。这就是瑞安航空开始下手之处——通过把机场转换到离城市中心更近的地方，让网上购票程序不再那么繁琐费劲。

　　品牌经理同时还关注定价和分销。价格下调能够使得你的产品更易获得，因而让你的品牌进入更多人的脑海之中。但是提高价格能够提高人们对其品质的意识，矛盾的是，这会使其更有价值。调整定价策略——实际上一点也没改变产品——能够给人们头脑中的品牌产生巨大影响。而分销也有类似效果：你是想让（产品）看起来哪里都有，或许成为一种日常购买的商品，还是作为一种稀缺的，得努力追踪才能购买到的东西？

　　不过大多数品牌经理还热衷于创新——主要是为了让他们

的品牌在人们头脑中保持新鲜感。一些人采用了一种叫作"品牌驱动创新"的方法。他们使用他们想要代表的观念去鼓舞激发新的产品概念，并过滤掉不利品牌创建的观点。比如，维珍公司想让其品牌代表"打破习俗惯例"，因此，当维珍大西洋航空公司设计了一种新的"高级舱"，公司的人就自问道："我们能打破什么样根深蒂固的惯例，从而更好地服务用户？"而且，现在让客户参与"共同创造"新产品已非常普遍了——如"乐高机器人"系列，即人们可用来制作程序机器人的工具包，就是一个用户创造新产品的成功案例。

## 根据你的体验

现在最时髦的品牌创建格言警句或许就是"体验设计"。这个概念要比仅仅解决问题或者调整价格或配销的意义更深，甚至要比引进新产品的意义还深刻。相反，品牌经理目标是要将客户体验的一切联系在一起，形成一段无缝的体验之旅。现在对几乎所有行业来说，这都意味着要将线上发生的事情与线下发生的事情统一起来——这不是一件容易的工作。通过给客户提供一种无缝而与众不同的体验，这类项目就会在人们的头脑中产生一个更加深刻的印象，并在理想状态下带来一种更加深厚、更加长久的公司与消费者之间的关系。

像这样的品牌创建计划常常应用原创技术，用于设计线上用户界面。他们界定了"人物角色"——想象中特定客户的典型，于是设计工作就是通过这些人物的眼睛完成的。他们绘制了这些人物所走的"客户之旅"图，从首次遇见产品或者公司，接着使用产品，然后推荐给其他人。然后他们界定"体验原则",时时刻刻地指导着他们要做出的设计决策。

当然,体验是随着时间的推移而产生的,因此通过旅程甚至是故事的比喻来设计客户体验是很自然的。为了创建它的品牌,爱彼迎公司以迪士尼风格的电影情节串连图板的形式,一步一步地详细描述了理想的客户体验。

## 广告的消亡?

改善产品或整体客户体验,常常是品牌创建项目的开始之处。但是世界需要了解这一伟大的新产品,因此营销传播——品牌创建的根本,依然至关重要。

为了让他们的形象或存在产生影响,让他们的广告词传遍世界,公司调动了整个媒体。最明显的,当然是各种形式的广告:品牌创建的传统阵地。尽管印刷广告处于急剧下滑状态,但线上已成为广告的前沿阵地,要使用复杂的技术,比如程序广告(其中要购买广告空间的是软件而不是人)。而且大家都熟悉的电视广告依然是影响力极大的方式,它将各种概念和情感与产品联系起来。

广告有时被看作"付费媒体",而且它是最昂贵的沟通联络形式。最便宜的方式被称作"自有媒体"——你的网站、你商店的展示柜、你的介绍,所有一切都完全在你的控制之下。还有一种"口碑媒体"——博客、社交媒体、电视和报纸上的报道。这几乎无法控制,但它如果以有利于你的方式产生作用,那么它或许就是最有成效的沟通联络形式——因为消费者越来越多地不相信你所说的话,而是其他人对你的评价。

实际上,因为人们变得非常擅长破解并低估、轻视传统的销售信息，所以许多公司大力投资"内容营销"。与销售鼓吹不同，他们创作并分享与消费者关注之物有关的实用内容。比如，帮宝适公司已成为婴儿护理指导的发起者。只要有可能，他们就会致力于制作人们想通过社交媒体相互分享的材料，因为人们对相互间听闻之事要比对从公司那听到的事情响应更加热烈。实际上，"红牛"现在似乎在制作内容和制作软饮料上所投入的精力一样多。多年来，贝纳通集团通过在其杂志《色彩》中富有煽动性的报道来创建品牌。运动相机公司（GoPro）通过在"油管"上播放的电影片段塑造其品牌，而不是通过传统广告。其他公司则把创建品牌化空间作为一种讲述方式，这能比广告讲述更加细腻的故事——就像在加利福尼亚和伦敦的"范斯"（Vans）极限滑板场或者伦敦牛津大街上的"特斯拉"店和"戴森"店一样。

　　这一切目前都存在争议。有些人认为，内容营销是正确的策略，尤其是作为与现有消费者加深关系的一种方式。其他人认为这是一种浪费资源的投资：在一个不忠诚、态度随意的消费者群体中，你需要不断吸引新的消费者来取代那些离开你的人，而最佳的方法依然是传统广告。品牌专家拜伦·夏普以大量数据作为证据证明：你需要让新客户注意到你，而不是与老客户成为朋友。

　　在这些场景的背后，另外一种沟通联络在品牌创建上至关重要。"利益相关者管理"的任务就是不断让最有影响的个体站在你这一边——政客、政策制定者和监管机构。比如，像"壳牌"这样的石油公司的健康发展更多地依赖该品牌在上述群体心中的地位，而不是普通消费者的看法。

## 文化即品牌

我们已讨论了许多种品牌创建计划,从目标到体验,从组合战略到内容营销。不过它们都依赖于人——依赖动员公司员工去赢得品牌。

因此,许多品牌创建计划的目标是在公司内部创造出适当的气氛——或者换种说法,改变其文化。尤其在服务行业,客户对品牌的印象依赖于他们对该品牌从业者的体验。大多数公司现在意识到,尽管一个品牌是一种外在现象,存在于客户的头脑之中,但品牌创建始于内部。你需要让自己的人理解你们想要代表的意义,并对之深信不疑,具备所有适当的技能,并利用好你的品牌身份,以便为客户做恰当的事。实际上,经营在线售鞋零售商"美捷步"(Zappos)的谢家华这样说道:"你的文化即你的品牌。"

因此,为了帮助孕育适当的公司文化,公司投资许多富有雄心壮志的"员工参与"计划,为的是获得尽可能多的人"践行品牌"。而且这种品牌思维能够变成一个企业的"曼怛罗"。在像约翰-路易斯百货商店、诺德斯特龙连锁商店、华为公司和美国奈飞公司(简称"网飞")这样的公司,品牌思想成为一种非常有用的领导力工具,指导人们的决策,并且在没有告诉他们确切做法的情况下提高他们的工作标准。这超越了传统的"指挥和控制"的管理方式,而是施加更加细微的影响力。一名谷歌员工曾这样跟我说过,"品牌在前,因此人们希望我们能够给人深刻印象,所以它肯定会让我们都提高自己的水平"。

公司常常任命有影响力的员工作为"品牌大使",甚至作为

"品牌传道者",将品牌信息传播给其他同事和外部世界。这个绰号很有趣——在一些文化中,可将其比喻为外交手段;在另一些文化中,可将其比喻为宗教信仰。最终的目的是让每个员工都成为一个品牌的倡导者,同时要消除潜伏在许多公司内部的"品牌破坏者"。

不过,仅有一种高能量的文化还不够:要出色地交付产品,一个公司还需要适当的技能。没有"文化"那么有魅力,但甚至比它更重要的则是"能力"。为了实现它"一直向好"的曼怛罗,像瑞安航空这样的公司必须在新员工招募、培训和技术(开发)方面进行投资。

自1961年起,麦当劳公司已通过位于芝加哥的"汉堡包大学"培训八万名门店经理基本技能。2001年,丰田汽车公司编撰了一套十四步方法作为"丰田生产模式"。沃达丰公司则利用在线系统快速拓展学习——员工常常通过录制短视频的方式相互传授最佳的做事方法。更具战略意义的是,许多公司意识到它们无法独自创造最有利的品牌,因而通过伙伴关系和联盟方式获得他们所需要的技术。比如,"维珍"主要通过与专业公司合资的方式创建其品牌:它与新加坡航空(以及最近与达美航空)合资创造"维珍大西洋航空",与"捷达"(Stagecoach)合资创建"维珍铁路",诸如此类。

## 设计的魔力

一些品牌创建项目纯粹为了设计——改变公司的外貌和言论依然是改变人们思考、感受和行为方式的一种有效方法。

不过,设计在每一类品牌创建项目中都有其作用。设计将逻辑转化成直觉，而且在最好情况下会把散文变成诗歌。设计因此能够使一个目标陈述人性化。它把一种主张和个性从平面纸张带入真实世界。它让一套品牌组合有了可视感。它激活了一种主动给予的行为，充实了一种体验。

这就是逻辑思想变得难以预料、非正式、个人化、突破规则或者具有煽动性之处。品牌创建可以运用反讽：比如，《慵懒镇》是冰岛一档电视节目，鼓励儿童要积极向上。品牌创建甚至会让人无法理解。大多数消费者都不知道"奥迪"标语"科技领导创新"的含义是什么，不过它依然形象地传达了一种强大有效的德国奥秘。通过这样的技巧，合理的也会变成不合理。用神经科学家的话来说，设计绕过理性思维，直接激发了人们的直觉或者说系统1的反应。

传统上，品牌设计师专注于品牌的视觉要素——最显著的符号（能指），比如品牌的标识、颜色和字体。不过，这些只是一个更大系统的一部分而已。除了视觉方面，设计者现在大量关注语言文字。这包括品牌名称、产品命名系统和口号标语，还包括品牌的"音调"或者每一样东西的写作风格。像"挚纯饮料"这样的公司就有一种非常突出的写作风格，而且其他许多公司现在也努力达到相同效果。"嘉士伯"品牌"可能"只要通过一个单词就能识别。

设计师们还仔细地在品牌的感官方面下工夫。气味、味道、姿态和纹理都能够非常有效地激发"系统1"的反应。凯宾斯基酒店集团在其酒店大厅喷洒一种与众不同的气味剂。汽车制造商确切地设计车门关闭时发出"沉闷的金属声"。西班牙美利亚酒店集团甚至鼓励其员工在向客户打招呼时将右手放在胸口,这是一种非常独特的品牌姿态。

但对许多公司来说,品牌设计还有一个更重要的方面:互动。设计师要仔细考虑在线用户界面每个像素、每一秒的细节——因为这是在客户头脑中培育正确的品牌印象的最有效方式。微信,这款中国人使用的通信软件,就是一个用户界面设计大师。

一些设计师讨论"接触点",即一个客户(或员工或投资人)看到或触摸到的一切不同之处,这些东西会影响他们对该品牌的感知。但是这可能是一种静态的、碎片化的思维方式——设计许多单独的接触点,而且就像我们已讨论过的那样,设计师把整个客户体验常常看作一种历时的"客户之旅",现在这种做法很普遍。

与任何创造性活动一样,品味、判断力和习俗惯例会随时间而改变。就像许多艺术家影响其他艺术家那样,品牌也会彼此获得暗示,相互借鉴。当下的时尚是纯粹主义,剥掉事物的外衣回归其本质。品牌视觉标识常常采用阴影、高光和纹理来产生一种三维立体的错觉。现在,这种时尚——从"苹果"到"可口可乐"——都转为简单的"扁平化"图片。而且品牌命名也由造词(如"谷歌""讯佳普""声田"等)转向简单的真实单词(如"优步""藤蔓""斯莱克"等)。

## 真实的实用性

设计在很多方面都是一切成功品牌创建项目中的关键工具。在一些项目中,设计就是创造出一个不可忽略的标识。在其他项目中,设计可能意味着要确切地界定一个用户点击"结账"时或者写下"一直向好"这样简单的曼怛罗时会发生什么。现在不再那么强调把设计看作造型,更多强调设计是用来解决问题——这是因为人们相信他们体验到的现实。品牌创建创造的神话越来越少,更多是去介绍(产品/服务的)良好真实的实用性(参见方框6)。

> **方框6 "极度干燥"(Superdry):英式日语**
>
> "极度干燥"是一个全球服装零售商,在过去十年里取得了快速成功,以其产品上印有显著的日语文字而闻名。但"极度干燥"并非来自东京,而是来自英格兰的切尔滕纳姆。这个品牌由朱利安·邓克顿在1985年作为"时尚衣物"品牌而创立,"极度干燥"为其内部品牌。但事实证明"极度干燥"更具影响力,因而在2012年所有的"时尚"店都更名为"极度干燥"。现在它在近五十个国家有五百多家门店。该公司表示他们专注于高质量产品——把复古的美式文化和日语灵感所激发的图形与一种英国风格相融合。这些日语文字大都没有意义且随机排列,但作为一个品牌设计,它的效果很好——当然,除了在日本本土之外。

第七章

# 品牌创建伦理

1988年,一家名为"禾众基金会"的荷兰发展机构创立了一套"公平贸易"的标准,想要保证生产商有一种体面的生活。禾众基金会的理念是利用品牌创建鼓励富裕国家的消费者改变购买行为:支付更多的钱购买符合伦理道德的产品。

这个理念迅速传播到荷兰之外。一家"公平贸易标签组织"得以成立,并且在2002年推出了一个新品牌"公平贸易"(参见图7)。生产者加入当地的合作社,然后就可从建议、培训和有保证的最低价格中受益。

这种方案并不完美。"公平贸易"产品的价格很高,因而批评家认为这种溢价的绝大部分都被零售商拿去了。而且这种制度将非"公平贸易"的农民置于一种严重的不利状态。尽管如此,截至2013年,消费者能够在三万种不同的"公平贸易"产品中进行选择,而且他们购买这些产品花费了五十五亿欧元。品牌创建计划已取得成效。该计划正在帮助七十四个国家的一百二十万名工人和农民。

品牌学

图7 社会变迁:"公平贸易"品牌鼓励人们选择有利于生产者的产品,而不是剥削他们

很明显，品牌创建是一种强大的力量。但它会一直是一种向善的力量吗？有许多理由让我们保持乐观。商业利润越来越取决于社会目标，因此，品牌创建要赚钱必须向善。

## 故事还是谎言？

再举一个超市产品的例子：如果你去英国玛莎百货商店购买三文鱼，你会发现包装上写有（比如）"缪尔湖（Lochmuir）三文鱼馅饼"。它听起来很美味。在英国，大多数人都知道"loch"是苏格兰语，表"湖"的意思，因此很容易想象这种三文鱼来自苏格兰高地某个漂亮的湖泊。但是，如果你用"谷歌地图"搜索"Lochmuir"，你会得到一个错误信息反馈："我们不能找到'Lochmuir'。请确保您搜索内容拼写正确。"为何会这样呢？因为根本不存在这样一个地方——这是品牌创建人员凭空捏造的一个地名，以产生一种原产地的感觉，从而增加产品的价值。

类似地，你可能觉得"极度干燥"来自日本——但正如我们已讨论过的那样，它在1985年成立于英格兰的切尔滕纳姆。你或许认为"哈根达斯"是北欧斯堪的纳维亚的牌子，但它却来自纽约。你可能猜想"瑰珀翠"（Crabtree and Evelyn）是一家有几百年历史的英国公司，但它却是由一个美国人和两个英国人1972年在马萨诸塞州创立的。那么，丰富多彩的故事讲述什么时候变成了对消费者的误导？倘若品牌创建意在改变我们的思考、感受和行为方式，那么它的影响何时会变得有害？

多年来，有许多批评家批评品牌和品牌创建。美国记者万斯·帕卡德曾在1957年写过一本引人入胜的书，叫作《隐藏的说服家》。他揭露了当时流行的动机研究做法，即广告推销人员悄悄渗透到人的潜意识心理过程中,去进行售卖(甚至使用现在被明令禁止的骗局,比如,潜意识广告)。"我们中很多人,"他总结道,"在日常生活模式中正受到影响和操控,远比我们想象的要严重。"因此,品牌创建以及它所涉及的一些实践都可能涉及对人系统性地欺骗或操控。

英国艺术评论家约翰·伯格在1972年录制了一系列电视节目,叫作《观看之道》,后来整理成了一本书。这是一种非常棒的马克思主义分析方式,分析了我们在艺术品中所看到的形象背后的意义、动机和经济情况;其中一个节目分析了伯格所说的"宣传"——他用来指广告和相关行为,一种我们今天可能会称作"品牌创建"的艺术。伯格总结道:"宣传的目的是让观众对其当前的生活略微不满意。"品牌创建故意让人们对其所拥有的感到不满意,为的是诱使他们购买更多。这是系统性地制造轻度痛苦。

其中最有名的,是加拿大记者娜奥米·克莱恩,她在2000年写了一本全球畅销书《拒绝品牌》。它探讨了品牌侵袭我们每个生活领域的方式,包括对学校的侵袭;探讨了大品牌拥有者的可疑行为,比如在发展中国家利用血汗工厂生产大量的世界品牌衣物。克莱恩预言,"随着更多年轻人发现全球标识网络的诸多品牌秘密,他们的愤怒就会激起下一场大型政治运动"。她的预言还没完全实现,但她已引发对品牌跨国公司史无前例水平的公开监督。

这些书攻击了比品牌创建更重大的东西:大型跨国公司傲慢自负的行为,又或者整个资本主义经济制度。它们对我们的青少年、叛逆者、阴谋理论家都有吸引力。但它们同时也猛烈地击中了品牌创建的欺骗性以及有时甚至是虚伪的本性——而且还揭露了它的本质：品牌创建不仅仅是许多一次性的欺骗行为，而且还是我们无法轻易摆脱的一种制度和一种环境氛围。

不过，这是看待品牌创建的唯一方式吗？显然不是。

## 国民之乐

品牌创建也有许多积极的效果。对消费者而言，它创造了多样性，并指导人们进行选择。为了保持他们的品牌在我们头脑中的新鲜度，公司会不断地开发提供新产品和新服务。而且若没有品牌创建，我们很难识别和找到要寻找的东西。如果我们想解渴、想油漆我们的房子，或者想获得一份贷款、想观看一个电视节目，品牌创建可指导我们，帮助我们获得我们想要的东西。设想一下：在一个没有品牌的超市内，每一类商品只有一种产品。

品牌让这个世界更有预见性，因而减少了日常生活中的焦虑。若没有品牌，我们可能不会知道该期望一款产品具有什么样的质量水准。我们不会知道信任谁或者信任什么。深夜，在一个陌生的城市，找到一家麦当劳餐厅会是一件非常令人安心的事。身为消费者是一件令人烦恼的工作，经常有做出错误购买决定的风险，而品牌创建的一个主要心理益处就是减少那种焦虑感。

品牌创建还会增强人们的渴望感，有助于让美好的东西变得更易获得：你可以认为这是一种民主化力量。企鹅出版社成立于20世纪30年代，为的是让新兴中产阶级能够买得起好的读物，而出版社的创立者艾伦·莱恩不仅将它视为一家出版社，也视其为一个品牌。在部分程度上，正是像伦敦的泰特美术馆和纽约现代艺术博物馆这样的品牌力量将现代艺术带给了更多人。你还可以说，正是因为品牌创建可以降低焦虑感，人们才会尝试新产品和新体验。英国乐购公司前首席执行官特里·莱希曾这样主张道，"英国工人阶级与我们一道迈向高端"，并主张"乐购"品牌鼓励人们尝试所有系列的外国新食品。比如，航空公司和酒店品牌给人的安心则鼓励我们去尝试新的国度和新的文化。

101　　品牌能让人自我感觉更好。不管对错，它们让我们感到已做出聪明的选择，或者认为我们就是我们一直想成为的那类人。品牌创建赋予产品和服务额外的意义、额外的价值——它们帮助我们向他人炫耀，或者只是静静地自我感觉更好。就像"乐高"品牌部落那样，它们也许给我们一种身份感和归属感；并且它们让我们参与到意义创造的过程中。而且一些品牌创建给我们一种别的方式所不能给予的力量。正是通过像"亿贝"和"易集"这样的电商平台的品牌力量，我们才能够把东西卖给全世界。

## 使之担责

品牌创建不仅会对消费者有好处，同时对工人也有好处。为一个好品牌工作，让人感觉工作更有价值。对于一家拥有强大品牌的公司，比如"约翰-路易斯"或者"诺德斯特龙"，员工会感受到一种更加强烈的归属感，认为他们的工作有价值。一个明确说明想要代表何物的主张有利于更好的决策。一个品牌能够指导工人们做什么以及如何做——就像"乐购"的曼怛罗"服务英国购物者，每天进步一点点"，或者印度联合企业"马恒达"的理念——让人"站起来"。

很明显,品牌创建对经济有好处。因为品牌创建的根本作用就是刺激购买(以及重复购买),很显然,它有助于创造销售额;而且你也可以认为在过去一百年,世界经济的增长至少部分程度上受到品牌力量的驱动。1920年世界生产总值不到两万亿美元,现在远超过五十万亿美元(以1990年价格计算)——若没有品牌创建,这有可能实现吗?

对于社会来说,品牌创建提高质量,因而让企业有了责任担当。因为品牌是某种质量水平的一种保证,他们(企业)会提高总体质量。由于一个品牌对其拥有者来说非常有价值,所以它会有动力去解决任何会破坏品牌的问题——比如,"普里马克"在2013年行动快速地改善了其在孟加拉的工厂条件,这就是其中的原因所在。品牌实际上成为有道德的消费者监督的一个重点——这种监督在一个没有品牌的世界里会困难得多。

诙谐一点来说,品牌给许多国民增添了快乐。设想一下,如果不允许"极度干燥"采用带有幻想色彩的日语表达,或者不允许"瑰珀翠"建立一种虚构的传统,没有品牌的世界将会多么单调——而且会多么地缺乏幽默感。这些故事为消费者增加了价值。而品牌则拉近了人们的距离。"苹果""三星""脸书""推特""耐克""阿迪达斯"都是当今的世界语:我们都共享的一个专门词汇。

## 无穷无尽的不满

不过,几乎所有这些论点都有消极的一面。对消费者来说,品牌创建会造成同质性,从而减少选择。尽管在某个层面我们有前所未有的商品和服务可供选择,但在另一层面,我们的选择其实变少了。大型全球品牌企业驱逐当地无品牌的公司,于是世界上每个城市现在都提供完全相同的商店、酒店甚至餐馆:"飒拉""假日酒店""硬石餐厅"。而在网上世界,品牌帮助产生网络效应,其结果就是准垄断状态——"谷歌""维基百科""亿贝""照片墙"。

品牌能制造一种错误的安全感。从某种意义上说,它们保证质量,但同时又鼓励我们停止思考——比如,想当然地认为品牌食品中的每一种成分都必然是健康的。

它们欺骗人们去购买他们并不需要的东西。你可以说这就是品牌创建的本质:制造欲望。品牌创建让人们支付比他们需要支付的更多的钱;购买和消费他们并不需要的东西;而且去购买对他们来说有害的东西,不管是香烟还是含糖饮料。对一些人来说,(购买品牌)变成了一种瘾癖,他们已成了品牌标签上瘾者。

就像约翰·伯格所主张的那样,品牌能让人们对其生活感到不满。因为品牌创建制造了欲望,它并不创造满意或幸福。就像一些令人上瘾的药物一样,它刺激我们的大脑产生多巴胺,使得我们不断要求更多的东西——下一款"苹果"手机、下一个"宝马"车型。人们可以这样认为,品牌创建会造成永久无法满足的欲望,就像奥斯卡·王尔德对香烟的描述:"一根香烟是完美的享受,它是高雅的,但留给人的是不满足。"

## 一切商业化

可以认为,品牌创建诱骗员工去服务股东的利益,而不是他们自己的利益。当今有许多员工为品牌公司精心效力,他们的工作时间若在维多利亚时代会让人惊讶不已,从早餐到就寝(以及就寝之后)都在回复邮件。你可以说,他们为之工作的品牌的光环让他们付出的劳动远远多于他们实际得到的工资。

对于经济来说,正如品牌创建会刺激经济发展,它同时也会激发不可持续的消费水平,因而导致不可持续的生产水平。它会造成这样一个时代:资源耗竭,海洋受到污染,生活环境遭到破坏,气候模式发生改变。

但是对于社会来说,品牌可能会成为企业做错事时的一个面具。熟悉的、令人尊敬的大品牌会让社会认定背后的一切都没问题,就像2015年世人所见的那样,当时大众汽车关于排放水平的系统性欺骗得到披露。

品牌创建或许可以增添色彩,但也会把一切都商业化,因而把一切事物都变得平凡庸俗。它助长了把宗教节日变成商业富矿的风气。它把商业带进了学校、大学、博物馆和展览馆。为了简明,品牌经理会简化一种生活方式,把城市这样的多维度实体变成一句粗鲁的口号:比如,爱丁堡变成了"鼓舞人心的首府"。

而且,尽管品牌把我们团结在一起,它们同时也把富人与穷人区分开了。它们突显出谁能买得起"苹果"手机,谁只能凑合着用古老的"诺基亚"手机。

## 为社会变革而创建品牌

那么,我们能得到什么样的结论呢?负面情况真实存在,我不想过于轻视这一点,也不鼓励大家对此漠不关心。但是品牌创建最有效之处是其道德伦理,因为它是一种真实的反映:撒谎的品牌创建不会持久。

而且，总体而言，品牌创建的作用就是迫使许多事情公开透明。通过运营品牌和使用这些有影响力的符号，公司的可见度变得很高。它们在人们的生活中很重要，因此自然成为受监督的对象。人们会意识到品牌创建以及它是如何起作用的——即使品牌创建已遵守其铁规。互联网文化的兴起增加了人们的品牌知识，增强了他们调查品牌的力量——同时激发了一种不恭敬、反建制的态度。通过社交媒体，个人已获得了要求公司承担责任的权力，而且近些年来消费者已抵制了像亚马逊、博柏利和雪佛龙这样的公司。这些抵制或许不会毁灭这样的品牌，但它们常常引起企业政策上的改变。因此，对大公司来说，无处可藏。

而且，如果品牌创建会改变人们的思考、感受和行为方式，那么它也会通过这样做而实现社会变革吗？品牌创建能够帮助人类和地球吗？很显然，品牌创建能够鼓励那些提高福祉的短期行为。"公平贸易"就是一个例子。联合利华公司创建"卫宝"香皂品牌，宣传其卫生质量，并在印度农村进行了一个健康教育项目，它声称影响了七千万人。

品牌创建还能产生长期的行为习惯，增加可持续性。比如，美国网上租车公司"链车"鼓励人们共享汽车，而不是拥有汽车；公司声称每一辆"链车"会把路上的私家车减少十七辆。法国拼车公司"巴拉巴拉汽车"和英国的"搭车族"旨在通过共享乘车而达到类似效果。美国环保清洁公司"方法派"制造吸引人购买的环保清洁产品。"维基百科"作为品牌，鼓励成千上万的投稿者通过义务工作给世界智力资源添砖加瓦（参见方框7）。

"女孩效应"是一个最初由耐克公司建立的组织，旨在利用媒体品牌的力量改变青少年女孩的态度和行为，尤其是发展中国家的女孩，引导她们获得更好的健康和教育。它的前两个品牌——埃塞俄比亚女子流行演唱组合"颜雅"和卢旺达的季刊杂志《美少女》，提供电台节目、女子乐队、杂志和网站，向青少年女孩展示新的社会标准。这项品牌创建吸引了几百万人，并且改变了过去被视为"标准"的东西。这些品牌开始展现出自己的生命力，因为观众开始把自己看作（比如）"颜雅"女孩，并开始感到一种更加强烈的自信。

**方框7　维基百科：一个有爱的劳工**

维基百科是一个并非由专业员工而是由志愿者运行的全球品牌。它由吉米·威尔士在2001年创立，并于2001年推向大众，其使命任务就是"编辑汇总人类的所有知识"。维基百科现在包含有二百五十种语言写的四千万个词条文章。尽管来源于大众，而非由学者撰写，但总体来说非常可靠，而且研究表明维基百科常常与《大英百科全书》一样准确，在许多方面已取代了它。英语版的维基百科现在大约有十二万个活跃的编辑。是什么让人们免费地创建了一个全球百科词典和一个全球品牌？这被称作"激励经济"——声誉、认可、对事实的一种渴望、对精确的执念。而且这也是许多新品牌的力量所在——仅仅为了那种参与并成为有价值之事的一部分的感觉。

## 优质商业

或许对品牌创建持一种积极观点最有力的理由,就是商业和社会影响力之间日益增强的相互依赖性。在一系列企业丑闻和垮台之后——安然公司（Enron）破产、英国石油公司承诺失误、雷曼兄弟公司的破产、大众汽车公司的丑闻等,人们对品牌要求更高的社会责任。为了赢得并维持相关重要人群的支持——消费者、员工、管理者、媒体,许多公司现在在追求商业影响力的同时积极追求社会影响力。像联合利华这样的公司还把社会目标看作激励创新、更有效地使用稀缺资源的一种方式。世界上最大的零售商"沃尔玛"把可持续性看作一种优质商业,而社会责任有助于它践行其品牌标语"省钱,让生活更美好"。对大多数世界级首席执行官来说,利润现在部分程度上依赖目标。因此,越来越多的公司不得不利用他们的品牌在实现其商业目标的同时,还要确保其社会目标（的实现）。

第八章

# 品牌创建的未来？

我们已看到，品牌创建尽管是一种非常古老的行业，最近已经变成一个重要的话题、高层会议室里的优先事项以及学术研究的一个领域。其范围已扩大覆盖了文化、政治、教育、各种城市、各个国家、名流界等。不过，品牌创建行业将如何改变？它是否已达到发展顶峰？或者说，它有一个长久的未来吗？

可以察觉出，有三个领域正在发生变化：品牌创建范围（给什么创建品牌）、品牌创建对象（为谁创建品牌）以及品牌创建精神（品牌创建如何发挥作用）。在每一个领域都没有发生由老到新的简单过渡。相反地，存在着一种辩证关系，两个力量之间的一种冲突。它有点像一个肥皂剧，有三条明显的故事线。就像所有好的故事线那样，这些故事线发展依赖矛盾：在每一故事线里都没有一个明确的赢家，只有对立的力量。但如果存在一种把这些故事情节连接起来的思想，那就是这样一个事实，即品牌创建现在受到一种更新的、非企业方案的挑战。

## 给什么创品牌？

商业界有一场现场辩论，辩论的是最佳的组织方式或者公司的最佳形式——因而也是关于什么样的组织实体需要创建品牌。

公有制公司依然是主导形式。这种公司对其股东负责并寻求利润上的不断增长，在过去一个世纪里经证明是一种非常有效的挣钱方式。苹果公司或许就是最好的例子：一个令人惊讶的财富帝国，坐拥两千亿美元的现金储备。在一个全球化的世界，规模比之前更加重要，因此公司持续并购，合并成更大的单位：比如，最近"卡夫"加入亨氏食品公司；壳牌公司并购了英国天然气集团。这些企业意图能够自给自足，能够自己解决问题，能够拥有它们自己的知识产权。在商业领域，他们是企业城堡。

不过，与此同时，许多其他公司形式也取得了发展。一些世界最大的公司是国有的（比如中国移动公司）或者私有的（比如"宜家"）。在一些市场中，员工所有的合作社（"约翰-路易斯"、蒙德拉贡联合公司）则非常成功。甚至中国的华为也在部分程度上是员工拥有的。有一种新型的社会企业，如"咖啡直达"；或共益公司，如"易集"、户外品牌公司"巴塔哥尼亚"以及英国食品公司"库克"等。还有更加松散但标识明确的各种运动，比公司更有"组织性"，比如"黑人的命也是命"运动。当然，过去十年里还出现了前所未有数量的初创企业。这些公司没有一个是由短期的股票市场需求驱动的；其中的一些公司受到一种反企业精神激发；几乎所有公司的目标都不仅仅是纯粹为了获利。

传统企业通过获得价格上的溢价并确保长期收益,把品牌创建作为股东价值最大化的一种方式。不过,公司的其他形式也可能具有其他目标。社会性企业也许想为某项特定的事业提供支持;数字世界的创业或许瞄准的不是即时的收益,而是网络效应。

而且许多公司——传统的和其他形式的公司,正以一种更加协作的方式运行。比如,当公司要依赖复杂且开发费用非常高昂的技术时,他们选择与那些拥有这些技术的公司合作,而不是自己去开发这些技术。这就意味着许多公司运行时不是像那些自给自足的城堡,而是更多地与其他公司合作。这种方式感受起来可能截然不同。一位公司研究专家菲尔·米尔维斯这样说道,"公司已不再是宇宙的中心"。不是居于舞台中央,控制着供应商和分销商网络,相反地,公司发现自己在一种公司生态系统中作为平等的伙伴与合作者(而且,经常与竞争对手)一起合作。

## 独立的城堡还是群星荟萃

这里所说的故事线其实就是两种哲学之间的冲突:独立的城堡与群星荟萃。你可以把苹果公司看作典型的城堡,而把谷歌公司看作一个非常显著的星座。不过,现实情况当然更为复杂。苹果公司的软件商城依赖于许多独立的开发商,而谷歌公司的母公司字母表公司现在正转变为一个貌似传统型的联合企业。开始创业时具有叛逆精神的公司在发展壮大之后,不可避免地会呈现出传统企业的特征。

品牌创建的结果很诱人。有时被称作"强力品牌"的传统全球品牌持续发展：如"苹果""百事可乐""梅赛德斯-奔驰""沃达丰"等。不过，其中的一些品牌偶尔会采用一种"去品牌化"的手段，试图显得规模小巧、非企业性质。比如，"星巴克"在西雅图有一家名为"罗伊大街咖啡茶品店"的社区咖啡店。它的网站写道，它"受到'星巴克'启发"，但实际上它就是"星巴克"所拥有的店面。

与此同时，矛盾的是，世界上的许多新品牌都试图让自己看起来更具企业特性。许多网络公司一开始就采用了非正式、简约且几乎是手工制作的品牌身份特征。对于这些公司来说，优先事项就是一款杰出的产品和一个让人难忘的名称，而不是一个华而不实的标识。像"照片墙"和"爱彼迎"这样一些公司的品牌名称都是手写的。其他的一些公司，像"雅虎"和"亿贝"的品牌名称则是跳跃状、卡通体。即使是强大的"谷歌"也采用了一种笨拙的印刷体标识。他们现在一个接着一个改变成设计更为精细、更符合传统常规、更具企业特性的品牌身份，为的是向用户和管理者表明，他们是合乎规矩、已发展壮大了的挣钱公司。

在这些现象的背后，所有权发生了变化：比如，美国网上租车公司"链车"被"阿维斯"收购，"雅虎"被美国电信公司"威瑞森"收购，而且依然可以看出这些第五版的品牌如何在新主人名下发展。一些网络品牌公司现在与传统公司合作：比如，字母表公司与葛兰素史克公司一道开始一项生物电子业务，叫"加尔瓦尼"。将来这些合资企业如何创建品牌呢？

与此同时，诸多大品牌已为许多公司共享。或许，世界上最大的品牌就是"安卓"，尽管它在法律上为谷歌公司所有，实际上却为几百家手机和平板制造商所共享。

## 作为联盟的品牌

现在新出现的模式就是各种目标明确的结盟——各公司联合到一起，追求商业目标以外的东西。通过社会媒体，各种"谜米"和"推特话题"可能在几小时内就会变成全球现象。这些是人们所采用的、认同的、赋予意义并分享的符号。尽管它们不被任何人所拥有，显然也不被任何商业机构所拥有，但它们却是品牌。在2015年法国讽刺类报纸《查理周刊》受到恐怖袭击之后，几百万人使用了这一口号"我是《查理》"。这个句子成为了一个联盟标识，一种临时性但强有力的非企业品牌。

因此，尽管品牌创建通常还是关于定位和拥有关系，但它同时也越来越多的关于目标和联盟关系。其主导作用还是让人们购买东西，但出现了一种新的作用：给人们和其他公司机构进行联盟的一种理由。会议组织公司TED的宗旨是传播"一切值得传播的创意"，它已在一定程度上放弃对其品牌的控制，允许世界上的各种组织加盟该品牌，组织他们自己的TED盛会。

这些公司性质上的变化会持续下去，于是我们会看到更多的品牌创建在以不同的方式达到非企业效果：表明社会目标，显得规模小且具本土性联合各个公司，展示魅力而不仅仅是权力。

当然了，如果一个品牌本质上就是一种企业行为，而世界又正向着非企业化发展，那将来就不会再有品牌的位置了。或许，在一个非企业化的世界，将只存在变化的、非正式的"各种组织"，没有一个组织会足够持久地存在，从而去创建一个品牌。

## 为谁创建品牌?

公司在形式上发生改变时,另外一场战役正在展开:在商品生产商(公司)和消费者(人民)之间的一场权力斗争。就品牌创建而言,谁处于掌舵地位呢?

在过去近十年来,尤其是通过其所拥有的消费者数据,生产商的权力已得到很大的加强。因为现在我们在线消费很多,都会留下一系列数据,精确地揭示我们所在的位置,我们所购买的东西,我们所阅读和观看的内容,以及我们的爱好如何随着时间的流逝而发生变化。当然,这种数据对生产商来说非常宝贵,于是,出售数据成了一种非常普遍的经济活动(尽管很大程度上隐蔽无形)。实际上,正是这些数据的价值支付了网上许多看似免费的服务。就像这句让人沮丧心寒的话所说的那样,"如果它是免费的,那么你就是它的产品"。

不过,与此同时,网络也给予了消费者前所未有的权力。消费者现在可以立即比较各种产品,从成千上万消费者那里获得公正无偏的产品评价,并可通过社交媒体进行公开投诉——所有这些直到几年前才有可能做到。或者,他们可以变成"合作消费者",拒绝旧的消费模式——我们每一个人都拥有自己的财产;拥护新的消费模式——商品可以在很多人之间共享。比如,目前在年轻人中间有一个很明显的变化,即从拥有汽车转向加入像"链车"这样的汽车俱乐部——这对汽车生产商来说是一个令人担忧的趋势,他们可能面临销量的大幅度下滑。

而且消费者从未像现在这样可以如此容易地进行投资、亲自生产或销售,完全取代了传统的生产者。比如,众筹公司"脚踏启动器"（Kickstarter）让我们都变成了商业投机资本家；"亿贝"让每个人都成为一个零售商；"爱彼迎"意味着任何人都可以成为小旅馆经营者；而有了"优步"，你可以开始自己的出租车业务。与此相伴的是小规模生产的巨大增长："生产者运动"包括越来越多的手工艺者对"易集"这类网站的利用；而"黑客文化"是一种亚文化，指的是聪明人通常使用软件编码（与入侵计算机系统的黑客不同）找到解决问题的新方法。

## 消费者演员

当然，其中许多现象只是少数人的行为，但思想深处的转变无疑是主流。研究表明，在2006年，90%的互联网用户是消极被动的，只是在消费（网络）信息。仅仅过了六年，这一比率就发生了转变，有87%的用户积极地贡献（网络）内容——即使只是在"脸书"上传发布最近的自拍照。互联网激活了消费者，于是法国人所说的"消费者演员"——一半是消费者，一半是演员——现在成了主流。

在某些方面，技术已让消费者变得更为个性化、原子化，而且每个人都已变成一个个人品牌。在其他方面，科技让消费者更容易聚合成各种团体、网络、社区，或者更时髦的说法——"部落"。

学术界把这种思想往前推进了一步，提出了一种名为"服务主导逻辑"的概念——它质疑了传统上对生产者和消费者泾渭分明的区分。它提出，在消费者购买一种服务时，他们在价值的生产过程中几乎总是起到一种积极的作用。通过使用这种服务，他们共同创造了它的价值。实际上，他们决定了他们那一部分的价值。当我采用像汉莎航空这样的航空公司时，我就要做一些工作：打印我的登机牌，携带我的随身行李等等。当我在"猫途鹰"旅游网站上贴一份评价，我就帮"猫途鹰"提供了一项更有价值的服务。

而且，这一理论又向前发展了一步，提出所有产品和服务的交换都是这样的——实际上最好把产品看作一种服务，这就是它的逻辑为何是"服务主导"的原因所在。它认为企业实际上不能产生价值。企业的权势局限于提供"价值命题"，消费者将其转变成价值。一辆"现代"汽车、一件"永远21"（Forever 21）的上衣甚至一块"奥利奥"饼干，在有人使用之前都没有价值可言。

再回到市场，品牌创建现已成为一场有趣战斗中的重要武器。生产者手中握有前所未有的大数据，能够更好地推出产品，利用品牌创建培育客户的忠诚，并且能更好地采取一系列方法在我们最可能购买的时刻向我们出售其商品。与此同时，消费者也变得更加精明、更加多疑，不那么忠实，并且更乐意抛弃传统的消费。而且这两种现象同时发生。我们中大多数人在某个时刻抵制品牌创建，而在另一时刻又受其引诱。

现在各公司的普遍做法就是承认权力上的一种变化，并认为他们的品牌现在为他们的客户"所拥有"，或者说由其客户"共同创造"。至少，这意味着公司认识到他们的品牌存在于他们之外，存在于外部人员的头脑之中，因此无法直接加以控制。你所能够做的一切就是轻轻地推动客户去创造"恰当的"意义。就像马蒂·纽梅尔在他的《品牌翻转》一书中所说的那样："一个品牌并非由公司所拥有，而是由那些从中汲取意义的客户所拥有。你的品牌并非是你说的那样。而是他们所说的那样。"这种思想现已落地，许多品牌经理现在从外部视角向内看待其品牌，并且把客户看作最重要的品牌创建人，争取其支持。

## 作为平台的品牌

这场战争中诞生了平台这一概念。"硅谷"现在公认的信条就是，公司不应生产销售给消费者的产品，而是提供人们可以做事情的平台：像"亿贝"、移动软件商城或者"优步"这样的平台。市场营销人员很少谈论建立情感上的"忠诚度"，更多地讨论生产那些只对人们"有用的"东西。品牌专家约翰·威尔夏巧妙地对比了传统品牌创建（他把它描述为"让人们想要某种东西"）和最新的模式（制造出人们想要的东西）。那些旨在制造欲望的广告人员已过时了，时兴的是那些只是想把某种东西变得有用的产品和体验设计师。品牌创建更加功能化，而品牌身份更具实用性。空气中弥漫着一种新的（或许常常是虚假的）谦虚朴实。

于是，这些平台品牌就存在这样一个问题，即：它们到底是谁的品牌？它们由一家"生产者"（比如"亿贝"）创造，却变成"消费者"的工具：它们变成了用户达成其目标的手段。一个"亿贝"卖主依赖的就是"亿贝"品牌的诚实正直。"优步"和"爱彼迎"品牌是"优步"司机和"爱彼迎"旅馆业主的基本标识。实际上，"爱彼迎"在2014年意识到了这一点，重新设计了其标识——被称作"贝洛"，作为"爱彼迎"旅馆业主能够采用、修改和重新画出的一种模板（参见图8）。截至2016年，已有十六万人制作了自己的"贝洛"。按照字面意义，该品牌由用户共享和制作，而非由其最初的拥有者。

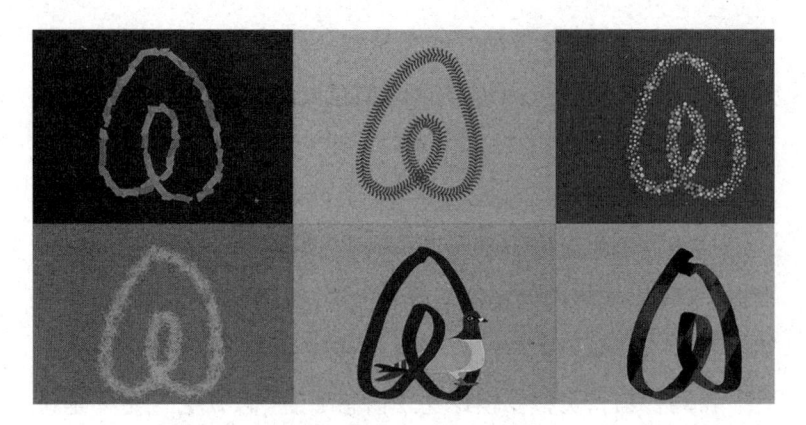

图8 一个共享的品牌:"爱彼迎"的标识被称作"贝洛",其设计供"爱彼迎"旅馆业主采用和修改,制作他们自己的标识

"平台"这一概念已经招致强烈反对。像"优步"这样的公司受到猛烈的批评,因其夺走了传统的、受到监管的出租车司机的工作。比如,在德国,这种高度个体化的"平台资本主义"被看作对更传统、更有组织的工作方式的威胁,在过去的工作方式中,工人之间团结一致,而非竞争关系。

因此,品牌创建虽依然是一种由生产者主张权力的劝解说服,但同时也在越来越多地建立一个有用的平台——消费者在此发挥影响力,并且实际上也变成了一个生产者。在此背景下,至少目前品牌的作用就是把越来越多的用户带到平台上,并让他们留在那里,从而产生网络效应。这就是我们在第三章所说的第五版品牌创建。

这种权力斗争的下一步会走向何方?一种观点认为技术会给予消费者而不是生产者更多的权力。有了足够的数据和有效的对比网站,消费者会拥有完整的市场信息,因而根据各种事实的完整知识做出他们的购买决定。根据这种观点,品牌就变得不那么重要了。在《绝对价值》一书中,伊塔马尔·西蒙森和伊曼纽尔·罗森举了一个非常明显的例证:"过去,你总是知道在赛百味或麦当劳那会得到什么。但当你通过点评网站'叫声'或者美食点评网站'萨加特'知道能从一个小餐馆那获得什么时,品牌名称就相对不那么重要了。"当然,你可能会持相反的观点:随着比较网站强制提高标准,同质性得到鼓励,这种非理性的东西、事实之外的特征会在我选择适合我的东西时显得更加重要。

未来的另一个版本是由"客户关系管理"(即大公司保存有关我们的数据库)转向"供应商关系管理"。在多克·希尔斯于《意愿经济》中形象勾勒出的新世界里,这个体系被推翻了:消费者现在对生产者密切关注,我们都有生产者的数据库。不是公司发起向我们销售产品的运动,相反地,我们会发起运动,向世界宣布我们的需求和目标(我们的"意图"),公司则投标满足我们的需求。如果我需要一台新冰箱,我会在网上宣布这一意向,于是"博世""倍科""卡迪""海尔"以及其他冰箱生产商相互竞争,给我最好的报价。这又再一次表明,这可能会使品牌创建变得无关紧要。或者,这意味着品牌成为公司提供给我们的部分内容即功能与意义。或者说,这甚至意味着我们自己的个人化品牌会有助于我们吸引公司提供最好的交易。

## 应如何看待品牌创建?

伴随着企业形态的变化以及消费者权力的变化,出现了与品牌创建文化有关的第三条故事线:品牌经理和品牌顾问如何看待他们要做之事。

这种传统的思考方式青睐忠诚专一。自广告大师大卫·奥格威开始讨论这种"大创意"以来，市场营销人员以及他们的顾问已成为联合统一者、简化者和合理化人员。企业身份设计学科，现在通常被称为品牌顾问，就是建立在一种冲动之上——将一大堆不同的品牌名称、标识和广告词混为一处，并将其打造成一个管理严密的组织机构的冲动。这种转变将由一种总体思想决定。这种方法最有影响力的提倡者沃利·奥林斯曾讨论过这种"中心思想"的重要性：每一份交流和设计都会遵从一个单一的概念。这种核心概念就是身份特征。一个机构要繁荣发展，需要拥有一种单一的身份特征，在时间和空间上一致；而标识就是那个身份的标记。

　　这种思维与商学院和管理顾问的传统方法非常吻合，公司机构被看作非常有纪律的实体，受总体战略支配。这是设计师或者大师级规划者所用的方法：一般的业务，尤其是品牌，最好是从一份蓝图开始构建。

　　公司机构思维的主流，按照托马斯·弗里德曼的说法，就是"世界是平的"。根据这种观点，资本主义的胜利以及智能手机和社交媒体极为快速的普及，意味着世界各地变得几乎相同。一个大创意能够普遍起作用，而且每一个企业的初创目标就是"按比例发展"其业务，因此同一款给一百个客户提供服务的软件也能够服务十亿个客户。

　　大多数全球性大品牌都采用了大创意方法。比如，宝马公司仍在使用1975年首次提出的标语"终极驾驶机器"。微软软件在世界上的任何地方都完全一致。而印度和中国的新品牌倾向于模仿这种思维，即一个品牌是通过一种连贯一致的标识、标语、颜色和交流联络方式而创建的。实际上,最新的研究表明,这些传统的品牌创建工具在将品牌深入人心方面依然非常有效。

## 反对公式准则

但过去近十年来出现了一种相反的观点:多元化、复杂性甚至杂乱无章可能是一件好事。该观点认为,世界运转太快,无法进行各种规划。各种五年战略和十年品牌布局定位一写出来就过时了。此外,客户不想要那些强加给予的思想。在塑造一个品牌的意义方面,他们会更高效,远不是品牌拥有者所能控制的。而且,该观点主张世界并非是平的:各种文化依然差异巨大,而且按照方案准则管理永远都无法完全奏效。实际上,吸引客户忠诚的秘方可能就是创造多样性、本土特性和保持不断的新奇性。

最后一点,许多从业人员现在对品牌创建有不同看法。他们对这种公式准则已产生了不信任,对品牌同一性感到一种厌倦,对大创意的追求感到疲劳。从业者谈论的不再是一种单一的品牌身份特征,而是设计一种多方面的客户体验。

这不是设计师的方法,而是学术界所说的用手头现成工具摆弄修理的人所采用的方法,即做零活的人、自己动手做事情的人,他们用手头一切可以用的事物来制作东西,并通过反复试验进行学习。

技术创业的爆发鼓励了这种新意向。这些公司抛弃了整齐、单一思想的战略和公司计划,青睐快速、复合多样的试验。成功并非来自整齐划一的智力思维,而是显得凌乱的创造性。119

软件工程所用的方法——灵活、快速定型、冲刺快跑、独立的团队——都被移植到管理哲学里，而这一概念的最高级形式就是一种极为分散的经营管理方法，被称作"无主管公司"——这是一个由许多既独立自主又相互依赖的单位组成的集团。

在品牌创建过程中，最显著的表现就是视觉上——出现了有变体且具有可生性并带有动画效果的各种标识。2000年，泰特美术馆发布了四种不同版本的"标识"，十年之后，麻省理工学院媒体实验室推出了一个有四万种变体的新标识——尽管这两个机构的标识后来都进行了简化。谷歌常常运行管理一种特殊的每日标识，叫作"谷歌涂鸦"。美国在线服务公司的标识就是白底上的白色图样，只有当背景色改变时才会显现出来：其设计并非静态，而是动态的。

## 作为风格特色的品牌

品牌创建专家讨论"流动品牌"或"移动品牌"，但他们的用意远不止流动的标识或者移动的标识。他们要表达的是，标识背后的思想本身并非是那样固定不变。体验设计专家马克·席勒姆认为，品牌创建就是"创造风格特色，而不是重复广告词"。这是许多小创意之间的相互作用，而不是一个大创意。"星巴克"已经不再对其咖啡店采用公式化的做法，而是倾向于"同一身份，但非完全一致"。

西方世界以外的品牌创建或许会（给我们）指明道路。但香港的文华东方酒店集团是一家摆脱西方公式化模式的酒店集团。"无印良品"通过摒弃更为炫耀浮夸的西方品牌创建模式而建立了一种零售品牌。中国富有创造性的"内容生态系统"公司

"乐视"正在创建一个兼具东西方风格的品牌。华为不是一个传统企业，因此可能会创造出一种不同的品牌。特别突出的是，非洲品牌正在世界舞台上崭露头角，比如尼日利亚电子商务公司"朱利亚"或者埃塞俄比亚鞋履生产商"索拉瑞宝"（Sole Rebels）。

这里具有戏剧性的是，许多公司由控制转向自由放开，然后再回归控制，不停地转换。可口可乐公司是公式化大师，但也支持自由放开，印刷有不同的标签，不仅印刷一种品牌名称，还有一系列名字——比如用可口可乐字体书写的"艾琳""凯莉""丽贝卡""蒂姆"等名字。当然，这只是一种更为复杂的公式准则。大型互联网品牌在某些方面是松散多样的，但依然依赖一种前后一致的名称、标识和用户界面去创造网络效应。而且大多数来自东方的新品牌尽管在管理风格上是东方特色，却在模仿西方品牌创建方式：就航空公司而言，阿联酋航空和靛蓝航空就是两个非常成功的例子。我们现在所看到的是，基于一种严格的品牌身份感的传统一致性与基于一种品牌体验多样化感觉的松散一致性之间的相互作用，正在不断地来回变动。

## 死与生

所有这三条故事线都对品牌创建的未来提出了疑问。如果公司变成更为松散的社会组织，那么他们还需要或者说还想要各种品牌吗？如果客户变得比生产商更强大，品牌会变得不再重要吗？如果由一致性向风格特色持续发展下去，我们所熟悉的品牌创建会逐步消亡吗？

我的观点是，品牌创建会继续成为必要之举，但它会变得不那么正式，不那么华而不实，不那么完整庞大，不那么具有制度规定性、纯商业性和企业性。在范围上，品牌创建会影响非正式的公司，而且甚至最大的公司也会试图看起来显得更小、更非正式。实际上，我们正处于向初创企业、社会性企业以及各种"开源"技术思想转变的初期。在作用上，品牌创建不再仅仅劝说人们去购买，而是邀请人们参与其中。而且在风格方法上，品牌创建将越来越不遵循西方模式：它在形式上将不再那么严格、受控、整齐、一致。亚洲和非洲品牌正开始兴起。

当然，这三条故事线密切相关：更松散的、不那么受控的公司适合强大而积极的消费者需求，因此最好通过更为松散、不那么一致性的品牌创建加以表达。这种动态将会加速发展。

换言之，品牌创建会一直持续下去。人类通过在物体上做标记来创造意义从而创造价值的实践，会永远与我们同在。

# 索 引

（条目后的数字为原书页码，
见本书边码）

## A

Aaker, David 大卫·艾克 19, 54—55, 66
Accenture 埃森哲 42
accountability 责任 102—103
Adbusters 广告破坏者 9
advertising 广告 18, 90—91
 Cadbury's 卡德伯雷 28
 company v. company 公司对公司 38—39
 deception in 欺骗 99—100
 manipulation of consumers 对消费者的操纵 35
 personalized 个人化的 70
 proposition and personality 主张和个性 35—37, 86
 reverse psychology 反常心理学 36—37
 slogans 标语 33, 35
 television 电视 36
advertising agencies 广告机构（公司）71—72
AEG 德国家电公司 38
affiliation 关系、联盟 111—112
Africa, advertisement for Coca-Cola 非洲，可口可乐广告 3—4, 12
agencies 机构、公司 71—73
 big four 四大（广告媒体公司）73—74
 expectations 期望 77—78

roles within 在……范围内的作用 74—77
Airbnb 爱彼迎 39—40, 49, 90, 111, 113, 115—116
Airbus 空中客车 42
Aldi 奥乐齐超市 49, 87
alliances 联盟 88
Alphabet 字母表公司 111
Amazon 亚马逊公司 20, 84, 88
Ambler, Tim 蒂姆·安姆伯勒 51
American Express 美国运通公司 37
Android 安卓 14, 111
animal branding 在动物身上做烙印标记 31
AOL 美国在线公司 120
Apple 苹果公司 38, 51, 61, 109—110
Ariel 碧浪 61
Aristotle 亚里士多德 46—47
art 艺术
 associated with branding 与品牌创建有关的艺术 9
 paintings on packaging 包装上的画作 32—33
 satirization of branding 品牌创建的讽刺 9—10
Arthur Andersen 安达信会计师事务所 58
Audi 奥迪 94
Avis 阿维斯 111
Aviva 英国保险公司"英杰华" 88

## B

B2B (business-to-business) brands

公司对公司品牌 39, 42
B2C (business-to-consumer) brands
  公司对消费者品牌 42
banks 银行 56—57
Bass "巴斯"啤酒 33
Bates, Ted 泰德·贝茨 35
BBC 英国广播公司 87
behaviourism 行为主义 71
Behrens, Peter 彼得·贝伦斯 38
Ben & Jerry's 本杰里 64
benefits of branding 品牌创建的好处
  101—103, 105—107
Benetton 贝纳通集团 91
Berger, John 约翰·伯格 100, 104
Bernays, Edward 爱德华·伯奈斯 35,
  71
Bernbach, Bill 比尔·伯恩巴克 36
Bettys teashops 贝蒂斯茶室 6—7
Bezos, Jeff 杰夫·贝索斯 20, 88
BG 英国天然气集团 109
big data 大数据 69—70, 72
big ideas approach 大创意方法 118—119
BlaBlaCar 法国拼车公司 "巴拉巴拉
  汽车" 106
Black Lives Matter movement "黑人
  的命也是命" 运动 109
BMW 宝马公司 118
Boeing 波音公司 42
Boston Consulting Group (BCG) 波
  士顿咨询公司 77
boycotts 抵制 105
BP 英国石油公司 21, 60—61
brain science 脑科学 49—50
brand 品牌

v. branding（动词）品牌创建 22—23
definition 定义 15—22
meanings 意义 3—6, 27—29
v. products 产品 16—17
as 'signified' "所指" 3
brand assets, social 品牌资产，社会
  的 58
brand associations 品牌联想 55
brand awareness 品牌意识 55
brand communities 品牌社团 52
brand consulting 品牌顾问 118
brand-driven innovation 品牌驱动创
  新 89
brand equity 品牌财产价值 54—56
brand identity 品牌身份（特征）
  72—73
  distinctive features as 作为显著特
    征 21
brand leadership 品牌领导力 66—67
brand-led philosophy 品牌引领的价
  值体系 66—67
brand loyalty 品牌忠诚（度）51—55
brand management 品牌管理 63—72
brand names, misleading 品牌名称，
  误导 99
brand orientation 品牌定位 66
brand strategy 品牌战略 85—86
branded house model "品牌化组合"
  模式 87
branding 品牌创建
  v. brand 品牌 22—23
  definition 定义 23—26
branding projects 品牌创建计划
  82—88

BrandZ "布朗兹"全球品牌排行榜 62
Braun 博朗公司 64
British Library 大英图书馆 7
British Museum 大英博物馆 29
Burberry 博柏利 21, 59, 71

# C

Cadbury 卡德伯雷 64
Cadbury, George 乔治·卡德伯雷 27—29
Cafédirect 咖啡直达 109
Campbell's 坎贝尔 33
Carlsberg 嘉士伯 94
Change.org 改革网站 23
changing brands, constant 不断改变的品牌 70
Chapman brothers 查普曼兄弟 10
*Charlie Hebdo*《查理周刊》111
China Mobile 中国移动 109
citadels and constellations 城堡和群星荟萃 110—111
cities 城市 11
client services 客服 74—75
Clifton, Rita 丽塔·克利夫顿 18
clothing labels 服装标签 43
Co-op 英国零售商"合作社" 22—23
Coca-Cola 可口可乐 3—6, 10, 12, 20, 33, 35—36, 50, 87, 121
Coca-Cola Company 可口可乐公司 64
collaborative consumers 合作消费者 113
colour in branding 品牌创建中的颜色 33
commercial branding 商业品牌创建 41
commercialization 商业化 104—105
commitment to brands 对品牌的忠诚 51—55
companies, ownership 公司,拥有关系 64—65, 111
company culture 公司文化 92—93
comparison sites 对比网站 117
computational aesthetics 计算美学 69
connections between products and ideas 产品和思想之间的联系 3—6, 27—29, 34—35
consistency 一致性 24—25
*consommacteurs* 消费者演员 113—115
constellations and citadels 群星荟萃和城堡 110—111
consultants 顾问 75
consumer neuroscience 消费者脑科学 49—50, 69
consumers 消费者
　boycotts 抵制 105
　brand communities 品牌社团 52
　choices 选择 45—46
　collaborative 合作(的) 113
　data on 消费者数据 112—113
　deception of 欺骗 99—100
　experiences 体验 89—90
　impressions on 对消费者的印象 68
　influence on behavior 对行为的影响 50—52
　inspiring innovation 鼓舞人心的创新 89

索引

137

opinion of branding 对品牌创建的观点
as owners of brands 作为品牌的拥有者 115—117
as producers 作为生产者 39—41
surveying 调查 61, 71—72
unconscious thinking 无意识的思考 48—49
contagion 感染 48—49
content marketing 内容市场营销 91
conventional meanings 常规意义 24
conventions, breaking 常规,打破 89
COOK 英国食品公司"库克" 109
copywriters 广告撰写人 76
corporate brands 企业品牌 37—39
corporate identity 企业身份 38—39, 72
countries 国家 11
Crabtree and Evelyn 瑰珀翠公司 99
creative designers 创造性设计师 76
creep factor 惊悚因素 70
critics of branding 品牌创建评论家（批评家）9—10
cultural branding 文化品牌创建 41
culture as brand 文化作为品牌 92—93

## D

data on consumers 消费者数据 112—113
De Beers 戴比尔斯公司 35
debranding 反品牌创建 110
deception of consumers 对消费者的欺骗 99—100
design 设计 93—95
designer labels 设计师（者）标签 42—43

digital agencies 数字机构 72—73
Disney 迪士尼 5
dissatisfaction 不满意 104
distinctive features 显著特征 21, 94
  见 logos
distribution 分销 89
Dove 德芙 64
*Downton Abbey*《唐顿庄园》48
Doyle Dane Bernbach 恒美广告公司 36
Dyson 戴森 67

## E

earned media 口碑媒体 90—91
Eastern brands 东方的品牌 120—121
eBay 亿贝 23, 39, 111, 113, 115
*Economist, The*《经济学人》杂志 21
education sector 教育部门 11
Ellis, Bret Easton 布莱特·伊斯顿·艾利斯 9
Emirates 阿联酋航空 88, 121
employees 员工、雇员 56—57, 68—69
  benefits of branding 品牌创建的好处 102
  in branding projects 品牌创建计划中 83—84
  company culture 公司文化 92—93
  happiness 幸福 34
  negative effects of branding 品牌创建的负面影响 104
  training 培训 93
endorsements 认可、批准 88
ethics of branding 品牌创建伦理

97—107

Etsy 易集 26, 109

experience 体验 119

experience design 体验设计 89—90

EY 安永会计师事务所 42, 53

## F

failure of brands 品牌的失败 58—60

Fairtrade 公平交易 97—98, 105

familiarity 熟悉 25

fans of brands 品牌粉丝（拥趸）52—53

fashion labels 时尚标签 43

feelings 感受 55

Ford 福特公司 69—70

formulas 公式（准则）120—121

franchising 特许经营（权）65

Friedman, Thomas 托马斯·弗里德曼 118

future of branding 品牌创建的未来 108—122

## G

Gallup 盖洛普 71

Galvani 加尔瓦尼 111

General Electric (GE) 通用电气公司 18, 56

geographical branding 地理品牌创建 11

gestures 姿势 94

Girl Effect 女孩效应 106—107

GlaxoSmithKline 葛兰素史克公司 111

global branding 全球品牌创建 6, 110

global management consultancies 全球管理顾问（咨询）77

*Good Wife, The*《傲骨贤妻》51

Google 谷歌公司 10, 14, 57, 62, 78, 92, 110—111, 120

GoPro 运动相机公司 91

Green and Black's "绿与黑"（有机巧克力）49

Gvasalia, Demna 丹姆纳·瓦萨利亚 43

## H

Häagen-Dazs 哈根达斯 99

habitual users 习惯性用户 53—54

habituation 习惯性 48—49

*Harvard Business Review*《哈佛商业评论》36

hashtags 推特话题 111

Havas Media 汉威士传媒 7, 62

healthcare sector 卫生部门 11

Heinz 亨氏公司 109

heraldry 纹章术 30—31

history of branding 品牌创建的历史 27—44

last thirty years 过去三十年 10—12

holacracy 无主管公司 120

homogeneity 同一性 103

Hoover 胡佛 59

house of brands model 品牌组合模式 87

Hseih, Tony 谢家华

Huawei 华为 59, 109, 120

索引

139

## I

IBM 美国国际商用机器公司 38, 41
ideas, connections with products 概念，与产品相关联 3—6, 27—29, 34—35
identification with brands 与品牌相一致 6, 8, 11—13, 47—48, 107
identity 身份
　　corporate 企业（身份）38—39, 72, 118
　　distinctive features as 身份的显著特征 21
　　v. image（动词）形象 19, 23
IDEO 产品设计公司"艾迪欧" 72—73
IKEA 宜家公司 17—18, 25—26, 86, 109
IKEA effect 宜家效应 48
image v. identity 形象与身份 19, 23
imagery 意象、形象 55
incentive economy 激励经济 106
IndiGo 靛蓝航空公司 60, 121
ingredient brands 成分品牌 87
Innocent Drinks "挚纯饮料" 64, 67, 94
Instagram 照片墙 111
Intel 英特尔 41, 42
internet 互联网
　　active contributors 积极贡献者 113—115
　　comparison and review websites 对比与评论网站 117
　　consumers as producers 作为生产者的消费者 39—41
Interpublic 埃培智集团 73—74
*Interstellar* (2014 film) 电影《星际穿越》(2014) 10

## J

J. Walter Thomson J. 沃尔特-汤姆森广告公司 71, 73
Jacobs, Kenny 肯尼·雅各布斯 80, 83—84, 86
Jobs, Steve 史蒂夫·乔布斯 70
John Lewis 约翰-路易斯 33—34, 60, 109
judgements 判断 55
Jumia 尼日利亚电子商务公司"朱利亚" 120

## K

Kahneman, Daniel 丹尼尔·卡内曼 48
Kalin, Robert 罗伯特·卡林 26
Keller, Kevin Lane 凯文·莱恩·凯勒 19, 24, 54—55
Kellogg's 家乐氏 33, 64
Kempinski 凯宾斯基酒店集团 94
Kenco 肯可（亿滋国际下属公司）64
Kenya, advertisement for Coca-Cola 肯尼亚，可口可乐广告 3—4, 12
Kickstarter 众筹公司"脚踏启动器" 113
Klein, Naomi 娜奥米·克莱恩 100
Komatsu 小松集团 84
Kornberger, Martin 马丁·科恩伯格 16, 19
Kraft "卡夫"食品公司 109

## L

Landor 朗涛设计顾问公司 72

Lane, Allen 艾伦·莱恩 101
language of brands 品牌语言 94
*LazyTown*《慵懒镇》(冰岛的一档电视节目) 94
Leahy, Terry 特里·莱希 101
LeEco 乐视 120
LEGO 乐高 60, 89
licensing 许可证(许可) 65
Lidl 历德(德国超市连锁企业) 49, 87
Liftshare 英国的拼车公司"搭车族" 106
logos 标识语符号、标识 21—22
　Airbnb 爱彼迎 116
　changing 变化的 23, 120
　improving 改善 111
　as 'signifiers' 作为"能指" 3, 9
London Transport 伦敦公交公司 38
London Underground 伦敦地铁 21
Lowenbrau "黑狮"啤酒 31
Lufthansa 汉莎航空 114
luxury branding 奢侈品品牌创建 42—43

# M

McDonald's 麦当劳 21, 24, 65—66, 93
McElroy, Neil 尼尔·麦克罗伊 63
McFadden, Cyra 希拉·麦克法登 9
McKinsey 麦肯锡公司 77
Mahindra 印度联合企业"马恒达" 102
Maison Margiela 马吉拉之家 43
Mandarin Oriental 文华东方酒店集团 120
Manet, Edouard 艾德华·马奈 9

market economics 市场经济学 11
market research 市场研究 71—72
marketing methods beyond advertising 广告之外的市场营销方法 90—92
　as sub-set of branding 品牌创建的子集 66
　见 advertising
Marks & Spencer 英国玛莎百货商店 99
Mars 玛氏公司 64
materialism 物质主义 11—12
Mattel 美泰公司 66
Maverick, Samuel 塞缪尔·马弗里克 31
MAYA (most advanced yet acceptable) "玛雅"(即"最先进超前但仍可接受的") 24
measuring brands 衡量品牌 61—62
media agencies 媒体机构(公司) 73
Meliá 西班牙美利亚酒店集团 94
memes 谜米 111
mergers 合并 109
Method 方法 106
Michelin 米其林 21
Microsoft 微软 118—119
Millward Brown 米尔沃德·布朗 8
Mindshare 传立媒体 73
MINI "迷你"(汽车) 21
Mirvis, Phil 菲尔·米尔维斯 110
mission 使命 84
MIT Media Lab 麻省理工学院媒体实验室 120
Moleskine 魔力斯奇那 59
Mondelez International 亿滋国际 64

Mondragon 蒙德拉贡联合公司 109
monopolies 垄断寡头 103
motivational research 动机研究 99—100
movements 运动 109
Muji 无印良品 79, 120
Museum of Brands, London 品牌博物馆，伦敦 8
museums 博物馆 11

## N

negative effects of branding 品牌创建的负面影响 103—105
Nescafé 雀巢咖啡 20
net promoter score 净推荐值 61
Neumeier, Marty 马蒂·纽梅尔 20—21, 115
News of the World《世界新闻报》58
ngram viewer 谷歌的"ngram 浏览器" 10
Nike 耐克 21, 106
Nokia 诺基亚 59
nostalgia associated with brands 与品牌有关的怀旧 8—9
Nurofen 诺洛芬 54

## O

Ogilvy, David 大卫·奥格威 18, 36, 73, 118
Olins, Wally 沃利·奥林斯 118
Oliver, Jamie 杰米·奥利弗 41
OMD"浩腾"媒体 73
Omnicom 奥姆尼康 73—74

Orange 手机品牌"橘子" 86
organizational branding 公司品牌创建 41
organizations 公司
　　culture as brand 作为品牌的文化 92—93
　　types 类型 109—110
owned media 自有媒体 90
ownership, marking 拥有关系，标记 29—32
Oxfam 牛津饥荒救济委员会 51

## P

P2P (peer-to-peer) brands 对等（或缩写为 P2P）品牌 40
Packard, Vance 万斯·帕卡德 99—100
paid media 付费媒体 90
Pampers 帮宝适公司 91
PanAm 泛美航空 37
Panasonic 松下公司 87
Patagonia 户外品牌公司"巴塔哥尼亚" 109
Pears Soap 梨牌香皂 33
Penguin Books 企鹅出版社 101
Pepsi 百事可乐 50
performance 性能 55
personality of the brand 品牌特性 36, 47—48, 86
personalized advertising 个人化广告 70
personas 人物角色 89—90
platform brands 平台品牌 115—117
Polaroid 宝丽来 59
Porsche 保时捷 49—50

portfolio 组合 86—88
positioning 定位 86
powerbrands 强力品牌 110
PR companies 公关公司 71
pricing 定价 88—89
Primark 爱尔兰服装零售商"普利马克" 102—103
Pringles 品客 64
Procter & Gamble 宝洁公司 63—64, 66, 87
products 产品
    v. brands（产品）与品牌 16—17
    connections with bigger ideas 与更大的思想相关 3—6, 27—29, 34—35
    importance of good service 良好服务的重要性 88—89
project managers 项目经理 75
promises of brands 品牌的承诺 60—61
proposition 命题、主张 35—36, 46—47, 86
prosumers 产消合一者 39—41
psychoanalysis 心理分析 35
Publicis 阳狮集团 73—74
purpose 目标 68
purpose statements 目标阐述 84—85
PwC 普华永道会计师事务所 42, 65

# Q

quality of products, branding as a mark of 产品质量，作为标记的品牌创建 32—33, 102

# R

Ratner, Gerald 杰拉德·拉特纳 55—56

rebranding 品牌重建 22, 80—84
Red Bull 红牛 91
Reed, Richard 理查德·里德 67
registered trademarks 注册商标 33
reputation 信誉 20
resonance 反响 55
Roman empire 罗马帝国 30
Ronseal 木材着色料品牌"朗秀" 33
Roy Street Coffee and Tea 罗伊大街咖啡茶品店 110
Ryanair 瑞安航空公司 19—20, 67, 80—84, 93

# S

Sabanci 萨班哲保险公司 88
salience 显著卓越 55
Samsung 三星公司 19—20
satire 讽刺 9—10
Schmidt, Eric 埃里克·施密特 57
scientific data 科学数据 69—70
Searls, Doc 多克·希尔斯 117
Seren 服务设计公司"塞伦" 77
service brands 服务品牌 37
service-dominant logic 服务主导逻辑 114
Sharp, Byron 拜伦·夏普 53, 91
Shell 壳牌石油公司 91—92, 109
Shillum, Marc 马克·席勒姆 120
Siegel+Gale 思睿高品牌战略咨询公司 77
signified and signifiers 所指与能指 3—4, 9
    见 logos

索引

143

Silicon Valley 硅谷 115
Simonson, Itamar and Emanuel Rosen 伊塔马尔·西蒙森和伊曼纽尔·罗森 117
simplicity of branding 品牌创建的简单化 60
Singapore Airlines 新加坡航空公司 21
slogans 标语 21, 33, 35, 118—119
　'Intel inside' 内置英特尔芯片 42
　reverse psychology 反常心理学 36—37
small business branding 小公司品牌创建 6—7
smells 气味 21, 94
social change 社会变化 105—107
social media 社交媒体 13, 51, 111
social responsibility 社会责任 107
social value 社会价值 58
Sole Rebels 索拉瑞宝 120
Solidaridad 禾众基金会 97
Sommerville, Lorna 洛娜·索姆维尔 5
Sony 索尼（公司）46—48
Sorrell, Martin 马丁·索罗 73—74
sounds 听起来 94
Southwest Airlines 西南航空公司（美国）38, 60
Spotify 声田 20, 51
stakeholder management 利益相关者管理 91—92
Star Alliance 星空联盟 88
Starbucks 星巴克 24, 110, 120
Stella Artois "时代"啤酒 31
success of brands 成功品牌 58—61

Superdry 极度干燥 96, 99
surveys 调查
　of consumers 消费者 61
　market research 市场研究 71—72
sustainability 可持续性 104, 106—107
symbols 符号 21
conventions 习俗惯例 24
system 1 thinking 系统1思维 48—49

# T

Target 目标 33
Tate galleries 泰特美术馆 24
tattoos 纹身 31
technologists 技术专家（技师）76
technology start-ups 技术创业 119—120
TED 会议组织公司 TED 112
Teflon 特氟龙 60
Tesco 英国乐购超市公司 85, 101—102
Thai Airways 泰国航空公司 88
Toffler, Alvin 阿尔文·托夫勒 39
TOMS 汤姆斯公司 60
touchpoints 接触点 95
Toyota 丰田 51—52, 93
training 培训
trends in brand design 品牌设计潮流（趋势）95
Tripadvisor "猫途鹰"旅游网站 114
troubleshooting 问题解决 88
Twitter 推特 51
Tylenol 泰诺 59
typefaces 字体 21, 33

## U

Uber 优步 113, 115, 116
Unilever 联合利华公司 23, 64, 105, 107
Uniqlo 优衣库 50
unique selling propositions (USPs)
　独特销售主张 35—36, 60
user interface design 用户界面设计 95

## V

value 价值
　of a brand 一个品牌 54—56, 62
　of branding 品牌创建 7—8
　social 社会 58
Verizon 美国电信公司"威瑞森" 111
Vetements 唯特萌 43
Virgin 维珍集团 38—39, 65, 93
Virgin Atlantic 维珍大西洋航空公司 89
vision 愿景 84
Vodafone 沃达丰 93
Volkswagen Beetle 大众公司"甲壳虫"汽车 36—37
Volvo 沃尔沃 5

## W

Waitrose 维特罗斯超市 53
Walmart 沃尔玛 107
Warby Parker 网上眼镜零售商"沃比帕克" 60
Warhol, Andy 安迪·沃霍尔 10
Watson, John B. 行为学派奠基人约翰·B.沃森 71
WeChat 微信 95
Wedgwood, Josiah 乔西亚·韦奇伍德 32
Wheaties 威蒂斯麦片 35
Whole Foods Market 全食超市 19—20
Wikipedia 维基百科 15, 21, 106
Wilde, Oscar 奥斯卡·王尔德 104
Willshire, John 约翰·威尔夏 115
WPP WPP传媒集团 73—74

## Y

Y&R's BrandAsset Valuator 扬罗必凯广告公司的"品牌资产标量" 61
Yahoo 雅虎 111
YouTube 优兔 39

## Z

Zappos 在线售鞋零售商"美捷步" 92
Zara 飒拉 55
Zipcar 链车 106, 111, 113

索引

145

Robert Jones

# BRANDING

A Very Short Introduction

*For Brian Boylan, friend and mentor*

# Contents

Thank you  i

List of illustrations  iii

Introduction  1

1  The triumph of branding  3
2  What is 'branding'?  15
3  The history of branding  27
4  How branding works  45
5  The branding business  63
6  Branding projects  80
7  The ethics of branding  97
8  A future for branding?  108

References  123

Further reading  127

# Thank you

I'd like to thank Mary Jo Hatch, who got this book off the ground by introducing me to its excellent editor, Andrea Keegan. Ije Nwokorie and Sairah Ashman at Wolff Olins have given me the time and space to write this book. Many people have helped along the way, including Val Allam, Hans Arnold, Deborah Cadbury, Hope Cooke, Anthony Galvin, Dan Gavshon-Brady, Tilde Heding, Kenny Jacobs, Nathan Jarvis, Peter McKenna, Chris Mitchell, Chris Moody, Jenny Nugée, and Jane Scruton. Craig Mawdsley gave me some particularly thoughtful feedback. My clients have expanded my ideas and horizons: Luqman Arnold, Dawn Austwick, Sally Cowdry, Michael Day, Stephen Deuchar, Cathy Ferrier, Danny Homan, Antony Jenkins, Stuart Lipton, Michelle McEttrick, Steve Morriss, Simon Nelson, Stephen Page, Farah Ramzan Golant, Fiona Reynolds, Chris Saul, Magnus Scheving, Nick Serota, David Souden, and James Tipple. My colleagues at the University of East Anglia have opened my eyes to many new angles on branding: in particular, I'd like to thank James Cornford, Paul Dobson, Nichola Johnson, Rose Kemmy, Ken Le Meunier-FitzHugh, Peter Schmidt-Hansen, and Nikos Tzokas. My students have constantly made me think. Brian Boylan has been my mentor for twenty years, and gave me his usual pin-sharp feedback. And my partner Neil McKenna has been generous as always, with warm encouragement and wise advice.

# List of illustrations

1. Branding at work: a poster in Malindi, Kenya, that suggests that Coca-Cola is not just a drink, but also a part of Africa's future **4**
   Photo by Dan Gavshon-Brady

2. Shopping at IKEA: an experience from which customers form their impression of the IKEA brand, including quality and price, but also design and lifestyle **18**
   Bloomberg/Getty Images

3. A brand pioneer: a Cadbury poster from 1888 that sells cocoa through the imagery of purity **28**
   Private Collection/© Look and Learn/Illustrated Papers Collection/Bridgeman Images

4. Getting people to buy: Sony's branding changes how people think and feel about its products—and also leads them to buy, and to keep buying **47**
   Helen Sessions/Alamy Stock Photo

5. Inside the brand business: ideas are developed jointly by clients and consultants in creative sessions, like this workshop at the brand consultancy Wolff Olins **75**
   Photo by Carl Baldwin

6. Rebranding that worked: Ryanair's project meant big improvements in customer service, summarized by this slogan—and led to a rise in the airline's profitability **81**
   Photo by Robert Jones

7. Social change: the Fairtrade brand encourages people to choose products that benefit their producers, rather than exploiting them **98**
   Ashley Cooper/Alamy Stock Photo

8. A shared brand: the Airbnb logo is called 'bélo', and it's designed for Airbnb hosts to adopt and adapt, making it their own **116**
   Airbnb

# Introduction

Every day, we're exposed to thousands of brand messages, whether we like it or not. The rise of brands has been phenomenal and unstoppable. Today, branding shapes and defines our world at every level, from the trivial to the profound.

Branding has been claimed as a science, as an art, and even as a dark corporate conspiracy. It's been studied by economists, marketers, designers, organizational specialists, psychologists, philosophers, social theorists, and cultural critics. Yet very few of these experts agree on what branding is, and how it works. It's important and exciting, but also amorphous, elusive, and ill-defined.

So this book aims to give you a quick guided tour. It suggests some straightforward answers to the big questions. What exactly is a brand? How did branding grow and spread? How do brands work on us? Who are the people behind the brands, and what do they do? Does branding guide us or enslave us? And where will branding go next?

Branding, as I hope to show, is more than it might appear. It's more than just an aspect of marketing: it's a broader activity, affecting most of the things an organization does. Following from that, its impact is not just on consumers: it's just as important as a force that guides and energizes employees. And, finally, branding has more than just a commercial impact. It's also a powerful social, cultural, and—in the widest sense—political force.

This Introduction is based not on textbooks, but on my twenty-five years' experience as a brand consultant. It's not the final word on branding—there never will be a final word—but I hope it will open your eyes to the extraordinary phenomenon of branding, and reveal a little about the work that goes on behind the scenes to shape the brands that surround us.

# Chapter 1
# The triumph of branding

In Malindi, Kenya, you'll find a poster painted on a bright red fence, showing a silhouette of a Coca-Cola bottle, and the slogan 'A billion reasons to believe in Africa'.

What it says is not that Coca-Cola will quench your thirst, but that Coca-Cola is somehow part of the optimism and growth of Africa. It suggests there are 'A billion reasons to believe in Africa'—which is presumably the billion people who live on that continent.

This African poster (see Figure 1) makes a fascinating snapshot of the strange phenomenon called branding. It shows, of course, that branding is everywhere, on every continent, urban and rural, rich and poor. And it shows how, in our globalized world, branding often tries to belong to a particular place too: this poster is aiming to make Coca-Cola feel distinctively African.

It shows that branding depends on signs—images that embody meaning. Brands are meanings ('signified'), recognizable through symbols such as logos ('signifiers'). And though it's part of a campaign launched back in 2012, the poster is painted, permanently, on a corrugated metal fence. Branding is not always ephemeral.

Though branding set out initially to sell consumer products, it often does more than that. It connects products with bigger ideas:

Branding

1. Branding at work: a poster in Malindi, Kenya, that suggests that Coca-Cola is not just a drink, but also a part of Africa's future.

sugary drinks, in this case, are connected with human progress. When you stop and think about it, this is a thought process that's bizarre, and almost magical. Coca-Cola's Global Brand Director Lorna Sommerville explains: 'When an idea taps into a fundamental human truth, there are no borders or boundaries to how far it can go'. Sometimes branding taps into 'truths': more often, perhaps, into universal hopes and aspirations.

So a brand is much more than just the name of a product. Around the world, mundane commercial products are plugging into bigger ideas, to make people feel good about the products, and to buy more of them. Every piece of branding hopes to get you to believe something. Branding aims to give us all 'billions of reasons to believe'.

Brands have been around for centuries, but the idea has become central to our lives since the 1980s. In the last thirty years or so, branding has become pervasive, reaching into even the poorest parts of the planet. In fact, it has become a defining characteristic of the modern world. How and why has this happened?

## A larger idea

Branding connects ordinary things with a larger idea. This larger idea has the power to change what people do: in particular, to buy more and pay more. Coca-Cola is just flavoured, sugared water. It's the brand that makes it possible to charge good money for it, and that therefore makes money for the company. Disney's larger idea is 'family fun'; Volvo's is 'safety'. That is the essence of branding.

It's a technique used by the owners—the Coca-Cola Company, for example—to create meanings that make us feel good about the product, so that we'll buy it. Coca-Cola invests in communication that connects its product with ideas of progress, optimism, and happiness. When this communication works, these meanings form the Coca-Cola brand. And in the end people buy more Coca-Cola. Branding changes how people think, feel—and act.

But it's also a method used by consumers to help make sense of the plethora of products in the world. Surrounded by thousands of choices, people assign them meanings, so that they can mentally file them and strengthen their sense of their own identity. We might, for instance, associate Coca-Cola with energy, perhaps with memories of childhood, and many of us define ourselves as Coca-Cola people, as opposed to (for instance) Pepsi people. Branding is a game kicked off by the big corporations—but it's a game where almost everyone joins in. The ideal, for the corporation, is when the ideas in our minds match the ones they try to project.

The Coca-Cola poster is one example of a phenomenon that, in the last couple of decades, has become pervasive. Branding started with products like Coca-Cola. Then it moved into services—for example, banks like Wells Fargo, or retailers like Carrefour, or airlines like Emirates. Next, it reached corporations, like Cisco or Unilever or LG Group. More recently, branding has expanded its reach into books, films, and television series. *Harry Potter*, Beyoncé, *Star Wars*, and *Game of Thrones* all are more than books, singers, films, or shows: they're big global brands. Whole genres can become a brand, like Bollywood. And over the last twenty years, a batch of huge online brands has come to dominate the world, from Alibaba and Amazon to Instagram and Uber.

Though branding started in the West, it has spread across the world. Global brands, as we've seen, try to establish a local resonance. Home-grown brands mimic the attributes of the global mega-brands, with shiny logos, catchy slogans, and glossy packaging.

Branding has spread into small businesses too. There's a small chain of teashops in the north of England, called Bettys, that's a model of branding: it uses its Swiss/Yorkshire heritage to add ideas of precision, daintiness, and warmth to the ordinary business of food and drink. As city districts get gentrified, even small shops get sophisticated design work done, and aspire to become brands. Every online start-up has an element of branding behind it. And everywhere we go, we see branding in action. I'm writing this in the British Library, in a space called not 'The Newspaper Archive' but, more excitingly, 'Newsroom'. This too is branding.

## The greatest commercial invention?

Branding is, of course, good at getting people to buy things. Brands play a role in many of our day-to-day buying decisions—both big decisions, like choosing an Apple tablet, or small ones, like believing my cat prefers a brand of cat litter called Thomas. Brands add excitement to, and reduce the anxiety in, shopping.

There are limits, though, to the power of branding. Many products actually have very little additional meaning. When we buy a pencil, or fill up with petrol, or take out an insurance policy, the brand we choose may well have no deep associations in our minds. One study showed that, though 80 per cent of marketing directors believe their products are 'differentiated', or have some distinctive meaning in consumers' minds, only 10 per cent of consumers would agree. For most products, most of the time, most people simply don't have time to care. Each of us has the mental space for only a few brands. For me, these might be Apple, the BBC, and the retailer Waitrose, but very few more. Underlining that, a study by the media agency Havas Media suggests that most people wouldn't care if 74 per cent of brands disappeared. People buy brands, and they buy into branding, but they like to be sceptical too. We find fanciful television advertising absurd: in fact, we probably fast-forward through it. We pride ourselves on seeing through companies' branding activities.

And yet brands are the primary source of value for many companies. When you look at the value of a typical business, you find that some of it comes from its buildings, equipment, and stock—its tangible assets—but a lot too from intangible assets, like customer goodwill, or patents, or its brand. In fact, the global market research consultancy Millward Brown reckons that brand accounts for more than 30 per cent of the stockmarket value of America's biggest companies, and we'll see why in Chapter 4. For some kinds of company, brand is less important: it matters relatively little to, say, an office cleaning business. But for others, such as luxury goods companies, it's worth up to 90 per cent of their value. Overall, around a third of all the corporate value in the world comes from branding. By any standards, this makes branding one of the most effective commercial inventions of all time.

## The most potent cultural form?

As we've seen, most people are aware of the phenomenon of branding. They discuss it, interpret it, and critique it. As well as an effective commercial technique, branding is also part of our shared culture.

Brands are a social reference point, something we all have in common. When my students meet each other for the first time each September, they bond within hours, at least in part because they have brands in common—whether it's Evian or Beats or Louis Vuitton, it's recognizable and means roughly the same thing everywhere, and people define themselves (and others) by the brands they like. There's even a board game, the Logo Game, where players compete on their knowledge of branding.

Brands are also one of the devices we use to remember the past. This comes across particularly strongly at the Museum of Brands in London, where visitors walk through a time tunnel of packaging and advertising, from about 1890 onwards. As they get closer to the present day, the overwhelming response is of nostalgia: the most common reaction among visitors is 'ah, I remember that'. Brands give an instant short-cut. For me, the

*Thunderbirds* brand takes me to the 1960s, Doc Martens to the 1970s, Audi to the 1980s, and so on.

Brand thinking pervades so much of our life. Brands have helped us sensitize ourselves to the interplay of signifier and signified. Signifiers—what things are called, and what they look like—really matter. Political correctness is an example of branding: carefully re-labelling things in order to shift how people think and feel about them. In one way, the liberal consensus is that labels shouldn't matter; in another way, they inevitably do.

Brands are frequently used or exploited by artists and writers. Indeed, there's an affinity between branding and art, as two parallel methods for making meaning. Edouard Manet's last major work was 'A Bar at the Folies-Bergère', an 1882 painting of a disaffected barmaid, one of those whom Guy de Maupassant described as 'vendors of drink and of love'. At the bottom right of the painting is a bottle of Bass beer, whose logo was the very first trademark to be legally registered, only five years before in 1877. Manet made an image that's interpreted by an audience to create meaning—and he included the Bass logo, which does exactly the same thing.

Many see brands as a negative force in culture. There's a Canadian group of anti-consumerists called Adbusters who describe themselves as 'artists, activists, writers, pranksters, students, educators and entrepreneurs'. Adbusters create powerful parodies of brand advertising, which they call 'subvertisements'. They use the techniques of branding to attack branding, and Adbusters has become a brand in its own right.

Perhaps the most powerful critics have been artists themselves. Brands are a quick way to signal people's status or aspirations, and an easy way to satirize a materialist society—a technique pioneered by Cyra McFadden in *The Serial* in 1977, and adopted by Bret Easton Ellis eight years later in *Less Than Zero*. More recently, artists such as the Chapman brothers have used brand imagery in a more savage critique of consumer culture, and one Chinese artist has painted the Coca-Cola logo onto ancient vases: a gesture that both vandalizes the vase and yet somehow beautifies the logo.

But at the same time, other artists have played along with branding, and see no conflict between commercialism and higher culture. Films lovingly embrace brands as a quick way to communicate information about characters and situations, from James Bond's Aston Martin onwards. And is it an accident that the heroine of the 2014 science fiction film *Interstellar* is called 'Brand', and the implication of the film's ending is that she is the future? Most famously, perhaps, Andy Warhol adopted the imagery of branding in works like his 1972 piece 'Campbell's Soup Cans'. Warhol was criticized for capitulating to consumerism, but wrote 'Making money is art, and working is art, and good business is the best art'.

## The last thirty years

Branding, then, is a pervasive system of signs, associated with products, services, organizations, cultural products, places, people, even concepts. These signs help give those things additional meanings not inherent in them. It's been around for centuries, as we'll see in Chapter 3, but it's become a central part of culture relatively recently.

Google's 'ngram viewer' is a clever bit of software that counts the occurrences of a given word in all the books that Google has digitized, and shows how the number of occurrences changes over time. The graph for the word 'brand' is flat until 1900, grows slowly until 1940, plateaus, then climbs again from 1980 onwards, accelerating rapidly at the end of the millennium. The academic study of branding, focusing on the concept of 'brand equity', also took off in the 1980s. Why has branding become such a pervasive concept, particularly in the last thirty years?

The triumph of market economics has created a world of global competition, where organizations must use branding to stand out from their rivals. Everywhere is now a market—including, in the last thirty years, China. And these local markets all merge into a global one. Shareholders demand that publicly quoted organizations constantly grow, which means increasing market share, or opening up new markets. Governments need state-owned organizations to hold their own, sometimes competing with foreign rivals in the home or export markets—so they too must play the brand game. Even monopolies are competing for something—to attract funding at the right price, or to attract the best possible employees.

And it's not just companies that are competing. Countries and cities compete to attract tourists, employers, students, and residents. Not-for-profit, sports clubs, political parties, and even religions compete to attract supporters. Branding is currently a hot topic in the world's two biggest industries, healthcare and education: hospitals, universities, and schools are taking their brands very seriously. In all these areas, in the last decade or so, it has become acceptable, and even fashionable, to use the language and techniques of branding. Ten years ago, people in museums, for example, rejected the notion of branding as commercial and reductive. But now, almost all museums readily talk about the importance of their brands. Because the internet is a global medium, all are competing across borders, which means that the same kinds of concepts and techniques rapidly expand everywhere.

This rise in the power of the market, this rise in materialism, has given people an increasing need for meaning in their lives, both as consumers and as employees. Human beings have always needed meaning, a dimension beyond the utilitarian, beyond the mundane things we all have to do from day to day. People need a sense of identity (who am I?) and belonging (where do I fit?). In the past, these meanings came from family, village, religion, nation—but all have been undermined by urbanization, secularization, and globalization. Materialism creates a vacuum of meaning—and then branding tries to fill that vacuum. Consumers need not just 'value for money' but *values* for money'.

In response, a particular kind of branding has become mainstream—seeing brand as not a product but a concept. That Coca-Cola poster in Kenya (Figure 1) is a perfect example. Many companies have become excited by the idea that they can be more than just manufacturers of material products: they can also be purveyors of ideas or even *ideals* that enrich culture and give people new senses of identity. Apple, Virgin, and IKEA are clear examples—all businesses that were either born in, or took off in, the last thirty years.

## Identity and belonging

And, over the same period, consumers have joined in this game. Branding has shifted from something that companies do to us, into a game that most of us join in. Academics, over the same timescale, have shifted from a positivist to a constructivist view of branding—in other words, they see brands as things we all help to construct.

As people have become richer, with more access to more goods, they've started to define themselves partly through seemingly mundane choices: the shoes they wear, the shop where they bought their furniture, the box sets they watch, the companies they admire, or even their favourite sugary drink. They use brands to help construct their identity, their sense of who they are. For good or ill, millions, perhaps even billions, of people—from an African village to a Shanghai penthouse to a mid-west mall—use brands to help form their self-image, or to help define the 'tribe' they want to belong to.

Of course, brands aren't the only option. Clearly, many identify themselves with the charities they support, the sports clubs they follow, the political parties they vote for, the places they visit, or the celebrities they admire. Many people resist branding, and a few are immune. Brands, for them, have none of this glamorous power. And—after a decade of company scandals and financial crashes—there's an increasingly anti-corporate spirit in the world.

Yet for many, particularly younger people, branding has become so pervasive, so *normal*, that it's lost its sting. They find it natural to play the branding game, and also to see branding as more than just a commercial phenomenon. They pick and mix ideas from a whole range of brands—not just Adidas and Apple but also Vimeo and Vice—and use them as components to create senses of identity. They do this through social media, so it's a shared activity, and one where fashions constantly move on, so that their identities morph.

By taking part in the magical activity of branding, people add value to the things around them, they become more than themselves, they acquire meaning—not least because everyone around them is doing it too. Often that meaning sits between me and you. I'm a customer of a British bank called First Direct, and if I see another customer with a First Direct card ahead of me in the checkout queue, I feel an odd sense of affinity. I feel that because we've both chosen the same bank, he or she must be a bit like me.

And in the age of social media, where it's instinctive to share things minute by minute, it's no surprise that brands—an easy token for sharing meaning—have become so central to our lives and our imaginations. Sharing of 'content' has become an almost universal habit. It's now normal to post on Facebook the moment something has happened, or even while it's happening. In this new culture of sharing, it's easy for brands to thrive and grow. And the phenomenon goes further: every time someone posts something on Facebook or Twitter or Instagram, they are nurturing ideas about who they are. Deliberately or not, they are building their own personal brand. In this sense, the world now contains almost two billion brand marketers.

## Both commerce and culture

The modern world is defined by a whole range of phenomena, from social media to climate change, from urbanization to obesity, from mass migration to the cult of celebrity. But one of them—so pervasive that we take it for granted—is branding.

Because the logic of the market is now so ubiquitous, and the need for a shared sense of identity has become so urgent, branding has become a defining characteristic of the modern world.

Through branding, boring things like detergents, everyday things like soft drinks, and intangible things like websites have acquired personalities and meanings, so that people recommend them, feel partisanship, forgive them their failings—all because organizations need to compete, and people need to feel and share meanings.

Branding is now one of the most potent forces, commercial and cultural, on the planet. But what exactly is it? (Box 1)

> **Box 1 Android: no-one's and everyone's**
>
> Android could be the biggest brand on earth, with a billion users and a 90 per cent market share. But it's not a company: it's a brand that's shared by 400 companies. And that's the secret of its success. Google released Android in 2008, as an operating system for mobile devices that would be customizable, accessible, and above all open, and now it's used in phones, tablets, watches, cars, and more. Legally, the brand belongs to Google, and manufacturers buy a licence. But emotionally, the brand belongs to everyone and no-one. And rather than enforcing consistency among all the manufacturers that use it, it encourages variation. Its slogan 'Be together, not the same' captures a lot about current trends in branding.

# Chapter 2
# What is 'branding'?

To define 'branding', we need to start by defining 'brand'. When we talk about 'the Netflix brand' or 'the H&M brand' or 'the Alibaba brand', what do we really mean?

Perhaps a brand is simply a name: 'Netflix' or 'H&M' or 'Alibaba'. But not every trade name is a brand. Think about your local back-street car repair business, for instance. It has a name—'Webster's Autos', or something like that—and locally it might be well-respected. It might have 'a good name', as people say. But we wouldn't naturally call it a brand. We tend to think a brand is deliberately designed in a more sophisticated way than the work of the local sign-painter.

So is it the design that makes the difference? Is a brand a logo, or a particular colour, or perhaps a slogan? The swoosh of Nike, the red of Manchester United, the 'Power of dreams' slogan of Honda? This is how Wikipedia defines 'brand': 'a name, term, design, symbol or other feature that distinguishes one seller's product from those of others'. But this definition doesn't account for the power of brands—if they were just decorative items that we see around us, they'd be much less interesting.

So maybe a brand is more about the product itself? Indeed, it's often very hard to separate 'brand' and 'product' in our minds.

What is it that people love, the Apple product or the Apple brand—or are they the same thing? The Al Jazeera news service is very close to the Al Jazeera brand. But they're not identical. It's possible to like the brand but not the product, or vice versa. My favourite car brand is Audi, but I actually decided to buy a BMW.

## Bigger than a product

Indeed, a brand is somehow bigger than a product. We sometimes see it as the aura around a product, or the ethos beneath a product, or the provenance behind a product. People sometimes use the word 'make' to mean 'brand'—'Aga is a good make of cooker'—meaning not just that it's a good cooker, but also that the company that made it is widely admired. Fans of Apple tell you that they admire the products, but they also admire the vision behind the products—and some worry that, after the death of Steve Jobs, the vision will slowly fade. A contestant on the British version of the reality television show *The Apprentice* called himself 'Stuart Baggs the brand', meaning that he was more than just a person, he was somehow a bigger set of ideas. And clearly, that's what Coca-Cola is trying to do with its poster in Kenya (Figure 1).

So a brand is something extra to a product. The branding expert Martin Kornberger has said that a brand is 'functionality + meaning': that is, the product plus an idea. In his view, the brand is the whole thing—the Toblerone brand is the chocolate bar, plus meanings to do with Switzerland, the Alps, and so on.

Conversely, the marketer Phil Barden suggests that 'brands are frames: they implicitly influence the perceived value of products and product experiences through framing'. On this view, the product is like a picture, and the brand is an additional frame round that picture, giving it context and potency. The chocolate bar is the picture, and the Swissness is a frame that makes the chocolate bar more interesting, memorable, and valuable.

This additional meaning is key to the power of brands. Brands get us to do things, they change behaviour, they create value, and that's because they're not static images on paper, they're dynamic ideas in our minds. A simple way to put this is: a product's brand is what it *stands for*. Webster's Autos doesn't stand for anything, beyond just being a car repair place, so it's not a brand. The Nike swoosh is not what Nike stands for, so it's not a brand either—it's just a signifier of that larger meaning, about challenge and achievement. And Corona is a great product, but its brand stands for something more than the beer, to do with Mexico, the summer, and the beach. The product on its own is not a brand.

## Standing for something

Importantly, 'standing for something' can mean two different things, depending on your perspective.

Looking from inside the organization, it can mean your internal ethos, your identity: the ideas you *want* to stand for. IKEA wants to stand for the idea of 'creating a better everyday life for the many people'. That's its official vision statement, in its wilfully odd English (Figure 2). Most organizations elaborately define their brand, and actively manage it, as we'll see in Chapter 5.

But looking from outside, it can mean your associations, your meanings, your image: the ideas you *actually* stand for in people's minds. If you ask people what's in their heads when they think about IKEA, they will say obvious things like 'furniture', 'kitchens', 'flat pack', and 'store', but also aspects of the shopping experience like 'meatballs', 'day trip', or 'queue', and bigger thoughts like 'design', 'life', or even 'love'. This is the exciting reality of a brand: a cluster of potent ideas in people's minds that influence where they choose to go, and what they choose to buy.

These are two very different angles on 'brand'.

2. Shopping at IKEA: an experience from which customers form their impression of the IKEA brand, including quality and price, but also design and lifestyle.

Practitioners—the people who manage brands and the people who advise them—naturally tend to have an insider view. Some managers take their brand very seriously. General Electric wants to stand for the idea of 'imagination at work', and its CEO, Jeff Immelt, has said: 'For GE, imagination at work is more than a slogan or a tagline. It is a reason for being.' Advertising agencies often see a brand as the big idea that is the fount of all their communication work. The advertising guru David Ogilvy said: 'Unless your advertising contains a big idea, it will pass like a ship in the night'. Specialist branding consultancies see a brand as a set of ideas that should influence not only communication, but everything an organization does. Brand expert Rita Clifton champions it as 'the central organizing principle in successful businesses'. On this view, a brand is a set of ideas inside an organization.

Academics, though, looking analytically at brands as a phenomenon, tend to take the outsider view. Business school academics often see a brand as a group of associations in consumers' minds that influence buying behaviour. Of course, there are many variations on this: indeed, there are probably as many theories as there are academics. Across the campus, another breed of academics specializing in cultural studies tend to focus on brands as signs, performing a central role in consumer culture—but again they take an outsider view, and often a highly critical one.

Martin Kornberger's book *Brand Society* neatly links the two views, seeing brands as things that transform both management (the insider view) and lifestyle (the outsider view)—things that link production (insider) with consumption (outsider).

## Defining 'brand'

So a brand is what you stand for internally, and what you stand for externally. The branding academic David Aaker refers to the internal version as 'identity' and the external version as 'image'. 'Brand' means both identity and image. But which view should we take as the primary definition? Which view best captures the power of a brand? Which is the 'real' brand: the identity the company intended, or the image the rest of us see? Whose view is clearer: the practitioner's or the academic's?

Though my background is as a practitioner, I'm struck by the words of the branding academic Kevin Lane Keller: 'The power of a brand lies in what resides in the minds of customers'. So for this book, we're adopting the external view: a brand is primarily the 'ideas and feelings a commercial, organizational or cultural entity stands for in people's minds'.

The Whole Foods Market brand is a cluster of associations in people's minds about quality, healthiness, organics, and premium prices. The Ryanair brand brings ideas in people's minds about low prices, a no-nonsense attitude, and basic levels of service. The Samsung brand is ideas about clever new technology, shiny design, and mid-level pricing. And so on.

Amazon's Jeff Bezos seems to reinforce this view when he describes a brand as 'what people say about you when you're not in the room'. It's a neat definition—and a scary one for practitioners. But it may be that his formula is a definition of 'reputation' rather than 'brand'. The two concepts are very close to each other, but reputation tends to be more a rational, verbal thing, an account of what you've done, when brand is often more emotional, more visual, and a belief about what I'll get from you in the future. It's possible, indeed, for a company to have a bad reputation and a good brand at the same time. Consumers say bad things about it, but keep buying from it. Ironically, Amazon is itself a great example of this phenomenon.

Brand expert Marty Neumeier captures the more emotional side. He defines brand as 'a person's gut feeling about a product, service or organisation'. This raises the question of which person he has in mind, and maybe therefore it's best to conceive of a brand as the combination of everyone's gut feelings. Or, to be more complete, because brands aren't only emotional, the sum total of everyone's thoughts and feelings: in a word, their ideas.

## Not just ideas

But a brand is not just ideas. Brands are founded on material things. The Whole Foods Market, Ryanair, and Samsung brands don't come from nowhere: they're shaped by what those organizations say and do. Our ideas about Nescafé are partly shaped by decades of advertising—by what Nescafé says. Our ideas about Spotify depend on the quality, day by day, of the user experience—by what Spotify does. Coca-Cola isn't just an abstract idea about progress in Africa—it's also a sweet, fizzy drink. Behind the ideas there's the substance.

And the fascinating thing about brands is that they all seem to have a symbol, badge, or label—a distinctive style. Going back to

Wikipedia's definition, brands do have interesting names, terms, designs, symbols, and other features. Every brand has a brand name, and almost every brand has a logo. BP has its green and yellow colours; Burberry, its check pattern; Michelin, its tyre-man; London Underground, its typeface. Nike has its slogan, 'just do it', and *The Economist* has a distinctive writing style. Singapore Airlines even has its own smell. Confusingly, this is often referred to as 'brand identity': in branding, 'identity' can mean both 'what we want to stand for' and 'the symbols we use'. These symbols often appeal directly to the more intuitive or more emotional parts of our minds—to what Neumeier calls our 'gut feeling'.

So for the purposes of this book, a brand is:

- a set of *ideas* and feelings about a product or other entity
- shaped by what that product *says and does*
- and recognized through a distinctive *style*.

For example, the McDonald's brand is a set of ideas about burgers, children, comfort food, 'happy meals', and many other things. It's shaped by our experience over many years of its restaurants and of its advertising. And it's symbolized by devices like the golden arches and the Ronald McDonald character.

The MINI brand, to take another example, is a set of ideas about individuality, clever design, urban driving, and adventure. It's shaped by years of advertising, as well as by the very distinctive small cars with a wheel at each corner—and also by films featuring the cars, like *The Italian Job*. And it's symbolized by the MINI logo and the particular shape of the MINI radiator grille.

This, then, is our working definition—one that starts to explain the power of brands in our minds, and how those ideas lodge themselves in our minds. But however we choose to define 'brand', people actually use the word much more loosely.

Very often, it's used to mean 'a branded product or company'—for example, 'the British Airways brand is struggling against its lower-cost rivals'. Sometimes, it's used to mean just the logo: marketing directors often ask their advertising agencies to 'make our brand bigger on this advert'. And sometimes 'brand' is used to mean the activity of branding. Marketing people say things like 'the goal of the Hyundai brand is to increase market share'.

The truth is that the word is a complex one, useful because its meaning is so fuzzy. The concept, in fact, bridges all sorts of gaps. A brand sits at the interface between the concrete and the abstract: between a product and an idea. It links the internal and the external: the 'identity' a company wants to stand for and the 'image' it actually stands for. It bridges the employee's world of production and the customer's world of consumption. It combines form and function: the logo and the product. And it embraces both commerce and culture.

## Brand and branding

What's the difference between 'brand' and 'branding'? Branding, simply, is the set of things a brand owner does to establish a brand. If a brand is 'what you stand for', branding is a technique through which a company gets its product to stand for something in the minds of millions. 'Branding' is the activity, 'brand' the result: 'branding' is the cause, 'brand' is the effect.

When people talk about branding (or 'rebranding') something, they normally mean trying to impress a new set of ideas into people's minds about it. They might also mean giving it a new style (name, logo, colours, or whatever), as a way of accelerating that change of mind. When the British retailer the Co-op rebranded, it wanted to change how people think and feel about the business—and it signalled that change through a new logo.

In doing this kind of thing, brand managers are trying to close the gap between 'image' and 'identity': to get what their product actually stands for as close as possible to what they want it to stand for. For strong brands like Apple, the gap is small; for weaker brands, it's much wider. Sometimes this means returning to the past: the Co-op chose not to design a new logo but to return to a previous one, aiming to rekindle in consumers' minds old ideas about local convenience, ethical trading, and value-for-money.

All of this, of course, is done to improve the business's commercial performance. Branding aims to get people not just to change their ideas but also to change their behaviour—most obviously, to buy more—and we'll explore this in much more detail in Chapter 4. The branding efforts of eBay are designed to get more and more people to go to eBay for new products—to see it as a retailer, not just an auction site. For not-for-profit organizations, branding might aim for social rather than commercial goals. Change.org, for example, uses its branding to encourage people to join campaigns that change government policy. And more and more commercial organizations aim for social goals too—Unilever is a prime example. Indeed they see social and commercial impact as a virtuous circle—the better citizen you are, the happier consumers will be to buy from you.

So we can start to define branding: shaping what the product or organization says and does, in order to change how people think, feel, and act, in a way that creates commercial (and sometimes also social) value.

## Same and different

Branding, then, starts by changing how people think and feel: it's about creating, or changing, meanings. And this is a delicate task.

To create meaning, you have to start by conforming to convention— to be similar to others—or people won't understand you at all.

Language and symbols work through conventional meanings. An airline needs to look a bit like other airlines. Fashion retailers like New Look, Primark, and Top Shop have surprisingly similar logos. When setting out to brand anything—from a fruit juice to a university—you have to conform to some extent to the conventions of fruit juices or universities, in what you do, what you say, and how you look. Otherwise people won't understand what you are, and they won't trust you.

But you have to be different too, and maybe even break conventions, or you'll fail to say anything new and people won't notice you. And branding tends to push towards difference, towards standing out from the crowd, away from conformity. 'Branding is all about creating differences', as Kevin Lane Keller says. The more different, the greater the risk, but also potentially the higher the reward. When Tate's new branding designs were presented to trustees in 1999, they were resisted: 'That's not what a proper art gallery looks like'. But the designs did get used, got noticed, helped Tate double its visitor numbers, and now seem normal, a new convention. Some branding experts aim for what they call 'MAYA', meaning 'most advanced yet acceptable'.

So brands are in some ways the same as their rivals, and in other ways different. They're also fundamentally the same from one country to another. Consistency matters: otherwise, whenever we travel, our expectations would be confounded and our trust would be broken. But even chains like Starbucks or McDonald's, which appear to be almost identical everywhere, in practice differ to suit local tastes. Hotel chains aim for a reassuring global consistency, but most also encourage local variation. Part of a good global brand's meaning is about familiarity and predictability and reassurance, but part too is about variation and surprise and local colour.

As well as being similar from one place to another, brands mostly stay the same from one year to the next. We rely on continuity:

most brands get their power from familiarity, going back into childhood, like Disney, Heinz, Mars, or Johnson & Johnson. But equally, no brand can stand still. Consumers change, attitudes change, technologies change, and branding must subtly morph too. The speed of change varies: a fashion brand may shift quickly, an infrastructure brand much more slowly. But all branding creates meaning that's partly about permanence and heritage and maturity, partly about dynamism and the future and youthfulness.

The task of branding, then, is a lot to do with deciding just how much to be the same as your competitors, and the same from one country to another, and the same as you were last year—and just how much to be different.

## Making meaning, making value

So branding helps a product or organization to stand for something, and therefore to stand out. For example, IKEA creates advertising carefully designed to suggest a particular lifestyle. It designs products and stores that make design affordable to everyone. It carefully manages its symbols, such as its blue and yellow colours, its logo, and its quirky product names. And all of this helps it to stand for 'a better everyday life for the many people'. This is the height of contemporary global branding.

Branding does all of this for a reason: to change how we act, in ways that create value. Branding creates brands—meanings, ideas in our minds—in order to influence what we do. It gets consumers to buy, and employees to work hard, in order to achieve the commercial goals of profit and growth—and also sometimes social goals like wellbeing and sustainability. IKEA's branding attracts customers, encourages them to visit often and buy more, and supports the growth of IKEA into more and more countries round the world. But it also nudges consumers into greener ways of living, by making low-energy light-bulbs the norm, and by moving towards what it calls the 'circular economy', where customers can not only buy new furniture but also sell back old items for others to re-use.

So branding changes minds in order to create many different kinds of value (Box 2). But its contemporary scope and power, illustrated by the IKEA example, is a recent thing. Over the centuries, branding has changed, grown, and expanded dramatically.

> **Box 2   Etsy: a platform for makers**
>
> Etsy is a platform that helps craftspeople sell their products worldwide—and so to build brands themselves. It was founded in 2005 by Robert Kalin in Brooklyn, NY, as 'an online community where crafters, artists and makers could sell their handmade and vintage goods and craft supplies'. More grandly, Etsy says its mission is 'to reimagine commerce in ways that build a more fulfilling and lasting world'. Etsy now connects 1.6 million active sellers with 26 million active buyers, selling $2.4 billion worth of stuff every year. Like eBay, it's a great example of a platform brand, giving sellers a marketplace on a scale never before possible. Unlike eBay, it plays to another great trend of our times: the desire not just to consume things but also to make them.

# Chapter 3
# The history of branding

It's 1865, and George Cadbury is in the Netherlands inspecting a new machine that makes cocoa. His family has sold tea, coffee, and drinking chocolate in Birmingham since 1824. He's a Quaker by religion, an idealist who wants to give people healthy, non-alcoholic drinks. He's also a businessman who needs to make money, because Quakers who go bankrupt have to leave the sect. Later, at the end of the century, he'll introduce progressive innovations for his workers too—airy factories, holidays, schools, even a whole village, called Bournville.

But back in 1865, he's fascinated by this new Dutch machine, because it solves the great cocoa problem. Cocoa is naturally full of fats, which make for an unpleasant drink. Traditionally, those fats are stripped out using additives, including harmful things like sawdust. But this machine hydraulically presses the cocoa beans, and squashes out much of the fat. For the first time, Cadbury can offer the people of Britain a chocolate drink that really is pure (Figure 3).

And over the succeeding years, Cadbury made not just a product, but also a brand. As early as 1867, he started advertising (which didn't come naturally to plain-living Quakers). He used a bold slogan: 'Absolutely Pure, Therefore Best'. He launched the slogan in an unmissable campaign on London's horse-drawn buses.

3. A brand pioneer: a Cadbury poster from 1888 that sells cocoa through the imagery of purity.

Cadbury promoted not just cocoa but the idea of *purity*. He commissioned advertising that showed children, the symbols of purity. He even launched a campaign for purity in food products. Decades ahead of his time, Cadbury was a natural at branding.

Fast-forward, and his company introduced Dairy Milk, its first big product brand, in 1905—and that was another imaginative leap, characteristic of branding, to link chocolate with the imagery of the dairy. Through the 20th century, Cadbury became one of the great confectionery brands, and in the 21st, it was snapped up by a conglomerate called Mondelez International.

George Cadbury helped make branding what it is today. Through huge commercial imagination, he found a new way to do the extraordinary thing that branding does—to associate an ordinary product with a larger idea, partly through what the product does, partly through what it says in its advertising, and partly through the distinctive visual style of its packaging and posters.

But, though he was a founding father of modern branding, the story goes back years, indeed centuries, before him. Cadbury's brilliant strategy was just one of a series of extraordinary creative leaps, as people have discovered new, bigger, bolder ways of using the techniques of branding. In fact, over the years, there have been five different versions of branding. The first dates back to the dawn of civilization.

## Marking ownership

In the galleries of the British Museum, there's a rather delicate bronze object, found in Egypt, perhaps from near Thebes. It's not much bigger than a pen, but instead of a nib, it has a flat disk, made in a complex abstract pattern. It's 3,500 years old.

Ancient Egyptians heated up objects like this in a fire, until they were red-hot, and then used them to burn a mark on their cattle. Everyone had their own mark, and the branded sign proclaimed ownership. This particular iron has a lioness symbol, signifying that these cows belong to a temple of the goddess Sekhmet.

Branding began with fire—and the word comes from a Viking word, *brandr*, meaning 'to burn'. The link between 'brand' and 'fire' is interesting. Like fire, branding has always included a sense of excitement, of danger even, but also of warmth and comfort. You could think of the power of modern branding as the way it burns ideas into our minds. And we still talk about 'brand new', meaning straight from the fire, a phrase so familiar that our sense of 'brand' is closely connected with the idea of novelty and newness. So brands, particularly the newest, are described as 'hot'—though at the same time, oddly enough, they're also referred to as 'cool'.

Back in ancient Egypt, the branding of cattle was a clear example of branding as we see it now: using signs to give an object (a cow) deeper meaning (its ownership), in order to change people's behaviour (not stealing it) in order to create value. When invented, this practice involved a remarkable invention—making a little mark convey a big meaning—though of course it now feels completely natural. It's the earliest form, the first version, of branding.

For thousands of years, people have burned, etched, inscribed, and carved marks to attach meaning to inanimate objects—the precursor to modern branding. Builders have always etched their mark in stone, potters on ceramics, painters on cave walls. These marks say 'this is mine' or 'I made this'. The Roman empire had a logo—SPQR, Senatus Populusque Romanus, the Senate and People of Rome—which you see on coins, and inscribed in stone on Roman remains across the empire. Here, the mark has a more social meaning: 'this is ours'.

In the middle ages, the complex techniques of heraldry spread across Europe—signs that included a logo (the coat of arms) and often a slogan (the motto). Each noble family had its own mark: a mark of lineage and pedigree, a mark of membership for the family, and a mark of affiliation for all those economically intertwined with that family. And during the middle ages, the modern company started to emerge, using a trade name and often some kind of imagery too. A handful of modern brand names date back to this time—Stella Artois, for instance, to 1366. Löwenbräu's lion symbol can be traced back to 1383.

The practice of branding had a darker side too: the burning of marks onto slaves, again to signify ownership; or onto criminals, to signify their transgression. Though we generally no longer burn marks on each other, this negative sense of 'branding' is still very common, particularly in newspaper headlines. Government policies are 'branded a failure', politicians' promises are 'branded as gimmicks', hospitals are 'branded as inadequate'.

Of course, if one farmer brands his or her animals, then very soon all farmers must do the same: so branding quickly spread and became the norm. One Texan rancher, though, became famous in the 1850s for refusing the burn marks on his cattle. His name was Samuel Maverick, and the word 'maverick', meaning someone who's stubbornly independent-minded, comes from him. Maverick explained that he didn't want to inflict pain on his cattle: others pointed out that he could claim any unmarked animal as his. Then, as now, trying to escape the system of branding was futile. Not branding is just another form of branding.

Animal branding still happens today, though often marks are frozen rather than burned. I recently saw branded horses at a stud for Lipizzaners in Transylvania, and here the complex system of marks signifies not ownership but heredity.

People, thankfully, are rarely branded, but the practice of tattooing is on the rise: a way of branding yourself, of signifying your passions, which sometimes, oddly enough, involves tattooing commercial logos like Harley-Davidson's.

And organizations still brand their property: the Rothschild family marks its estates with the family logo, and every company displays its logo on its offices, factories, and warehouses.

## Guaranteeing quality

Back in the 18th century, the practice of branding property was well-established. And for craftspeople, there had been a long tradition of applying maker's marks to their work. Guilds of craftspeople used marks to try to eliminate fakes, and the law required goldsmiths and silversmiths to have their work marked by an independent 'assay office'. But with the industrial revolution, and the emergence of mass production, came a new insight: if you were a factory owner, you could put a mark not on your property, but on your *products*. You could turn a mark of provenance into an explicit mark of quality. You could morph the meaning of your mark from 'this is mine' and 'I made this' to 'this is a product you can trust'. In an era of shoddy mass-produced products, and often adulterated foods, these marks could win the trust of consumers—and command higher prices. This is the second version of branding.

The techniques of branding began to shift. Burned marks evolved into marks impressed onto products like pottery, and then into those printed onto packaging. The great pottery entrepreneur Josiah Wedgwood was a pioneer of this idea, stamping his products 'Wedgwood' from 1759 onwards. A decade later, he started adding the word 'Etruria' (the classically inspired name he gave his factory). He knew that this kind of branding could speak to the rapidly expanding middle classes, reassuring them that they were spending their hard-earned money wisely, on products that would last.

By the 1820s, the word 'brand' was being used explicitly in this new sense. The focus was on brand names and on brand reputations, and a new expertise emerged: the design of trademarks and packaging. Most of this work was done by commercial artists, now long forgotten, but occasionally companies used the work of famous painters. Pears Soap used for many years a painting called 'Bubbles', originally entitled 'A Child's World', by John Everett Millais.

Branding gained huge new power in the 1870s, with the idea that you could protect these new assets as 'registered trademarks'. Design and law made a potent combination, and many of the earliest registered trademarks are still effective value-creators now, like Bass, Campbell's, and Kellogg's. (And it was the Bass trademark, of course, that Manet depicted in his 1882 painting, 'A Bar at the Folies-Bergère'.)

Coca-Cola started in 1886 (with, in its early days, 9 milligrams of cocaine as an ingredient), Campbell's in 1898, and Kellogg's in 1906. All, of course, are still big brands now: branding can have extraordinary longevity. All use the colour red, a colour that stands out, a colour that expresses warmth and energy—the colour of fire. And all use a typeface that resembles handwriting. They all look like signatures, like personal guarantees of quality.

By now, manufacturers routinely used advertising to promote their products, usually offering simple, functional benefits like 'delicious' and 'refreshing' for Coca-Cola. This kind of branding is designed to nurture fairly simple ideas in people's minds, mainly about quality and functionality. And this approach is still prevalent today: a famous example is the wood stain Ronseal, whose slogan has been since 1994 'It does exactly what it says on the tin'.

In fact, most branding operates in this way still: burning a name into our minds, making us remember that name, and associating the name with a limited range of mainly functional associations. For example, most household product branding works this way. And the primary meaning of a retailer brand like John Lewis (see Box 3) or Target is the quality of the products it makes or sells.

> **Box 3 John Lewis: happy employees**
>
> John Lewis is not just a retailer but a British institution, almost universally admired. Breaking all the rules of marketing, it aims first not for the happiness of its customers, but of its employees. And yet it's consistently voted Britain's favourite retailer. Set up in its present form by John Spedan Lewis in 1920, the company is a kind of cooperative, owned by a trust on behalf of its workers. Together, these 89,000 'partners' run over forty department stores and over 350 Waitrose supermarkets, offering exceptionally good customer service. The partners get an annual bonus, in some years as much as a fifth of salary. John Lewis's brand proposition, written by its founder back in 1925, is 'Never Knowingly Undersold'—odd English that reassures its mainly middle class shoppers that they won't find better value elsewhere. The company's secret is simple: happy staff make happy customers. Or, to put it slightly differently: branding starts from within.

## Promising pleasure

But the story doesn't stop there. Around the start of the 20th century, mass production became amplified by the arrival of mass media. Factory owners realized they could combine with media owners to give their trademarks even more power. They saw that through advertising in newspapers, then cinemas and radio, they could do more than guarantee quality. They could associate their products with powerful ideas—as Cadbury did with the idea of 'purity'.

This is the kind of branding that we saw with Coca-Cola in Kenya, back at the start of this book (Figure 1), and it's another bold leap, though it seems a normal practice now. Branding could do more than guarantee quality. It could promise much bigger ideas, bolder metaphors, poetic associations: not just functional quality but also much deeper pleasure. In that way, you could create desire for things people didn't know they wanted, which would propel the sales figures, and ideally make people feel an emotional bond with, and ideally be loyal to, your brand. This is the third version of branding.

Coca-Cola, for example, moved its advertising slogan from the prosaic and functional 'delicious and refreshing' to the startlingly poetic 'ice cold sunshine' in 1932. Wheaties become 'the breakfast of champions' in 1934. And De Beers suggested that 'a diamond is forever' in 1947.

Once again, the techniques of branding shifted, into the new arts of advertising and public relations. Cultural forces like psychoanalysis played a role in this. Sigmund Freud's nephew, Edward Bernays, was a founding father of PR, and saw how we could tap into unconscious forces to manipulate people. (He thought manipulation was a good thing.)

People like Bernays saw that you could associate products with abstract ideas that went much further than the product's functional benefits. He persuaded American women to smoke cigarettes by photographing female film stars on their own on the streets of New York, linking cigarettes with a kind of private pleasure, and, even more importantly, with the idea of independence. Now, a cigarette could make you independent. An ordinary product could make you look better to others, and feel better about yourself.

## Masters of branding

Advertisers started to perform this trick by defining brands through a *proposition* and a *personality*, in order to create powerfully persuasive communication. The proposition expressed the benefits the product offered consumers. Its apogee was the idea of the 'unique selling proposition', or USP, invented by the advertising agency Ted Bates in the 1940s: the concept that your advertising should communicate a benefit for the customer that was (as far as possible) unique to your product. Then a 1955 article in the *Harvard Business Review* introduced the concept of the 'brand personality', making a more emotional or subliminal appeal. Branding could now appeal to the mind and the heart, and deliberately aim to change how people think and feel.

Large manufacturers of consumer goods—Coca-Cola, Procter & Gamble, Ford, and many more—became masters of branding, and the practice began to be seen as a long-term strategic investment. The ad-man David Ogilvy's credo was that 'Every advertisement is part of the long-term investment in the personality of the brand'. Advertising was not just about selling in the short term, but about brand-building in the long term, and the advertising agencies became the champions, the guardians, the priests almost, of their clients' brands.

This version of branding turned direction, and grew in power, in the 1960s, with the arrival of television in almost every home, and of the 'creative revolution' in advertising, which produced hugely more sophisticated brand messaging, often using television as its medium. Coca-Cola no longer advertised its thirst-quenching functional powers, but its ability to make you look good to your friends, through slogans like 'The sign of good taste'. Later on, it promised to make you feel like an optimistic citizen of the world, through the famous 'I'd like to buy the world a Coke' campaign.

Bill Bernbach, at his agency Doyle Dane Bernbach, developed subtle, ironic advertising that flattered its audience's sense of their own intelligence. A famous 1959 advert for the Volkswagen Beetle shows a stark black-and-white image with a headline that reversed the received wisdom in the American car trade into the phrase 'Think small'. The advertisement is mostly white space. The headline ends with a full stop, making it sound like a definitive statement, not a sales slogan. The text is witty and knowing, spelling out all the ways that small is good (fuel consumption, parking space, price) and suggests that if you want to be different from the crowd, and smarter, then of course you'd choose a VW.

Alongside product brands, service brands started to appear: American Express, Hilton, PanAm, and many more. Naturally enough, advertisements frequently showed the people who delivered these services. Branding a service became an art in itself, more complex than branding a product. Somehow, you have to make the intangible into something people can grasp. AmEx focused on the tangible part of its service: the card itself. Others dramatized the customer's (ideal) experience. 'Halfway to Europe between cocktails and coffee', proclaimed one PanAm advert.

And building an airline brand, or a hotel brand, or a bank brand depended on getting the company's employees to do the right thing, to keep the promises made in the advertising. For the first time, branding was the job of more than just the marketing department: branding now reached across the whole company. In these ways, branding started to touch not just the product, but also the people behind it: the corporation.

## Inviting belonging

Through the mid-20th century, a new force was emerging in society: the post-industrial corporation. Companies became huge supra-national centres of power. Big corporations, and their institutional investors, saw that they could broaden the impact of brand from their individual products to the company itself. This was another bold leap, and branding started to work on new audiences, beyond the consumer: on employees, investors, and opinion-formers. Companies could now be 'corporate brands', and this kind of branding could do more than promise pleasure. It could invite all kinds of stakeholder to feel a sense of belonging. By feeling they belong, employees would work harder, and customers would stay loyal for longer. This is the fourth version of branding.

The practice of branding shifted into defining an organization's purpose (or 'vision' or 'central idea'), expressing it through visual design—the logo and its supporting paraphernalia—and sharing it through the various mechanisms corporations use to build their internal working cultures. And a new kind of expert took centre-stage: the design-based brand consultant.

This concept was originally called 'corporate identity', and early pioneers included Peter Behrens at AEG in Germany before the first world war, then London Transport in the 1920s, then IBM in the 1950s. But it took off in the 1980s. Reaganism and Thatcherism glamorized the corporation still further, and created a new cohort of privatized companies—organizations like British Airways and BT. This was the golden age of the corporate.

Interestingly, at the same time, the personal computer gave individuals a new sense of power, culminating in the Apple Mac, and the 1960s generation started identifying with a new kind of apparently anti-corporate company, like Apple, Virgin, or Southwest Airlines. These new phenomena felt like consumer brands, and the old terminology of 'corporate identity' switched to 'corporate brand'—though in some ways 'uncorporate brand' would have been more appropriate.

## Company v. company

Apple was a master of this art. It launched the Apple Macintosh with a famous advert, directed by Ridley Scott, which showed a female athlete (representing the Mac) running into an auditorium and throwing a sledgehammer at the Big Brother face on the screen (representing the old world of corporate computing). The advert dramatized a new kind of hip corporate brand that displaced the older model of corporate identity, epitomized by IBM. It invited consumers to belong to a movement—to help defeat 'big brother'.

These new-generation corporate brands could even expand from one industry into others, using their brand to bring their customers with them. Virgin grew from record label into airline into financial services then trains, mobile phones, and many more.

Corporate brands like Virgin appeal to consumers, but branding also became a powerful tool for companies that sell to other companies. Alongside B2C (business-to-consumer) brands, a new breed of B2B (business-to-business) brands emerged, many in the world of information technology, like Accenture, Cisco, Oracle, SAP, Goldman Sachs, 3M, and Reuters.

And it's at this point that the techniques of branding started to spread beyond the corporate world, into not-for-profits, sports clubs, political parties, cities, countries, and celebrities. More and more people talked about, and wrote about, 'brand'.

## Enabling action

At the end of the 20th century, patterns of consumer behaviour were transformed by the arrival of the internet. Consumers could, as never before, become producers too. Writers like Alvin Toffler had talked about the producer-consumer, or 'prosumer', back in the 1980s, but the internet made prosumers mainstream. Suddenly, people had more knowledge and power than ever, and gained huge new scope to make and sell things, as well as buying them.

Entirely new businesses transformed industry after industry: Amazon, eBay, Google, YouTube, Skype, Facebook, Wikipedia, Airbnb, Uber. None promised pleasure, or (in any deep emotional sense) invited belonging, but they all offered people a platform on which they could do new things. They enabled action. With eBay, you could sell your stuff to the world. With YouTube, you could upload your own films, as well as exploring a giant database of video clips. With Airbnb, you could 'list your space', renting out your home to travellers from across the planet. This is the fifth version of branding.

These new businesses used branding not to sell but to encourage network effects: the more people used these products, the more useful they became. The techniques of branding therefore changed once again. The new platforms think in terms of their role in people's lives, and of the principles behind the user experience—and their success depends on how well that experience works. The old arts of advertising and logo design are much less important in this world—and in fact most of these new brands were built without expert logo design or advertising campaigns. Instead, the expertise lies with the tech companies themselves, and with new kinds of specialists like service designers.

And these platforms led to the creation of a new kind of brand, the peer-to-peer or P2P brand: the brand of the individual seller on eBay, or the video blogger on YouTube, or the property 'host' on Airbnb.

## Where we are now

All five versions of branding still happen, side by side. Animals are still branded. Many of the most mundane products are still branded for their quality and functionality. Probably the dominant kind of branding is still the technique of giving products deeper, more emotional associations, promising pleasure or enhanced self-esteem—and the advertising agencies who make this happen are still the most powerful force in the brand world. Meanwhile, most big corporations now take their corporate brand very seriously, and brand consultancies are still very influential.

The most recent kind of branding, version 5, is still very young. It's impossible to predict how it will play out, and it's unclear who the new breed of experts will be. And the story is not linear.

The start-ups behind several of the biggest internet brands have now become large global corporations, have started running brand advertisements, and have redesigned their logos to look more traditionally corporate, as we'll see in Chapter 8. They are hovering between the new kind of branding that tries to enlist participants, and the older kind that promotes a corporation.

## Degrees of control

With all these different kinds of branding in play, almost anything can now be branded. What varies is the degree of control and complexity involved.

Commercial branding—of products, services, and content (such as Spider-Man or My Little Pony)—is very tightly controlled by the owners and their lawyers, and relatively simple: it helps a company sell something to a consumer, in order to extract the maximum value from the product.

Organizational branding—of companies, not-for-profits, sports clubs, political parties—is more complex. The aim is to encourage the maximum support for the organization, but that means reaching many more kinds of people (managers, employees, owners, investors, supporters, members), and is often, of necessity, less tightly controlled and policed.

Cultural branding—of places, people, movements, concepts—is the most complex of all, and may be impossible to control in any kind of corporate way. Here, the aim is to create maximum buzz around an idea, often an idea that belongs to no-one.

And the truth is that many brands straddle more than one of these worlds. IBM is a product brand, a service brand, and a corporate brand. Jamie Oliver is both a product brand and a person brand. Intel is a corporate brand and a product brand. Branding is a dynamic, opportunistic activity that constantly breaks across the conceptual categories that academics and consultants try to construct. Its role and its methods keep morphing.

## B2B

Intel, in fact, is a good example of a B2B brand that broke into the B2C world too, through the 'Intel inside' campaign. Intel made advanced computer chips and sold them to computer companies, but in the late 1980s it found it hard to compete with cheaper competitors. So it started paying its customers, the computer manufacturers, to put an 'Intel inside' sticker on their products, to suggest added value. Sales of those computers rocketed. Consumers felt that 'Intel inside' conveyed quality (and an element of mystique), and Intel—though a B2B company—rapidly became famous among consumers.

Many B2B brands are now using some of the techniques of B2C branding, to appeal over the heads of their clients to their clients' customers. Airbus and Boeing sell their products to airlines, but their brands are well-known to passengers too: the latest Boeing plane can attract customers to an airline that flies it.

Traditionally, branding mattered less in the B2B world: clients bought your product or your service or your expertise, not your brand. But that's changing. Even such rational organizations as the big audit firms, like PwC and EY, now invest heavily in brand-building, not least to attract the brightest new graduates. The pioneer, in many ways, has been the consulting firm Accenture, which has invested seriously in brand-building from the day it was created, consistently using the slogan 'high performance delivered'.

## The paradoxes of luxury

At the other end of the scale—where customers happily pay a huge premium for your brand—is the luxury brand. Most of the value of (say) a Ralph Lauren shirt or a Mont Blanc pen or a Cartier bag or a pair of Christian Louboutin shoes or a Ferrari car is in the brand as opposed to the product. But luxury branding, too, is on the move. Instead of selling to a few rich people in the West, these companies are selling to a vast new middle class in China. Rarity has become abundant. Many luxury businesses are broadening their appeal, for instance by collaborating with mass-market retailers: Lanvin, Versace, and Alexander Wang, for instance, with H&M; and Lemaire with Uniqlo. Burberry makes what it calls an 'entry level' perfume, cheaper than its clothes.

In the fashion industry, in fact, branding traditionally appeals to those who love labels, want to be seen wearing labels, and want to look good to their friends. But more recently it has started to work in a different way on those who are tired of labels, who avoid ostentation, or who want to feel good about themselves. So alongside the labels are the anti-labels: the newest form of branding is a very self-conscious kind of anonymity. Maison Margiela clothes often have blank labels—though the stitching of the label is visible on the outside of the garment, so they still proclaim themselves, to those in the know. New entrants like Vetements don't carry a designer name or a visible logo, and are aimed at customers who don't want to be walking adverts for brands: founder Demna Gvasalia says 'The ultimate designer, for me, is the woman who wears it'.

## Wherever there's a market

What we see around us, then, is a universe of branding. Five different versions, all in play. Commercial, organizational, and cultural branding, each involving different levels of control. B2B branding, where you might think brand counts for least, and luxury branding, where it probably matters most.

Branding is also powerful in labour markets. There's tough competition for the brightest new employees, and the most compelling version 4 branding attracts the best new talent. Organizations also compete to attract finance, and a strong brand can make you more valuable to investors, and may even secure better terms from banks. Organizations increasingly work together, and this trend creates another marketplace: a strong brand can help you attract the best possible partners. Wherever there's a market, there's branding.

Is there anything that can't be branded? Are there human activities so un-corporate, so un-designed, so homespun perhaps, or so invisible, that branding could never work? Water? Air? Happiness? Even illegal products like drugs are often branded.

## A constantly morphing force

We're so familiar with the idea of brand that it all seems natural to us. But branding has grown through a series of audacious leaps: from property to product, from product features to wider emotional associations, from product to organization, and from consuming to participating. Branding has expanded its scope from the commercial world, into the broader world of organizations, and then into the wide open spaces of culture. And it's exerted its power not just in the glamorous sectors you'd expect, like luxury, but also in the greyer markets of B2B. Over the years, branding has found ever more ways to change how people think, feel, and act.

# Chapter 4
# How branding works

Think back to how your day started today. As a consumer, you've been consuming since you woke up. You'll have made a lot of passive choices, particularly among the things you use, and the things you do by habit or default—your radio station, coffee, shower gel, phone, social media app, browser, even the company you go to work for—though at some point in the past, you made a conscious choice about all of these things. And others may be more active choices: the things you buy, your coffee shop, your lunch place. Some things, of course, you can't affect: your bus company, your computer at work.

For most of us, most of these choices are influenced at some stage by branding. We choose the cereal that tastes good, or that's nutritious, or that's cheap—but maybe also that reminds us of our childhood. We choose the radio station that best suits our mood, or gives us the most accurate news—but also that reflects who we like to think we are. We might choose the first cash machine we come across—or the one belonging to the bank we think is most ethical.

In other words, we choose things not just for functional reasons, but also because of how they make us feel about ourselves, and about our relationships with others. We make decisions based not just on the product, but also on the things that product stands for—its brand.

Brands—from Tropicana to Colgate, Illy to Shiseido, Nintendo to PowerPoint, the *New York Times* to Buzzfeed—are not just a passive phenomenon, sitting out there in the world. They get deep inside us. They are a set of ideas, feelings, memories, and images that make us do things.

Branding works on our rational brains—but also at a more profound level, on our intuitive, pre-conscious reasoning, and on our emotions. By changing how we think, and more deeply how we feel, branding changes how we act. And it reaches not just consumers, but employees too.

## Branding changes how we think and feel

Through our experience with using a product, and through the messages conveyed by its advertising, we build up a set of beliefs about it. This is the rational side of branding. Aristotle, the ancient Greek philosopher, anticipated the techniques of branding in his book *Rhetoric*, and talks about this as *logos*: the word, or the rational argument. (*Logos* is also the origin of 'logo', the term we use to mean 'brand emblem'.)

For example, I've heard of Sony, I know it's a Japanese business, I know that it makes games machines, televisions, mobile phones—and also that it makes films and other forms of entertainment. I believe that its technology is good, though maybe not as advanced as (say) LG's. I think a Sony product will be well made, carefully engineered: it will be reliable and offer reasonable value for money. In these kinds of ways, branding appeals to our conscious, rational minds. It offers a 'brand proposition', and helps us calculate the benefits of buying, say, a Sony product (Figure 4). This is how branding version 2—the guarantee of quality—operates.

**4. Getting people to buy:** Sony's branding changes how people think and feel about its products—and also leads them to buy, and to keep buying.

But the real power of much modern branding is that it goes deeper. It also appeals to our intuitive, unconscious, irrational, and emotional selves. Through the pleasure a product has given us, through the memories it evokes, through the attitudes we've picked up from friends, through the storytelling in its advertising, through the colour of its logo, we build up a set of feelings. In these ways, branding creates a 'brand personality', and helps us to feel that a particular decision is right. Aristotle would probably analyse this aspect of branding as *ethos* (the character and credibility of the speaker) and *pathos* (the emotions of the audience). And this is branding version 3.

For example, I've enjoyed thousands of hours of television entertainment through Sony. In fact, it was the first television I ever bought, so to some extent I'm a Sony person. I trust Sony. Expert friends tell me that its picture quality is superior. I've seen Sony products looking good in countless films (some of them, no doubt, made by Sony Pictures). I like its communication style, and even its clunky little logo: they're understated and reassuring. These are all feelings, and writing them down like this is slightly misleading, because they exist in my mind in a pre-conscious, pre-verbal form.

## Thinking fast

In fact, branding appeals very strongly to what the Nobel prize-winning scientist Daniel Kahneman calls 'system 1' thinking. He describes the differences between intuitive 'system 1' and conscious 'system 2' thinking in his book *Thinking, Fast and Slow*. We all use system 1 thinking constantly in our lives. For example, when we're driving, we don't deliberate about every gear change or every adjustment of the steering wheel: we drive largely on autopilot. Branding frequently appeals directly to our autopilot brains, getting us to pick a product on a supermarket shelf without any conscious thought. It uses logos, symbols, colours, images, music, smells, tastes to go direct to our intuitions. By creating a brand personality in people's minds, and expressing that personality through the brand's style, branding targets system 1.

Branding often works through irrational phenomena like 'habituation' and 'contagion'. For example, the *Downton Abbey* brand worked on me in both these ways, and every year I watched the programme because I always had (habituation) and because so many other people did (contagion). As human beings, we're subject to a whole range of cognitive biases like these, and branding often depends on them. There's even a cognitive bias, recognized by social psychologists, called 'the IKEA effect', which is our tendency to feel attached to things just because we've assembled them.

Habituation is an important contributor to the goal of brand loyalty—one of the aims of branding versions 3 and 4. And contagion is vital in branding version 5. Many online businesses depend on network effects: the more users a service like Airbnb or Uber has, the more useful it becomes. Here, the interplay of functional and emotional is critical. 'Contagion' becomes a complex thing, and I chose Airbnb, for example, not just because so many other people do, but also because it benefits me to behave like them.

Most branding, in fact, gets its power by mixing the intuitive and the rational. Sometimes, branding has an automatic, intuitive effect first (system 1 thinking), and then we post-rationalize (system 2). In the supermarket, I might unthinkingly grab a bar of Green and Black's chocolate because I'm drawn subliminally to the sophisticated, dark packaging. I'll then tell myself I chose it because it's healthily organic.

At other times, branding starts with a purely functional appeal, but as we get used to it, we tell people about it, we feel warmer towards it, and it gains emotional dimensions. For example, the discount supermarkets Aldi and Lidl took off by simply being cheap, but they became brands that Britain's middle classes now feel proud to identify with. Offering your dinner-party guests a bottle of Aldi wine shows just what a savvy shopper you are.

## Inside the brain

Some experts use brain science to analyse the interplay between rational and irrational. They believe that decisions get made first in those primitive parts of our brains that we inherit from our reptilian predecessors. We then justify them in our limbic brain, the part that deals with our social feelings, or in our cortex, where we do our rational thinking. So, for example, I might buy a gas-guzzling SUV car—let's say a Porsche Cayenne. I tell myself that I chose the Porsche because it's practical for driving down muddy lanes to my country cottage: that's the cortex at work, post-rationalizing. I tell friends I bought it because the high driving position makes it safer for other road users: that's the limbic system, making me a good citizen. But the real reason remains a secret, buried in my reptilian brain: I chose it because it gives me a primitive sense of power.

More precisely, the new field of 'consumer neuroscience' is starting to show how branding works inside the brain. It uses machines called functional magnetic resonance imaging (or 'fMRI') scanners to watch how brains respond to stimuli. Scientists have looked to see the effects of branding stimuli (to being shown a logo, for example, or given a branded fizzy drink). There's evidence that branding produces activity in the ventromedial prefrontal cortex, which sits behind the forehead, and is associated with feelings of reward. Tasted blind, Coca-Cola and Pepsi do this equally, but when people can see the cans, Coca-Cola seems to produce this activity much more than Pepsi does.

Branding also produces activation in the hippocampus, much deeper inside the brain, and in the dorsolateral prefrontal cortex. Both these areas are associated with memory. So branding seems to stimulate brain activity to do with reward and memory. All this is interesting, but unsurprising: it tells us where things happen in the brain but not why they happen. And it's based on what people do in the highly artificial surroundings of the fMRI lab. We have a long way to go before we can understand branding at the level of brain cells.

## Branding changes how we act

So how does all of this influence people's behaviour? Obviously enough, branding gets us, as consumers, to buy. Uniqlo's branding, for instance, makes us *think* that its products offer good design at an amazing price. The branding also makes us *feel* things: perhaps that we like Uniqlo's slightly quirky, but also very neat and tidy, Japanese ethos. And so we *act*: we buy this t-shirt (and, probably, half a dozen other impulse purchases as we go round the store).

But there's more. Branding attracts more customers in. It gets them to buy more things. It gets them to buy things from you more often. It gets people to buy things in new ways. In the field of music, for example, the Apple brand got us to switch from CDs to downloads, and then the Spotify brand got people to switch from downloads to streaming. And in many cases—again, Apple is a good example—it gets people to pay more, to pay a 'brand premium'.

If you're a charity like Oxfam, branding gets people to donate to you. If you created a television show like *The Good Wife*, it gets people to watch it. Even if your service is (apparently) free, like Twitter, it gets people to use it. And good branding can get retailers to sell your product, comparison sites to push it, agents and brokers to favour it—all of which propels sales.

Branding, then, gets people to buy—which means that good branding, one way or another, increases the company's revenue.

But the really deep power of branding is that it gets us to keep doing things, into the future. Brands burn themselves into our minds. They create not a single act, but habitual behaviour. Branding gets people not just to *buy* you, but to *buy into* you: not just to pay money, but also to make an emotional investment. As a result, in the words of the branding expert Tim Ambler, 'a brand is an upstream reservoir of future cashflow'. Good branding makes your future more predictable.

To take a specific example, Toyota in recent years has had a spate of quality problems, which has forced it to recall cars for repair. But Toyota's branding helps it survive. Customers believe that, in spite of recent faults, these are good cars. People like Toyota's rather serious brand personality. And so they buy Toyota again.

Indeed, Toyota still sells nine million cars a year, even after several major product recalls.

This kind of commitment is conscious and deliberate, but branding also creates a less deliberate behavioural commitment: we often buy the same brand of (say) ketchup out of mere habit.

So branding gets people outside the organization to keep buying, and often to recommend the product to friends. It can turn customers into unofficial salespeople. It can even, in some cases, encourage them to get together in 'brand communities'—groups of fans. These brand communities seem to form particularly around products that are toys, either for adults or children. Harley Davidson, JEEP, Barbie, and LEGO all have fan groups, official and unofficial.

Good branding gets the media to praise you, policy-makers to support you, and perhaps even gets regulators to smooth your path. And it gets investors to stay with you, through bad times as well as good.

All of this means that, in financial language, your 'risk' goes down: your future is more secure. Through the downturn following the 2008 crash, the market value of America's largest companies declined dramatically. But if you look instead at the value of just the companies with the most valuable brands, their performance dipped much less. They also returned to growth by the summer of 2009—almost three years before their less well-branded rivals. If you have a big brand, you recover much faster, and your risks are therefore much lower.

## Loyalty is for dogs

This kind of consumer commitment is often called 'brand loyalty'. But loyalty, when you analyse it, is a complex thing. It can be a matter of attitude, or a matter of behaviour, or both. Sometimes people are both attitudinally and behaviourally loyal: I have to admit that I both love, and keep buying, Apple. In cases like this, brand experts often talk about 'brand love' and even 'lovemarks'—and these kinds of consumer are the true 'brand fans'. But there are limits. Though some of us may feel something akin to love towards one or two brands, very few have room in our hearts to love more than one or two. Brand love will always be the exception rather than the rule.

As consumers get more and more choices, and become better informed about what's on the market, they tend to become less loyal. Many people now do some of their shopping at premium supermarkets, and some at discount stores: they're too canny to be loyal to one or the other. In the supermarket, shoppers often choose the store's own-label products over the traditional branded ones. Most of us carry a stack of 'loyalty' cards from various stores and hotel groups. We're not really loyal to any of them, we just make multiple, and partial, commitments. As someone once ruefully said, 'loyalty is for dogs'. A study by the management consultants EY in 2012 suggested that only 40 per cent of consumers worldwide buy things out of brand loyalty, and only 25 per cent in the USA.

Waitrose is my favourite supermarket, and I'd always recommend it to people, but in practice I shop at all the main supermarkets. I'm attitudinally, but not behaviourally, loyal. The brand expert Byron Sharp suggests that the market is now dominated by promiscuous consumers like me. These people may *feel* loyal to, say, Dell, but they actually buy Lenovo or Asus. He calls them 'loyal switchers'.

In other cases, people stick with a product even though they don't like it. It's hard to switch bank, for instance, so most consumers are behaviourally but not attitudinally loyal. We use the same broadband, the same browser, the same search engine, and probably the same online retailer day after day, without loving any of them. In these cases, consumers are 'habitual users'.

So branding today, while aiming ideally to create brand fans, knows that in most cases its best result will be loyal switchers or habitual users. Yet these kinds of half-loyalty are still complex commitments to brands—and branding still helps reduce the risk of losing customers.

## The pay-off of branding

In the 1980s, two writers, David Aaker and Kevin Lane Keller, wanted to describe more precisely these powerful effects of branding. They developed the concept of 'brand equity', by which they mean the value of a brand—of the ideas out there in people's minds—to the company. Specifically, a product's brand equity is the additional value it can create, compared with a similar product with fewer or no associations in people's minds. Keller describes it as 'the added value a product accrues as a result of past investments in the marketing activity for the brand'. The goal of branding, then, is to maximize brand equity.

For example, I can go to a pharmacy and buy ibuprofen from a company called Value Health, and it costs me 35p. Value Health means nothing to me: it's an anonymous manufacturer, not a brand. Next to it on the shelf is a product called Nurofen. It has the same active ingredient, but it's also a brand, owned by Reckitt Benckiser. Nurofen has been built up over the years through millions of pounds of advertising. And Nurofen costs £2. The price difference hints at Nurofen's brand equity—the brand is so powerful that the retailer can charge £1.65 extra per pack.

That's a simple case, but brand equity is often more complex. In the case of a low-cost airline, or a discounter supermarket, the price is actually lower: brand equity for IndiGo or Lidl comes from not a price premium but greater sales volumes or faster growth. And equity may not always be about money. A brand's equity, or its relative advantage, could be measured in longevity, growth rates, or even social impact.

Aaker analyses brand equity into three components, brand awareness, brand associations, and brand loyalty. Brand *awareness* is the most basic: people's level of familiarity with the product or organization. Brand *associations* are all those other ideas and feelings—the ideas people associate with, for example, IKEA—that make people choose to buy, or not to buy, including importantly the product's perceived quality. And brand *loyalty* is the pinnacle: people's feelings of commitment to a particular product or organization—the greater the commitment, the less the company has to spend on marketing.

Keller takes the thinking a stage further, labelling his version 'customer-based brand equity'. Keller starts with *salience*. For Zara, for example, this would mean 'I've heard of Zara, and when I think of fashion, Zara is top-of-mind'. Then he talks about the product's meaning, divided into *performance* ('Zara clothes are well made and low priced') and *imagery* ('Zara is Spanish, on trend, fast fashion, and for people like me').

Up another level is the customer's response, divided into *judgements* ('it's good quality, I prefer it to Primark, I'd always look in there') and *feelings* ('I feel excited about Zara, it makes me look good, I feel good about myself'). And at the top, much like Aaker's loyalty, is *resonance* ('I feel loyal to Zara, I always shop there, I'm a Zara fan').

Keller visualizes all this as a pyramid, with 'salience' at the base and 'resonance' at the peak. This is probably the most widely used diagram by brand academics, and it's been adapted for use by many brand-owning companies too.

Brand equity can be strong or weak. Indeed, you can have negative brand equity. This happens when a branded product gets sold for less than its generic or own-label equivalent, or when no-one will buy it at all. In 1991, Gerald Ratner, chief executive of his family jewellery business, joked that his stores' earrings were 'cheaper than an M&S prawn sandwich but probably wouldn't last as long', and his comment immediately sent the Ratners brand into negative equity.

## Branding on the inside

So branding builds (we hope) positive brand equity. It appeals to consumers, in both the short term and the long term. That's all obvious. And many writers on branding leave it here. They talk about the need to take consumers up a 'ladder' or through a 'funnel' from brand awareness to preference to loyalty.

But less visible is the internal effect of branding: it operates too on the people behind the brand, the employees. In a branded organization, people are normally strongly aware of the brand they work for. At a place like GE, where, as we've seen, the brand is officially about 'imagination at work', they might think about bringing their imagination to work, they might feel that they like this spirit of inventiveness, going right back to GE's founder, Thomas Edison. And so they work hard to invent. That, at least, is the theory.

Branding gets good recruits to apply to, and join, the organization. The glamour of the brand brings new employees in, and though the reality is usually more mundane and imperfect, the brand sustains them. Once inside, it can focus people's efforts, so that they work harder. It can help people feel more united, and so collaborate with their colleagues, rather than fighting them. Branding can make people feel more positive, more 'engaged', to use the management jargon—and in fact there's a whole sub-set of branding called 'employer branding'. The result is that there's less effort to hire people, fewer mistakes in hiring, more productive workers, less wasted effort, less internal conflict or duplication of work.

And branding can work not just on employees but also on others who help the company produce what it produces: banks, for example, and suppliers. A strong brand, for instance, makes you more attractive to your bank and could help you negotiate lower interest rates. And it can certainly extract the best possible prices from your suppliers, who are keen to be associated with your brand.

In all these ways, branding can make the organization much more efficient—which means that costs go down.

For insiders too, the brand has effects which last into the future. In a business like Google, the brand encourages people not just to do today's job, but to help create tomorrow's success. It's the thing you have to live up to. Google's brand is about organizing the world's information, and its view, in Eric Schmidt's words, is that 'big problems are information problems'. Everything—education, healthcare, transport, finance, crime—is soluble by data, so as a Googler you're constantly challenged to use data to solve a new big problem (and so create a new big business). Branding can encourage people inside their organizations to grow, in lots of ways: at a minimum, to stay with the company, to learn new skills, to develop new methods, to invent new products, to expand into new markets.

All of which means that good branding helps employees to maximize the organization's future opportunities.

## A corporate asset

So branding works on us at a rational level, changing how we think; and more deeply at an intuitive and emotional level, changing how we feel. It affects our knowledge of products and our judgements about them; but it also affects our feelings, sensations, and memories. And in these ways, it changes how we act—both our conscious purchasing decisions, and our autopilot reflexes in the supermarket.

Branding affects the behaviour not just of consumers, but of employees too. And the results are not just short-term blips but long-term patterns that last into the future.

In the short term, good branding increases revenues and decreases costs, which generates profit. In the long term, it minimizes risk and maximizes opportunity, which leads to long-term growth prospects. Combine profit with growth, and you get commercial value. So brand is amazingly powerful commercially, and as we saw in Chapter 1, for many organizations, their brand is their biggest asset.

But there's another dimension too. Not-for-profit organizations have always aimed at a different kind of value, social rather than commercial. And many corporations are now aiming at both. It's possible to analyse social value in the same way as commercial value, from the consumer and the employee perspective, looking for short-term and long-term effects. We'll explore the idea of social value in Chapter 7.

## Secrets of success

So branding, at its best, creates huge value. But what exactly does successful branding look like? Some brands, like Johnson & Johnson, have an ethical impact, holding the company to generally high standards. Some brands lead through engineering, like Dyson or Huawei (see Box 4); others through customer service, like Nordstrom or John Lewis. Some score on recognizability: Mastercard, for instance, is visible and distinctive everywhere. Others, like Stella Artois—almost 700 years old—simply last longer. Douwe Egberts dates back to 1753, C&A to 1841, and Levi's to 1850.

Yet, of course, brands fail too. Businesses like Arthur Andersen or the *News of the World* are accused of malpractice, so their brands become tainted in people's minds, and they no longer attract

> **Box 4  Huawei: hitting with a pillow**
>
> Huawei is possibly the next big global brand, the next Apple or Samsung. This huge Chinese telecoms manufacturer has 170,000 employees, and a third of the world's population uses its products (though it's treated with suspicion, and seen as a security risk, by some in the US). Huawei's red logo now appears in Interbrand's league table of the world's 100 most valuable brands. But it's not a great state-owned powerhouse: founder Ren Zhengfei has shared ownership among 80,000 employees, and Huawei rotates its CEO every six months. It's not a short-termist money-maker: it plans ten years ahead, and half its people are in research. And it puts a lot of emphasis on its people, called Huawei-ren: they work ferociously hard, but in a culture of gentle self-criticism, which Zhengfei compares with hitting colleagues with a pillow. The big new brands from the East may turn out to be subtly different from the old ones from the West.

customers. Others, like Blackberry, Borders, or Woolworth, get to feel old or irrelevant. Some, like Blockbuster, Kodak, and Polaroid, get overtaken by technology. Companies with good brands can make terrible mistakes and survive. Tylenol hit a crisis in 1982 when seven people in Chicago died after taking capsules that turned out to contain cyanide. But the brand was so strong that, only six months later, sales had returned to normal. Hoover ran a disastrous promotional competition in 1992, which forced it to give away £50 million of free airline flights. The business was sold, but the brand continues. And failing brands can come back to life. The fashion company Burberry restored its fortunes by reinventing its original design principles in contemporary ways, making pioneering use of digital technology and social media—and in that clever way rebuilt its brand. The Nokia brand has lived through several cycles of decline and revival. The Moleskine and Polaroid brands have been revived by new owners. Indeed, to borrow the name of yet another durable brand, you could say that brands themselves are like Teflon: bad news seems not to stick to them for long.

So what's the secret of success? Sadly, there's no neat formula, no guaranteed method. But common sense, and my own experience in branding, suggest three themes.

First, successful branding stands out. Great brands are different. The companies behind them do their own thing, rather than copying others. Southwest Airlines pioneered low-cost point-to-point air travel. LEGO is not like other toys. No other shoe company is quite like TOMS, the company that, for every pair it sells, donates a pair to an impoverished child. The online eyewear retailer Warby Parker has a similar programme. Rather than just meeting existing consumer needs, great branding tends to lead the market: Chobani, Tesla, and Tencent have all brought new things to people. The best branding is radical, and its ideas are big. But the companies behind the greatest brands are not necessarily the inventors of new technologies. Like Apple or Sky (in very different ways), they're the popularizers.

Which leads to the second theme: great branding belongs to all of us. It's simple enough to be widely understood and shared, and to become part of everyday culture. Indeed, it may sometimes help lead and shape that culture. Great branding comes naturally to the companies that do it: it's authentic, human, and not corporate or mechanistic. It's easy to understand, share, and even join in. For the British middle classes, John Lewis is a great example of branding that's easy to like and easy to spread. The best branding is social, and its ideas are simple.

And to become a social property like that, to be credible, successful branding does what it says. Great brands are built on reality, not mere image. The Indian airline IndiGo promises to be on time, and is. BP, on the other hand, promised to go 'beyond petroleum' and didn't, which damaged its brand. Successful companies know how to mobilize their people to keep their brand promise, day after day—which often means keeping this as simple as possible. The best branding is tangible, and its ideas are true.

For all three of these reasons, successful branding depends on strong leadership. It happens through conviction, rather than consensus—that's the only route to simplicity. It depends on substance: not just a nice logo, but a thoughtful design of the whole customer experience. And, like everything else in life, it also depends on luck: being in the right place with the right product at the right time.

## Branding by numbers

So branding aims to build brand equity, and more widely to create commercial and social value. How can all this be measured? Broadly, you can measure three things: how people think and feel, how they act, and the value that's created.

Measuring the thoughts and feelings in people's minds is traditionally done through surveys and focus groups. Big brand-owners commission market research themselves, or buy into databases like Y&R's BrandAsset Valuator, which is constantly surveying thousands of consumers about thousands of famous brands. Many use a very simple measure called the 'net promoter score', which asks people how likely they are to recommend your brand. The maximum score is 100, and the minimum is minus 100. A brand with very committed customers, like Apple, usually scores around 60.

Measuring behaviour means tracking data like customer numbers, frequency of purchase, repeat buying, overall sales, and market share. More recently, companies have started measuring online behaviour such as Facebook likes and Twitter re-tweets. These measurements are more objective than brand perceptions, but harder to interpret: it's often very hard to say how much of this month's sales growth, for instance, is actually the result of branding activity.

Some companies go a stage further, and try to measure the value that all this behaviour creates. They aim to put a dollar value on their brand, based on its ability to generate future revenues. Every year, four organizations—Interbrand, BrandZ, Brand Finance, and *Forbes* magazine—produce league tables of brand valuations. Currently, the most valuable brands are, unsurprisingly, technology brands, like Apple, Google, Microsoft, and IBM. The numbers are astonishingly high. In 2016, BrandZ valued the Google brand, for example, at $229 billion, which was roughly the GDP of Portugal. But this is not a precise science—the four different firms produce wildly different valuations—and you only get a truly accurate measure of your brand's value (as with the value of your house) if you sell it to someone.

## The many dimensions of brand impact

These measures tend to focus on the external and commercial impacts of branding. But increasingly, as we've seen, businesses are interested in the effect of branding on employees, and also on its potential to achieve social benefits. So new, broader measurement techniques are emerging, such as the 'MeaningfulBrands' index produced by Havas Media.

And it's this multi-dimensional impact that accounts for the world's current fascination with branding. Branding changes how people think, feel, and act, in both the short term and the long term, both inside and outside the organization. And it creates value, both commercial and social.

It's a big job, and creating all these effects depends on whole armies of people. The footsoldiers in those armies are the people known as 'brand managers'.

# Chapter 5
# The branding business

On 13 May 1931, deep inside Procter & Gamble—a giant consumer-goods company—a junior marketing manager called Neil McElroy wrote a memo that launched the whole branding business. McElroy was in charge of Camay soap, which was performing less well than P&G's other soap brands like Ivory. So McElroy proposed that every P&G brand should have what he called a 'brand man'. The brand man, supported by a specialist team, would push that product's sales, using things like market research, advertising, and packaging design. That way, every brand would get the attention it deserved. McElroy's proposal was adopted, and 'brand management' was born. McElroy then rose through the ranks of P&G, and eventually, strangely enough, became the US Secretary of Defense. Or perhaps it's not so strange. Perhaps the essence of the brand manager's role is to defend their brand in the great war of commerce.

McElroy's memo invented a completely new job: the brand manager. And brand managers have become the central players in the business of branding. They almost always work inside the company's marketing department. Under them, or alongside them, are people working on all the other marketing activities: market research and analytics, marketing strategy, marketing communications (including advertising, PR, social media, sponsorship, and media planning), and product development.

Nowadays, though, branding goes miles beyond the marketing department, and depends on many more people than just the marketing team people, so brand managers influence, orchestrate, and coach their colleagues right across the organization.

Some of the time, these people aim to build brands scientifically, by collecting as much data as possible, by understanding what triggers people's behaviour, by experimenting with alternative methods, and by deploying the techniques that work. But human behaviour is almost impossible to pin down. It's hard to turn branding into a formula, and branding therefore depends also on creativity: on imagination, intuition, going beyond the evidence, and making something new. The business of branding is part science, part art—but in the end, art matters more.

## Not always what it seems

Behind the brands we know and love (or hate) are the millions of companies that own them: the manufacturers, service companies, media businesses, and so on, where all these brand managers work. And not just commercial companies but other kinds of organization: not-for-profits, schools, government bodies, museums, political parties, cities, countries, celebrities.

But beneath all the familiar names, all is not what it seems. In consumer goods—the original home of branding—most brands are actually owned by a much larger organization, like Nestlé, Pepsico, and Procter & Gamble. Dove and Ben & Jerry's, for example, belong to Unilever. Pringles belongs to Kellogg's. Whiskas belongs to Mars. Cadbury and Kenco belong to Mondelez International. Braun and Ariel belong to Procter & Gamble. Innocent Drinks is 90 per cent owned by the Coca-Cola Company. These and many other famous names look like companies in their own right, but are actually just properties of a handful of mega-corporations.

Going in the other direction, some brands that look as though they belong to a single giant organization are actually run by dozens of smaller companies. They operate under the protective umbrella of a big brand name, through franchising and licensing. Of all the McDonald's restaurants worldwide, 85 per cent are actually a smaller company operating a franchise. Most of the big chain hotels are owned by local property companies who use the brand name under licence. Virgin appears to be one thing, but is actually 400 separate companies. A few, like Virgin Galactic, are wholly owned by Virgin Group. Most are companies that Virgin part-owns. Some, like Virgin Media, are separate businesses that use the Virgin name under licence. In PwC, the accounting and consulting giant, each of the 159 national partnerships is a separate legal entity which through a legal arrangement is licensed to use the PwC brand.

So behind the brands we encounter every day, there's a much less visible, and much more complex, pattern of ownership. Brands, in other words, are themselves products that can be bought and sold, borrowed and lent.

## Managing or leading

The scope and power of the brand manager varies hugely from organization to organization. In a business-to-business company, or a not-for-profit organization, branding may be a relatively unimportant, tactical tool, and the brand manager normally sits a long way down the hierarchy, with a small team and little power. Their role is limited to managing communications or policing design.

But in consumer goods companies, in retailers, and in luxury products most of all, branding is central to the organization's success. Branding is seen as a strategic activity, encompassing all the ways the organization touches its customers. The brand team is usually large and powerful, and brand gets talked about a lot at the top of the business.

Many organizations now realize that branding can no longer be seen as just a sub-set of marketing: indeed, it's the other way round, and marketing is a sub-set of branding. Some companies, like Mattel, McDonald's, and Procter & Gamble, have created a new role, chief brand officer, which encompasses both traditional branding and some of the other functions, such as innovation and customer service, that are vital to brand-building.

And in some organizations, the only place where all those roles meet is the CEO. Particularly in those companies that believe in the internal power of branding, alongside its influence on outside consumers, many chief executives today see themselves as the steward of their organization's brand (or brands)—as, in a sense, the ultimate brand manager.

The writer David Aaker makes a distinction between tactical 'brand management' and the much broader, more strategic concept of 'brand leadership'. In his view, brand management has a short-term perspective, setting out to create the best possible brand image in the consumer's mind. Its impact is measured (if at all) in sales and market share. Brand leadership has a much more strategic perspective, aiming to maximize brand equity, juggling a whole portfolio of products, focusing on the employees too, and driven by a very clear statement of what the company wants its brand to stand for. You could go further and say that brand management polices the world as it is: it's mainly a top–down, process-heavy control mechanism. Brand leadership, in contrast, tries to shape the world as it could be: it's more a lateral, experimental, creativity tool. Brand management focuses on individual products; brand leadership aims to use the brand idea to direct the whole organization.

## Brand-led or not?

How many organizations are brand-led in this way, adopting an approach the academics call 'brand orientation'? CEOs differ in their views on this subject. Richard Reed, founder of Innocent Drinks, declares that 'the brand is the business, the business is the brand'. Sometimes, as with Innocent, the brand-led philosophy started because the CEO had a marketing background, but often—as in many continental European organizations—it was more cerebral in spirit. And often CEOs elevate the brand concept into the grander notion of 'purpose'.

But others see brand as just one of many factors in their business life, and see it not as the driver but as the consequence of good decision-making. Some commercial organizations hold the idea of branding at arm's length. Dyson likes to say that it's an engineering business, not a marketing operation. Ryanair says it's too pragmatic for airy-fairy big ideas. Others feel that the excitement of branding has passed. Until recently, it was the biggest source of intangible value for many organizations, but now there are other contenders, such as the customer data they hold.

The truth is that practice varies, and organizations hold different views—deep enough perhaps to be called 'theologies'. Some adopt brand leadership, where the brand identity is seen as a strategic asset, used constantly in decision-making, and shaping innovation. Others are driven by more commercial or pragmatic objectives. Some manage their brand explicitly, others rely on creating an implicit climate. Some control everything from the top, others allow much more freedom. Some push relentlessly to be consistent, others welcome variation and innovation.

## Philosopher and coach

So the organization may be brand-led or brand-supported. And the brand manager may be a lowly functionary, or a senior marketing person, or one of the new breed of 'chief brand officers', or even occasionally the CEO. But whatever their status, their role—the task of brand management—is changing.

The role used to be relatively easy to define: writing the brand strategy, achieving consistency in the branding work, policing every piece of design, and tracking the brand's performance. But the scope of branding in many organizations is much less clear-cut than it was twenty years ago. At one moment, big long-term questions of meaning and purpose are central to the CEO, while at the next moment, the pressure shifts to short-term results, and branding is little more than a sales gadget. Brand managers therefore increasingly have to hold the high ground, to remind their CEO of the long-term value to be derived from investing in the brand. They argue for the importance of values, meanings, and ideas in the minds of consumers—and of employees too. Often it's the head of brand who is reminding the organization's leaders how critical it is to building purpose, confidence, conviction, and unity among employees. Their current keyword is 'purpose', which has more currency for many chief executives than 'brand'. As the champions of meaning and purpose, and the posers of 'why' questions, brand managers are almost the *philosophers* of their organizations.

At the same time, the reach of brand managers is widening. When branding was essentially about communicating, the job could be done within the brand department. But increasingly, customers believe deeds not words: the whole customer experience, rather than the latest advertising campaign. And this means influencing colleagues in many other departments, including product design, engineering, and customer service. Many organizations, as we've seen, are keen to build the right brand in the minds of employees, just as much as among consumers. They use branding to change how employees think, feel, and act. Often, they produce a set of guidelines for how employees should behave—even in meetings that no consumer will ever see.

So the brand manager's task becomes an educational one. In some cases, this means teaching the whole organization to collectively deliver the best possible customer experience, in order to build the right brand for consumers. In others, it goes even further, and means building the right brand for employees too, getting them to 'live the brand'. To control communications, brand managers used to deploy brand manuals and guidelines. Now, they're much more likely to talk about practical tools and online learning. The brand manager has become, in effect, the organization's *coach*—its teacher and trainer—using an array of educational media and practical toolkits.

## Scientist and creative director

Today, brand managers are also learning the habits of the *scientist*. This is because CEOs increasingly demand 'scientific' data from their marketing people—not just impressions and instincts but evidence and quantification—to justify their budgets. Brand managers are therefore getting interested in a range of new scientific disciplines. As we saw in Chapter 4, consumer neuroscience is still too young to be of much practical use. There's an emerging science called computational aesthetics, which aims to be able to predict which designs will work best just by measuring their features (line widths, curve angles, colours, brightnesses, and so on)—but that's still a long way behind the effectiveness of the human eye.

But another kind of data—often described as 'big data'—now plays a central role in branding. Much of what a company does in the market—communicating, selling, and delivering its product or service—now happens online, which means it gets tracked, which means there's data about it. Big data can tell a brand manager which online campaigns get most clicks, which tweets get most re-tweets, which discounts work best, which sales channels are most efficient, who the customers are, where they are, what else they like, how much they use your product, and what they say about it on Facebook.

Using this data, the brand manager's goal is to build a brand that's ahead of people's changing needs. Ford, for instance, is monitoring its customers' driving habits from its R&D centre in Silicon Valley. Big data can help you identify new trends and new needs, for example by analysing what people are searching for on Google. Big data can help you get pricing right, and to experiment with new products. And of course it can help you target communication at exactly the right people—for example, showing people advertising based on what they've been writing about in their emails. This kind of personalized brand-building is now commonplace—and so easy to do that brand-owners worry about 'the creep factor', the tendency for consumers to feel intruded on by brands that know too much about their lives—and therefore to reject the companies that do that.

So brand people are increasingly becoming data scientists. In fact, in many companies, the marketing department is now the biggest buyer of IT. The only trouble with big data is that it's big—there's far too much of it for it to be quickly useful. A 2013 IBM study suggested that 40 per cent of companies don't yet have the tools to understand all this data.

And the truth is that branding will always depend on creativity. Branding now depends as never before on innovation: constantly offering the next flavour, the latest store format, the newest technology. Brands that don't change die—in other words, companies have to keep trying to update the ideas about them in people's minds. Steve Jobs used to quote his favourite Bob Dylan line: 'he not busy being born is busy dying'. Many brand managers therefore focus on stimulating the organization to constantly renew itself. They push for rapid experimentation, and they often try and speed up the organization's body clock. Indeed, it's often the brand manager's role to push for renewal—to be the organization's *creative director*.

So brand managers today are a fascinating combination of philosopher, coach, scientist, and creative director.

## Bringing in experts

In a few companies—Burberry is a good example—the brand managers do all this branding work in-house. And there are signs that others are moving in this direction: design, for example, is being brought in-house at places like IBM. But to increase their chances of success, most brand managers rely on outside agencies—advertising agencies, design consultancies, PR companies, and so on. Often, an agency works for a company for far longer than any individual brand manager or marketing director: the agency becomes the fount of knowledge, the keeper of the brand.

Originally, brand managers hired advertising and public relations agencies to get the message out. The advertising business dates back well into the 19th century (J. Walter Thompson, for instance, was founded way back in 1864) and PR began in the early 20th century, with Edward Bernays, who we met in Chapter 3, as one of its founding fathers.

These pioneers, working in the age of scientific management, often saw themselves as scientists. J. Walter Thompson set up its own 'University of Advertising' and worked closely with the psychologist John B. Watson, founder of the behaviourist school. There was a belief that you could study, understand, and then control human behaviour, however irrational it might be.

In this scientific spirit, brand managers felt the need to understand their customers better, and the market research business grew to meet that need. One of its founders was George Gallup, who started his business in 1935. Over the years, they developed a range of techniques, 'quantitative' (surveys), and 'qualitative' (focus groups). More recently, market research has focused on what consumers do, rather than what they say they'll do, using 'ethnographic' techniques (observing people's behaviour), and analysing 'big data' on their buying behaviour. Some neither talk to nor observe consumers: instead they use the techniques of semiotics to analyse the cultural artefacts—films, music, design—that surround consumers and shape their lives.

## Buying creativity

At the same time, brand managers brought in design and brand agencies to create or renew their 'brand identity' or 'look and feel'. Initially, they used packaging design companies, and then—as branding spread from the branding of products into the branding of companies—they worked with corporate identity companies, of which Landor, founded in 1941, was one of the first.

By the 1960s, these design companies, together with the proponents of the new 'creative revolution' in advertising, had tipped the balance away from science towards art. Brand managers no longer attempted to control consumer behaviour, but to stimulate it through the power of imagination, in graphic design, photography, illustration, film-making, and copywriting.

These advertising, PR, market research, and design agencies dominated the scene until the 21st century, when the digital revolution changed everything. Brand managers had to quickly master the digital world, and 'digital agencies' emerged, of many different kinds, from advertising agencies specializing in online advertising, like AKQA, R/GA, and SapientNitro, to 'search engine marketing' companies that helped make sure that people searching on Google would find you.

At the same time, brand managers needed to design more than just their brand identity. To shape how their customers saw their brand, they had to get the whole customer experience right, particularly the online experience. The product design company IDEO moved into this area, joined by specialist service design businesses like Livework and Foolproof. 'Experience design' became one of the hottest buzz-phrases in the branding business.

Meanwhile, increasingly sceptical consumers became less interested in sales talk and more interested in broader 'content', through corporate blogs, social media, and magazines, and 'content marketing' agencies emerged to create all this material, like Redwood and Cedar (both, oddly, named after trees).

Media, which used to be very simple (television, radio, press, posters), became, in the digital world, very complex, and 'media agencies' (formerly the least exciting departments of advertising agencies) became big and powerful agencies in their own right. Specialists like Mindshare or OMD were the people who knew enough to get your content to the right people at the right time, using the right channels, at the best possible price. The scientists had returned.

## The big four

These forces hugely multiplied the number of agencies on the scene, but at the same time agencies were consolidating too. Just as the world's big consumer brands had clustered into companies like Procter & Gamble and Unilever, so the agencies started to cluster into groups big enough to serve them. Four giant groups—Interpublic, Omnicom, Publicis, and WPP—now dominate the industry.

The biggest, and best known, is WPP, built from scratch by the British entrepreneur Martin Sorrell. Bizarrely, WPP stands for Wire and Plastic Products: its original business was making wire shopping baskets. Sorrell bought the company in 1985 as a platform on which to build an empire of marketing agencies. Within a few years, he had bought two advertising giants, J. Walter Thompson and Ogilvy, and the group now employs 120,000 people. It includes advertising agencies like JWT and Ogilvy; brand agencies like

Brand Union and Landor; the market research company Kantar; the digital agency AKQA; and the media agency GroupM.

While Sorrell was shaping WPP in London, three US-based advertising agencies merged to form another giant called Omnicom, which is now WPP's biggest rival. Omnicom has three large advertising agencies, all with rather anonymous initials as their names: DDB, BBDO, and TBWA. Over the years, the group has also bought brand agencies (such as Interbrand and Wolff Olins), market research specialists Flamingo, content company Redwood, media agency OMD, and many more: around 70,000 people now work for Omnicom.

WPP and Omnicom have two slightly smaller competitors. The French group Publicis has around 60,000 people, with agencies like BBH and Saatchi & Saatchi. And Interpublic, also US-based, has 50,000 people: its most famous agencies are McCann-Erickson and FutureBrand.

Generally, clients interact with individual companies in these groups, rather than with the group itself. The groups need to maintain the separate identities of these member firms in order to attract creative people, and also to minimize client conflicts. But WPP pulls them together frequently, to serve big clients like Vodafone jointly. Omnicom has a consortium called Team Nissan to serve one of its biggest clients. The trend across the industry is probably towards closer collaboration.

Alongside the big groups, there are still thousands of independent agencies, with more starting up every year. Consolidation and fragmentation happen side-by-side.

## Life in an agency

In most of these agencies, the most visible people are the account managers, sometimes called 'client services'. Their role is to make

5. Inside the brand business: ideas are developed jointly by clients and consultants in creative sessions, like this workshop at the brand consultancy Wolff Olins.

the best possible working relationship between client and agency, meeting clients' needs, and keeping clients happy. Behind the scenes, they also have to keep the agency's own team happy, and to make sure their work is done on time and to budget. In design and brand agencies, where the focus may be less on the relationship and more on the work, these people may be called project or programme managers (Figure 5).

Alongside the account managers are consultants, sometimes called strategists or planners. Their job is to make sure that the agency's branding advice achieves its client's business objectives. They'll speak business language (up to a point, at least), and use PowerPoint and Excel. Some will focus on the client's organization, and facilitate workshops that get its people to shape its brand. Others may be more interested in its customers, they may commission market research, or run focus groups themselves. Yet others may be numbers people, experts on data analysis, or on brand valuation, which we explored in Chapter 4. They'll organize all the thinking that emerges during the project, make sense of it, and aim to find new ideas, new insights, and new opportunities.

At the heart of any creative agency are the 'creatives' or designers: the people who make the ads, create the packaging, design the logo, or even specify the whole user experience. Most will have art or design school educations. Many will specialize in the visual side of design; others in the verbal side, and may be known as copywriters. For all these people, the goal is to make the creative leap from idea to form, from rational to emotional, from logical system 2 thinking to intuitive system 1 thinking, so that their client's branding stands out, gets noticed, gets remembered, and changes how people think, feel, and act.

Many agencies now also have a fourth kind of person: technologists. In a world where the main and sometimes only experience of a brand is through a phone or other computer, the technologist has a dual role. They are responsible for helping to create the experiences that people will interact with (using a tap, a swipe, their voice, or a click). And they are responsible for helping colleagues and clients understand how technology continues to change what is possible. They are advocates for the possibilities that technology can bring.

In some agencies, work gets handed from one department to the next, but much more often, people mix together, and everything's done in a way that's as interdisciplinary as possible. Agencies tend to operate in an informal, non-hierarchical way (at least on the surface), but there's always someone in charge. In some agencies, the account manager choreographs everything; in others, creativity matters most, and it's a designer who runs the project; in some (the minority) it's the business thinking (and therefore the strategist) in the lead.

And though most agencies offer a wide range of services, they all have a specific heritage, a home territory. Some, for instance, come from the world of product brands, where packaging was their original skill, and will probably have a sharp commercial focus on product sales. Others may come from the world of corporate and service brands, and their original craft was logo design.

Sometimes these companies are therefore less interested in short-term sales figures, and more in long-term things like identity, ethos, and purpose.

Branding, of course, is a fashion industry. To keep clients interested, to stay relevant, to stimulate new business, to attract the best recruits, to keep themselves on their toes, most agencies frequently change the story they tell, or the proposition they offer. There are exceptions—Siegel+Gale, for instance, consistently talks about 'simplicity'—but many agencies are, paradoxically, better at managing their clients' brands than their own.

## Beyond marketing

The big four are essentially marketing services organizations, but branding, as we've seen, these days reaches way beyond marketing. So the global management consultancy firms, like McKinsey or Boston Consulting Group, advise clients on branding too. They've moved beyond their traditionally hard, numbers-led approach into the softer arts of brand-building.

BCG, for example, bought a specialist consultancy called Lighthouse to bolster its ability to advise clients on defining their 'purpose'. And the consulting firm EY, for example, bought the service design agency Seren, because it knows that successful brand-building increasingly depends on the nitty-gritty details of the customer experience.

At the same time, branding consultancies are moving into the world of strategy, and offering clients creative, as opposed to analytic, ways to shape their future success.

## New expectations

Branding, then, depends on companies and agencies working effectively together. This happens best when the two sides share an ambition for the project, have a deep understanding of the issues, and trust each other.

But there can be fractures too—particularly when new expectations don't match old assumptions. Recent research suggests that clients now expect to work with agencies in ways that are very different from traditional 20th-century practice.

Branding today is complex, and many companies prefer to break the problem up into chunks, with a specialist agency for each. Traditional agencies, though, want to be in the lead, to be at the top table, to be the 'agency of record', to somehow control the work of other agencies. Instead, they have to get used to being one of many. Google's new brand identity, launched in 2015, was designed in-house, though Google's many agencies may have suggested ideas indirectly. Increasingly, agencies need to think of themselves as contributors, not authors.

Branding, as we've seen, now relies on data as well as creativity. Agencies used to prize creativity above everything; brand managers no longer do. That's one of the reasons that media agencies have become more powerful in recent years. Brand agencies need to get brilliant at quantitative evidence, as well as qualitative imagination.

And branding is no longer just about communication. Consumers believe not what you say, but what you do. What matters, therefore, is the quality of the whole customer experience—and that should now be the primary focus of branding. In a 2015 survey, one brand client said: 'Agencies are largely behind pace. It's now all about putting customers first and designing seamless experiences—driven by tech and innovation.'

## Marketing and more

Branding is, in many ways, a curious business. Its origins are the creative worlds of marketing and design, but it has outgrown those worlds, and now deals also in strategy and data. It used to focus on a sales 'proposition', but is now obsessed with a deeper corporate 'purpose'. It's a collision between imagination and commerce, between philosophy and pragmatism, between intuition and evidence, a constant tug between art and science.

People working in branding deal constantly with tensions. Do we try to change the whole company, or focus on marketing first? Do we pursue our internal organizational ambition, or the external customer need? Do we follow our convictions (which encourage us to be bold), or the research (which often pushes us to be conservative)? Do we aim for the long term, or accept that these days it's impossible to predict more than a few weeks ahead? Do we construct a single organizing idea for all our work, or launch many parallel small ideas? These are some of the conundrums that you'll find inside every branding project (Box 5).

### Box 5  Muji: no brand

Muji is a global retail brand, but its name literally means 'no brand'. Started in 1980 by the Japanese retailer Seiyu, Muji now has 650 stores globally, selling around £2 billion of housewares and clothing a year. Founded, in its own words, as 'an antithesis to the habits of consumer society at the time', Muji aimed to make simple, useful products from natural materials, to 'maintain an ideal of the proper balance between living and the objects that make it possible'. Though high in concept, Muji is unpretentious in its products, stores, and communication, and its leading light, Ikko Tanaka, was famous for his humility. Muji is a pioneer of a fascinating, paradoxical law of branding: that, for many consumers, the less you behave like a conventionally ostentatious brand, and the more you appear to reject branding itself, the more seductive your brand becomes. Less brand is more brand.

# Chapter 6
# Branding projects

In February 2014, an Irish marketing expert called Kenny Jacobs joined the low-cost airline Ryanair as the company's first chief marketing officer. In thirty years, Ryanair—with low fares, minimal service, and an aggressive attitude—had become the biggest airline in Europe, carrying eighty million passengers a year. Ryanair didn't do conventional branding—it didn't seem to care about the customer experience, or about its image, or about design—but it had become a huge brand. Ryanair was almost universally known, and almost universally disliked, with a bad press that would have destroyed many other brands (Figure 6).

Jacobs's brief was to change things. With a pledge to listen more to customers, he launched a programme called 'Always Getting Better'. Fares would stay low, but the website and app would become user-friendly, service levels would rise, and Ryanair would fly to more convenient airports at better times of day. The airline would launch a new slogan, promising more than just a price benefit: 'Low fares. Made simple.' Jacobs says that the programme 'galvanised incredibly fast change', generating an impressive 6 per cent increase in Ryanair's 'load factor' (how full its planes are), and that it's been 'the best ride of my life'.

This was a fast, and effective, rebranding project. Jacobs reshaped what Ryanair does, what it says, and (a bit) how it looks, in order

6. Rebranding that worked: Ryanair's project meant big improvements in customer service, summarized by this slogan—and led to a rise in the airline's profitability.

to change the ideas in people's minds. And he did it in a typically Ryanair way. 'We just got on with it,' he reports, 'with no nonsense, and no consultants. We do have a brand strategy, but we don't navel-gaze. I just wrote down the brand on a page and gave it to the CEO.' The rebranding goal was, in a way, modest: 'I have no pretentions to "brand love". We have a functional brand offering a functional product—we're not a high-brand business like Virgin.' And he's more interested in measuring the change in reality than the change in image: 'We track Ryanair the experience, not Ryanair the brand'.

For a high-flying airline, this branding project could not have been more down-to-earth. This is Ryanair's own, authentic way of doing branding. And the best, and longest-lasting, branding is honest. It starts with an internal truth about a product or service or company, and makes that truth external. It nourishes that idea in the minds of consumers. Like all nourishing, this is a continuing daily task, not something that can be done once and for all—so branding keeps refreshing those ideas, and sometimes has to encourage a more profound rethink. For some organizations, branding is a central philosophy, a way of being. For others it's merely one tool among many. But for all, the fake tends to be ephemeral, the authentic lasts.

## Just getting on with it

The Ryanair story exemplifies a great deal about current branding practice. Brand managers aim increasingly to listen to customers, and even to involve them in branding projects. Every business, it seems, aspires to be 'customer-centric'. Branding is still driven by the corporation's own agenda, but these priorities are tempered by what customers say they want.

Branding projects today tend to be fast, aiming to produce results in weeks rather than years. Sometimes their aim is highly ambitious—to transform the business, or even to change the world—but often their spirit is more modest and pragmatic. As Jacobs says, 'we just got on with it'. In many industries, the ground feels as if it's constantly shifting, and brand managers therefore have to get something done quickly: there may not be time to achieve perfection in everything. Though a project may be fast, the task of brand-building never ends, so each branding project tends to be just part of a bigger journey.

Branding projects today are rarely linear. There was a time when projects progressed in a logical fashion through a series of stages: first research, then strategy, then design, then implementation. Nowadays, commercial deadlines often demand that items are implemented while the strategy is still being developed. Branding, in any case, is a creative task, and creativity rarely conforms to linear plans. The best work is often done through rapid prototyping—constantly developing, testing, and improving ideas—rather than a traditional stage-by-stage approach.

Twenty years ago, if organizations used outside consultants, they would work in these phases, presenting their work at each step to be signed off by the client. Now, the task is much more interactive, and organizations and their advisors develop ideas in collaboration. Agencies meet their clients at workshops, not at presentations. This is partly because it's the best way to bring the client's first-hand knowledge into the project, and partly because it helps the organization to buy into the emerging ideas. The agency stimulates, provokes, encapsulates, and visualizes thinking, rather than being its author.

## Always getting better

Critically, branding projects today focus more on what the organization does than on how it looks or what it says. In this project, Ryanair didn't change its logo or its colours, but its routes, its timetable, and its online booking system. Brands are built through the smallest details of the online and offline experience that customers get. Jacobs measures this constantly and precisely: 'We track Ryanair the experience'.

To make these changes happen, Jacobs created the slogan 'Always Getting Better'. This slogan was aimed not at Ryanair's customers but its employees. Branding projects now almost always start from the inside, because to get the reality of the customer experience to improve, you have to encourage colleagues to change how they do things. Branding projects today aim first to change how employees think, feel, and act.

So branding projects today are increasingly customer-driven, fast, pragmatic, and employee-focused. They're about deeds rather than words, performance rather than philosophy. But they still depend on the power of ideas. Almost all branding projects start by writing something down, some kind of thought that will become the touchstone for everything else. 'I just wrote down the brand on a page,' Jacobs reports. But for all his modesty, this was a very important page for Ryanair: a definition of what the businesses wanted to stand for.

So if this is the overall flavour of branding projects, what do they specifically aim to do? And how do they go about it?

## On purpose

Branding, as we've seen, often starts from the inside, and many branding projects aim not to attract customers, but to galvanize the organization's employees. If an organization's performance is slowing, or if its competitors are accelerating, it often uses the disciplines of branding to energize its own people. A re-organization or an acquisition (or a series of acquisitions) may fragment the business, and leave people wondering 'who are we?' A branding project can help create a renewed sense of identity.

Organizations used to talk a lot about their 'vision' (the future state they wanted to work towards) or their 'mission' (their corporate objective), but today, these ideas can seem self-serving. Amazon's vision is to be 'earth's most customer-centric company'. The Japanese earth-moving equipment company Komatsu famously had as its mission 'beat Caterpillar'. But workers today tend to want to make a difference to the wider world, rather than just to win a corporate battle, so purpose statements try to answer the more worthwhile question 'why do we exist?'

This is the most fundamental kind of question, and projects like this usually get kicked off by the CEO—but they're often run by the company's most senior brand experts. Here, branding clearly extends beyond marketing, and indeed projects like this usually invade the territory of strategy: it's hard to be clear about why we exist without also thinking about what we do and where.

Ryanair spent very little time worrying about such philosophical questions, but many organizations believe that a clear answer leads to a whole range of benefits. As well as motivating existing employees, an exciting purpose can attract the best new talent. It can guide and accelerate decision-making across the organization. And for some organizations, it can also attract outside investment.

Most organizations see a value not just in the outcome of a project like this, but also in the process. Often they involve all their senior managers, or even the whole company, in formulating a purpose. This can be complex and time-consuming, but it makes people feel valued, trusted, and influential. And often the 'wisdom of the crowd' is greater than that of the CEO on his or her own.

These projects are tricky. Involving many people can lead to compromise rather than conviction: a watered-down purpose that offends no-one and excites no-one. At the other end, you can end up with a purpose so grand that it's hard to put into practice. The best purpose statements are radical (they want to change the world) but also doable (they're credible and practicable) and useful (they're specific enough to guide day-to-day decisions). The supermarket company Tesco recently changed its purpose from 'to make what matters better together' (preachy and vague) to the much more practical statement 'to serve Britain's shoppers a little better every day'.

## What to stand for

Kenny Jacobs wrote the Ryanair brand quickly on a page, but many organizations devote a great deal more time and effort to 'brand strategy'. Branding projects like this aim to define what the product or company wants to stand for in people's minds, and how it's going to make that happen. This is sometimes referred to as 'positioning' the brand.

Often, positioning can be pinned down through two concepts from the world of advertising: proposition and personality. The proposition states what customers get for their money—IKEA's, for example, is 'affordable solutions for better living'. It's the more rational side of branding. The personality, on the other hand, is more emotional: it defines how the product or company should feel to people. When the mobile phone brand Orange was first launched, it described its personality as 'the world through the eyes of a seven-year-old', high on wonder and optimism, with no anxiety or cynicism.

Brand strategy projects are almost always guided by market research, exploring customers, their lives, their needs, and their desires. As Kenny Jacobs says, listening is important. And, increasingly, brand managers see consumers not as one group, or a number of 'segments', but as a set of individuals, whose worldviews can't easily be aggregated—making the task of finding a single proposition much harder.

## One or many

Brand strategy projects often explore another complex topic, also beginning with the letter 'p': portfolio. Most large organizations operate with more than one brand. In pursuit of growth, they buy brands, or create new brands to appeal to new markets, and they end up with a portfolio of brands—often complex and hard to manage.

The strategic choices quickly become fascinating. Do we simplify our portfolio, and reduce the number of brands? This option can help focus the organization on high-growth activities. Do we go further and connect our brands together, as Virgin does through the Virgin name? Or do we unify everything under one brand, like IKEA? This can encourage employees to collaborate more, rather than fighting for their own brand. And it can make the marketing operation much more efficient: it's cheaper to build one brand than a hundred. This approach is sometimes called 'branded house': one company with one brand.

But there are also advantages to keeping many brands in play, each looking to customers like an independent business. If one hits problems, the others aren't tainted. And when your customers live in many different cultures, with many different aims in life, you can reach more by spreading your branding bets. This is the 'house of brands' model, exemplified by Procter & Gamble.

Business today is complex, and the desire for simplicity often drives organizations towards the 'branded house' model. But equally, consumers today aren't uniform, and their changing needs are hard to predict: these forces drive businesses towards the 'house of brands'. It's perhaps not surprising that organizations rarely settle for one extreme or the other. Many are on the move, unifying or decentralizing. And others adopt hybrid positions. Coca-Cola, for example, has apparently independent brands like Fanta, plus brands like Dasani that are labelled from Coca-Cola. And its four main products—Coke, Diet Coke, Zero, and Life—look increasingly like flavours of one brand.

As well as sub-brands and product names, some companies deploy special kinds of brands. Ingredient brands convey a special skill or technology. Panasonic, for example, uses 'Lumix' to look good at photography. The BBC has a range of channel brands, from BBC ONE to BBC Radio 4. Many retailers have 'own-label' or 'private label' brands, for products made especially for them. Some use range brands to indicate quality and price, from 'basics' to 'best'. Others invent seemingly independent brands that are carefully designed to look a bit like the big familiar brands, or even like small craft brands, with names like 'Ocean Sea' or 'Rowan Hill Bakery'. The discounters Aldi and Lidl are famous for this.

The brand team also looks at architecture outside the company—what other brands do we want to be associated with? Companies use 'endorsements' to add value to their brands—for example, some L'Oréal products are endorsed by the singer Cheryl Cole. They use sponsorship to reach new customers: the airline Emirates became famous to British consumers by sponsoring Arsenal. They use alliances to extend their reach. Thai Airways, by joining Star Alliance, can offer more routes and more lounges. And they get into new markets by starting joint ventures, often with competitors: Aviva entered the life insurance market in Turkey by teaming up with local insurer Sabanci to form AvivaSA.

## Getting the product right

These branding projects—defining purpose, proposition, personality, or portfolio—largely produce words, strategies, plans. But as we've seen, the emphasis is increasingly on deeds. Projects like Ryanair's start with the 'offer'—the product or service that customers get. This is the best way to generate rapid increases in revenue or profitability. Jeff Bezos, founder of Amazon, says, 'In the old world, you devoted 30% of your time to building a great service and 70% of your time to shouting about it. In the new world, that inverts.'

There's always a trade-off here between improving what exists, and introducing something new. Often the quickest way to improve your brand—to upgrade the ideas in consumers' minds—is to find out what they most dislike about your current offering, and fix those problems. This was where Ryanair started—by switching to airports nearer to city centres, and by making the online purchase process much less arduous.

Brand managers also look at pricing and distribution. Pushing the price down can make your product more accessible and get your brand into the minds of many more people. But pushing the price up can increase people's sense of its quality, and paradoxically make it more valuable. Adjusting the pricing strategy—without actually changing the product at all—can make a big impact on the brand in people's minds. And distribution has a similar effect: do you want to be seen as universally available, and perhaps a daily purchase? Or as rare and special—something you have to make an effort to track down and buy?

But most brand managers are also keen to innovate—not least to keep their brand fresh in people's minds. Some adopt a method known as 'brand-driven innovation'. They use the idea that they want to stand for to inspire new product ideas, and to filter out ideas that won't build the brand. Virgin, for instance, wants its brand to stand for 'convention-breaking', so when Virgin Atlantic designed a new Upper Class cabin, its people asked themselves 'What ingrained conventions can we break to serve the user better?' And it's now common to involve customers in 'co-creating' new products—LEGO's Mindstorms, kits from which people can make programmable robots, are an example of a successful user-generated new product.

## In your experience

The most fashionable phrase is branding now is probably 'experience design'. The idea is to go deeper than just fixing problems with the product, or adjusting pricing or distribution, and deeper even than introducing new products. Instead, brand managers aim to connect together everything the customer experiences, into one seamless journey. For almost every business, this now means unifying what happens online with what happens offline—not an easy task. By giving the customer an experience that's both seamless and distinctive, this kind of project creates a much deeper impression of the brand in people's minds, and ideally leads to a deeper and longer relationship between company and consumer.

Branding projects like these often apply techniques originally created to design online user interfaces. They define 'personas'—imaginary people who typify particular kinds of customer—and the design work is done through the eyes of these personas. They map the 'customer journeys' these personas take, from first encountering the product or company, through to using it and recommending it to others. And they define 'experience principles' that guide the second-by-second design decisions that they make.

An experience is, of course, something that plays out over time, so it's natural to design customer experiences through the metaphor of the journey, or even the story. To build its brand, Airbnb specified its ideal customer experience, step by step, in the form of a Disney-style film storyboard.

## The death of advertising?

Improving the product, or the whole customer experience, is where branding projects often start. But the world needs to know about the great new offer, so marketing communications—the original home of branding—are still critically important.

To influence their image or presence, to get their message into the world, organizations deploy the whole range of media. The most obvious, of course, is advertising, in all its forms: the traditional home of brand-building. Though print advertising is in steep decline, online has become the front-line in advertising, where complex techniques are deployed like programmatic advertising (in which software, rather than people, buy the advertising space). And the familiar television commercial is still an immensely powerful way to associate ideas and emotions with a product.

Advertising is sometimes referred to as 'paid media', and it's the most expensive form of communication. The cheapest kind is what's called 'owned media'—your website, your shop displays, your presentations, where everything is entirely under your control. Then there's 'earned media'—coverage in blogs, social media, television, and the press. This is almost impossible to control, but when it works in your favour, it's probably the most effective form of communication—because increasingly consumers believe not what you say, but what others say about you.

In fact, because people are getting so good at decoding, and discounting, traditional sales messages, many companies are investing heavily in 'content marketing'. Instead of sales talk, they create and share useful content on the things that matter to consumers. Pampers, for instance, has become a source of guidance on childcare. Wherever possible, they aim to make material that people want to share with each other through social media, because people respond much more warmly to things they hear from each other than to things they hear from companies. Indeed, Red Bull now seems to put as much effort into making content as it does into making soft drinks. For years, Benetton built its brand through provocative reportage in its magazine *Colors*. The camera company GoPro has built its brand through films on YouTube, not conventional advertising. Others create branded spaces as a way to tell a subtler story than advertising can—like the Vans skate parks in California and London, or the Tesla and Dyson stores in London's Oxford Street.

This is all currently controversial. Some say that content marketing is the right strategy, particularly as a way to deepen relationships with existing consumers. Others say this is a wasted investment: in a world of disloyal, promiscuous customers, you have to keep attracting new consumers to replace those who leave you, and the best way to do that is still traditional advertising. Brand expert Byron Sharp, with a great deal of data as evidence, argues that you need to get noticed by new customers, not to become friends with old ones.

Behind the scenes, another kind of communication is vital in branding. 'Stakeholder management' is the task of keeping the most influential individuals on your side—politicians, policy-makers, and regulators. The health of an oil business like Shell, for instance, may depend much more on the brand in these people's minds than it does on consumers' perceptions.

## The culture is the brand

We've looked at many kinds of branding project, from purpose to experience, from portfolio strategy to content marketing. But they all depend on people—on mobilizing the organization's employees to get with the brand.

Many branding projects therefore aim to create the right climate inside the organization—or, to put it another way, to change its culture. Particularly in service businesses, customers' impressions of the brand depend on their experience of the brand's people. Most organizations now realize that, though a brand is an external phenomenon, out there in the minds of customers, branding starts with the internal. You need your own people to understand what you want to stand for, to believe in it, to have all the right skills, and to use your brand identity well, in order to do the right things for customers. Indeed, Tony Hseih, who runs the online shoe retailer Zappos, says 'your culture is your brand'.

So, to help nurture the right company culture, organizations invest in ambitious 'employee engagement' programmes, in order to get as many people as possible to 'live the brand'. And the brand thinking can become a corporate mantra. In companies like John Lewis, Nordstrom, Huawei, and Netflix, the brand idea becomes a very useful leadership tool, guiding people's decisions and raising their standards without telling them exactly what to do. It moves beyond the traditional 'command and control' style of management, exerting a subtler power. A Google employee said to me: 'The brand goes before us, and therefore people expect us to be impressive, so that certainly makes us all raise our game'.

Organizations often appoint influential employees to be 'brand ambassadors', or even 'brand evangelists', spreading the branding message to colleagues and the outside world. The label is interesting—in some cultures, diplomacy is the right metaphor, in others, religion. The eventual aim is to have every employee as a brand advocate, and to eliminate the 'brand saboteurs' that you'll find lurking inside many organizations.

But it's not enough to have a high-energy culture: to deliver its product brilliantly, an organization also needs the right skills. Less glamorous than 'culture', but even more important, is 'capability'. To achieve its mantra of 'always getting better', a business like Ryanair must invest in recruitment, training, and technology.

Since 1961, McDonald's has inculcated over 80,000 restaurant managers in essential skills through its 'Hamburger University' in Chicago. In 2001, Toyota codified its fourteen-step methodology as the Toyota Way. Companies like Vodafone use online systems to spread learning rapidly—often with employees teaching each other how best to do things, by making short videos. More strategically, many organizations realize they can't create the right brand on their own, and bring in the skills they need through partnerships and alliances. Virgin, for example, has largely built its brand through joint ventures with specialists: with Singapore Airlines (and, more recently, Delta) for Virgin Atlantic, with Stagecoach for Virgin Trains, and so on.

## The magic of design

Some branding projects are purely about design—changing the way the organizations looks and talks is still a powerful way to change how people think, feel, and act.

But design has a role to play in every kind of branding project. Design turns the logical into the intuitive, and at its best turns prose into poetry. Design can therefore humanize a purpose statement. It brings a proposition and personality off the page and into the world. It makes visual sense of a portfolio. It activates an offer, and fleshes out an experience.

This is where logical thought becomes unexpected, informal, personal, rule-breaking, or provocative. Branding can deploy irony: *LazyTown*, for example, is an Icelandic television show that encourages children to be active. It can even be incomprehensible. Most consumers don't know what the Audi slogan *Vorsprung durch Technik* means, but it still vividly conveys a powerful Germanic mystique. Through tricks like this, the reasonable becomes unreasonable. In the language of the neuroscientists, design by-passes rational thinking and directly triggers people's intuitive, or system 1, responses.

Traditionally, brand designers have concentrated on the visual elements—the most obvious signifiers—of the brand, such as its logo, colours, and typefaces. But these are just part of a much larger system. As well as the visual dimension, designers now give a great deal of attention to the verbal. This includes the brand name, product naming systems and slogans, but also the brand's 'tone of voice', or the style in which everything is written. Businesses like Innocent Drinks have a particularly distinctive writing style, and many others are now trying to achieve the same impact. Carlsberg can be recognized just by one word, 'probably'.

Designers also work carefully on the sensory dimensions of the brand. Smells, tastes, gestures, and textures can be very effective triggers of system 1 reactions. The hotel group Kempinski sprays its lobbies with a distinctive smell. Car-makers design the precise 'clunk' sound their car doors make when being closed. And the Spanish hotel group Meliá even encourages its staff to put their right hand on their hearts when greeting a customer—a distinctive brand gesture.

But for many companies, there's an even more important dimension of brand design: the interactive. Designers carefully consider the pixel-by-pixel, second-by-second details of the online user interface—because that's the most effective way of nurturing in customers' minds the right kind of impressions of the brand. WeChat, the Chinese messaging app, is a master of user interface design.

Some designers talk about 'touchpoints'—all the different things that a customer (or employee or investor) sees or touches, and that influence their sense of what the brand is all about. But this could be a static and fragmented way of thinking—designing many separate touchpoints—and it's now common, as we've seen, for designers to look at the whole customer experience, often as a 'customer journey' through time.

As with any creative activity, tastes, judgements, and conventions change over time. Brands take their cues from each other, just as artists influence other artists. The fashion at the moment is for purism, for stripping things back to essentials. Brand visual identities have often used shadows, highlights, and textures to give an illusion of three dimensions. Now the fashion—from Apple to Coca-Cola—is for simple 'flat' graphics. And brand naming has moved from made-up words (Google, Skype, Spotify) to simple real words (Uber, Vine, Slack).

## Honestly useful

Design, in its many dimensions, is a critical tool in every successful branding project. In some projects, it's about creating an unmissable logo. In others, it may mean defining exactly what happens when a user clicks on 'Checkout', or writing a simple mantra like 'Always Getting Better'. The emphasis now is less on design as styling, much more on design as problem-solving— and that's because people believe the reality they experience. Branding is less about myth-making, more about good, honest usefulness (Box 6).

**Box 6 Superdry: English Japanese**

Superdry is a global clothing retailer that has shot to success in the last ten years, famous for the striking Japanese lettering on its products. But Superdry comes not from Tokyo but from Cheltenham, England. The brand was founded in 1985 by Julian Dunkerton as Cult Clothing, with Superdry as an in-house brand. But Superdry turned out to be the more potent brand and, by 2012, all the Cult stores had changed their name to Superdry. Now there are over 500 stores in almost fifty countries. The company focuses, it says, on high-quality products that fuse vintage Americana and Japanese-inspired graphics, with a British style. The Japanese lettering is largely nonsense and random, but as a branding device it works brilliantly—except, apparently, in Japan.

# Chapter 7
# The ethics of branding

In 1988, a Dutch development agency called Solidaridad created a set of 'fair trade' standards that would guarantee a decent living for producers. Solidaridad's idea was to use branding to encourage consumers in rich countries to change their buying behaviour: to pay more for ethical products.

The idea rapidly spread beyond the Netherlands. A Fairtrade Labelling Organisation was set up, and in 2002 it launched a new brand, Fairtrade (Figure 7). Producers join a local cooperative and they benefit from advice and training, as well as a guaranteed minimum price.

The scheme is not perfect. Fairtrade products command a high price, and critics say that too much of this premium is kept by the retailers. And the system puts non-Fairtrade farmers at a serious disadvantage. Nevertheless, by 2013, consumers could choose from 30,000 different Fairtrade products, and they spent 5.5 billion euros buying them. The branding project had worked. And the scheme was helping 1.2 million workers and farmers in seventy-four countries.

Branding, clearly, is a powerful force. But is it always a force for good? There are reasons to be optimistic. Increasingly,

7. Social change: the Fairtrade brand encourages people to choose products that benefit their producers, rather than exploiting them.

commercial profit depends on social purpose, and branding has to be good in order to make money.

## Stories or lies?

Take another supermarket product. If you go shopping for salmon in Marks & Spencer in Britain, you'll find packages that say (for example) 'Lochmuir Salmon en croute'. It sounds delicious. Most people in Britain know that 'loch' is a Scottish lake, so it's easy to imagine that this salmon comes from a beautiful lake somewhere in the highlands. But if you go to Google Maps, and search for 'Lochmuir', you get an error message: 'We could not find Lochmuir. Make sure your search is spelled correctly.' Why is this? Because there's no such place—it's an invention of the branding people, to create a sense of provenance, and so to add value to the product.

Similarly, you might expect that Superdry comes from Japan—but, as we've just seen, it was founded in Cheltenham, England, in 1985. You might think that Häagen-Dazs is Scandinavian, but it's from New York. You might imagine that Crabtree and Evelyn is an old English company that goes back centuries, but it was set up by an American and two British people in Massachusetts in 1972. So when does colourful storytelling turn into misleading the consumer? Given that branding is designed to change how we think, feel, and act, when does its influence become pernicious?

There have been many critics of brands and branding over the years. The American journalist Vance Packard wrote an engrossing book called *The Hidden Persuaders*, back in 1957. He exposes the then-fashionable practice of motivational research, in which advertising people tapped into people's subconcious psychological processes to sell things (even using tricks, now banned, like subliminal advertising). 'Many of us', he concludes, 'are being influenced and manipulated, far more than we realize, in the patterns of our everyday lives.' So branding, and some of the practices it involves, can involve systematically tricking or manipulating people.

The British art critic John Berger made a television series in 1972 called *Ways of Seeing*, which became a book too. It's a brilliant Marxist analysis of the meanings, motives, and economics behind the images we see in art, and one programme analyses what Berger calls 'publicity', by which he means advertising and its related practices—an art that we might today call 'branding'. Berger concludes that 'the purpose of publicity is to make the spectator marginally dissatisfied with his present way of life'. Branding deliberately makes people unhappy with what they have, in order to induce them to buy more. It's the systematic creation of low-grade misery.

Most famously of all, the Canadian journalist Naomi Klein wrote a world best-seller in 2000, *No Logo*. This is an exploration of the way brands have invaded every area of life, including schools, and of the dubious practices of the big brand-owners, such as the use of sweatshops in developing countries to make a lot of the world's branded clothing. Klein predicts that 'as more young people discover the brand-name secrets of the global logo web, their outrage will fuel the next big political movement'. Her prediction hasn't entirely come true, but she has sparked an unprecedented level of public scrutiny of the branded multinationals.

These books attack something bigger than branding: the overweening practices of the big multinational corporations, or the entire economic system of capitalism. They all appeal to the teenager in us, the rebel, the conspiracy-theorist. Yet they do also hit hard at the trickery and sometimes hypocrisy of branding—and at the way that branding is not just a series of one-off deceptions but a system, a climate that we can't easily escape from.

But is this the only way to see branding? Clearly not.

## The gaiety of nations

Branding also has many positive effects. For consumers, it creates variety and guides choice. To keep their brands fresh in our minds, companies constantly develop new products and services. And without branding, it would be hard to identify and find the things we're looking for. If we want to quench our thirst, or paint our house, or get a loan, or watch a television show, branding guides us, helps us get what we want. Imagine a brand-free supermarket, with just one product in every category.

Brands make the world more predictable, and so reduce the anxiety of day-to-day life. Without brands, we wouldn't know what level of quality to expect from a product. We wouldn't know who or what to trust. Late at night, in a strange city, it can be very reassuring to find a McDonald's. Being a consumer is a worrying job, with a constant risk of making bad buying decisions, and one of the main psychological benefits of branding is to reduce that anxiety.

Branding also raises aspirations, and helps make good things more accessible: you could argue that it's a democratizing force. Penguin Books was founded in the 1930s to make good reading affordable to the new middle classes, and its founder, Allen Lane, spoke of it as not just a publisher but also a brand. It's partly the brand power of something like Tate in London or MoMA in New York that brings things like contemporary art to more people. You could also argue that it's through the anxiety-reducing power of branding that people try out new products and experiences. Tesco's former CEO, Terry Leahy, has argued that 'the British working class moved upmarket with us', and that the Tesco brand encouraged people to try a whole range of exotic new foods. The reassurance of airline and hotel brands, for example, encourages us to try new countries and new cultures.

Brands can make people feel better about themselves. Rightly or wrongly, they make us feel we've made the smart choice, or that we're the kind of people we've always wanted to be. Branding gives products and services extra meaning, extra value—they help us to show off to others, or just to quietly feel better about ourselves. They may give us a sense of identity and belonging, like LEGO's brand communities, and they get us to participate in the process of creating meaning. And some branding gives us a power we wouldn't otherwise have had. It's through the power of brands like eBay and Etsy that we're able to sell things to the world.

## Held to account

Branding can be good not just for consumers, but also for workers. Working for a good brand makes work feel more worthwhile. Employees feel a stronger sense of belonging, and that their work is worth doing, for a business with a strong brand like Nordstrom or John Lewis. And a clear statement of what you want to stand for makes for better decision-making. A brand can give workers guidance on what to do and how to do it—like Tesco's mantra 'to serve Britain's shoppers a little better every day', or the Indian conglomerate Mahindra's idea of enabling people 'to rise'.

Branding, clearly, is good for the economy. Because the primary role of branding is to stimulate buying (and repeated buying), it clearly helps create sales; and you could argue that the world's economic growth over the last century has been at least partly driven by the power of brands. The gross world product in 1920 was less than $2 trillion, now it's well over $50 trillion (at 1990 prices)—could that have happened without branding?

For society, branding improves quality, and makes corporations accountable. Because brands are a guarantee of a certain level of quality, they tend to improve quality overall. And because a brand is so valuable to its owner, it's motivated to fix anything that could damage the brand—which is why, for example, Primark moved so rapidly in 2013 to improve conditions in its factories in

Bangladesh. Brands in fact become a focus for scrutiny by ethical consumers—a scrutiny that would be much harder in an unbranded world.

At a less serious level, brands add to the gaiety of nations. Imagine how drab a brand-less world would be—and how humourless, if it didn't allow the Japanese fantasy of Superdry or the imaginary heritage of Crabtree & Evelyn. These stories add value for the consumer. And brands bring people closer together. Apple, Samsung, Facebook, Twitter, Nike, Adidas are today's lingua franca: a lexicon of meanings that we all share.

## Endless dissatisfaction

But there's a negative side to almost all these arguments. For consumers, branding can create homogeneity and reduce choice. Although at one level we've never had more goods and services to choose from, at another level there's less choice. The big global brand corporations drive out local, unbranded businesses, so that every city in the world now offers exactly the same range of shops, hotels, and even restaurants: Zara, Holiday Inn, Hard Rock Café. And in the online world, where brands help generate network effects, the result tends to be quasi-monopoly—Google, Wikipedia, eBay, Instagram.

Brands can create a false sense of security. In one way they guarantee quality, but they also encourage us to stop thinking—to assume, for example, that every ingredient in branded food must be healthy.

They trick people into buying things they don't need. You could say that this is the essence of branding: to create desire. Branding gets people to pay more than they need to; to buy and consume things they don't need; and to buy things that are bad for them, from cigarettes to sugary drinks. For some they become an addiction, they become label addicts.

Brands can make people feel dissatisfied with their lives, as John Berger has argued. Because branding creates desire, it doesn't create satisfaction or happiness. Like some addictive drugs, it stimulates the production of dopamine in the brain, making us constantly want more—the next version of the iPhone, the next BMW model up. Branding—it could be argued—creates permanently unsatisfied desires, rather like Oscar Wilde's description of the cigarette: 'A cigarette is the perfect pleasure; it is exquisite and leaves one unsatisfied'.

## Commercializing everything

You could argue that branding tricks employees into serving shareholders' interests, not their own. Today's employees, many serving carefully branded organizations, work hours that would have looked shocking in Victorian times, answering emails from breakfast to bedtime (and after). The glamour of the brand they work for, you could argue, leads them to put in far more labour than they're actually paid for.

For the economy, just as branding stimulates economic growth, it also fuels unsustainable levels of consumption, and therefore unsustainable levels of production. It creates a cycle in which resources are depleted, oceans are polluted, habitats are destroyed, and climate patterns are changed.

And for society, brands can be a mask behind which organizations can do wrong. Big, familiar, respected brands can make society assume that everything behind the scenes is OK, as the world saw in 2015 when Volkswagen's systematic deceptions about emission levels were revealed.

Branding may add colour, but it also commercializes everything, and makes everything banal. It helps turn religious festivals into commercial bonanzas. It brings commerce into schools, universities, museums, and galleries. In the interests of simplicity, brand managers can reduce a living, changing multi-dimensional entity like a city into a crass slogan: Edinburgh, for instance, becomes 'inspiring capital'.

And though brands unite us, they also divide the haves from the have-nots. They make it very visible who can afford an iPhone, and who has to make do with an ancient Nokia.

## Branding for social change

So what conclusion can we come to? The negatives are true, and I wouldn't want to minimize them, or encourage complacency. But the most effective branding is ethical, in the sense that it's the projection of a truth: branding that lies tends not to last.

And, overall, the effect of branding is to force things into the open. By operating under brand names, by using these powerful signs, companies are highly visible. They're important in people's lives, and therefore a natural object of scrutiny. People tend to be aware of branding and how it works, even while obeying its iron law. The rise of internet culture has amplified people's knowledge of brands and their power to investigate them—as well as fuelling non-deferential, anti-institutional attitudes. Through social media, individuals have gained the power to call companies to account, and in recent years consumers have boycotted companies like Amazon, Burberry, and Chevron. These boycotts may not destroy the brand, but they often do instigate changes in corporate policy. So for big companies, there's nowhere to hide.

And if branding changes how people think, feel, and act, can it also do that to achieve social change? Could branding help people and the planet? Clearly, branding can encourage short-term behaviour that leads to increased wellbeing. Fairtrade is an example. Unilever brands its Lifebuoy soap for its hygienic qualities, and runs a health education programme in rural India that it claims has reached seventy million people.

Branding can also create long-term habits that lead to increased sustainability. Zipcar, for example, encourages people to share cars rather than owning them, and claims that every Zipcar takes seventeen privately owned cars off the road. BlaBlaCar and Liftshare aim for similar effects, through ride-sharing. Method makes environmentally friendly cleaning products attractive to buy. Wikipedia is a brand that has encouraged thousands of contributors to add, through voluntary work, to the world's intellectual resources (Box 7).

Girl Effect is an organization—originally set up by Nike—that aims to use the power of media brands to change the attitudes and behaviours of teenage girls, particularly in the developing world, guiding them towards better health and education. Its first two brands, Yegna in Ethiopia and Ni-Nyampinga in Rwanda, offer radio programmes, girl bands, magazines, and websites that show teenage girls new social norms. The branding draws millions in

### Box 7 Wikipedia: a labour of love

Wikipedia is a global brand run not by expert employees, but by volunteers. Founded in 2001 by Jimmy Wales, and launched in 2001, its mission is 'to compile the sum of all human knowledge'. Wikipedia now contains forty million articles in 250 different languages. Though it's crowdsourced, rather than written by scholars, it's generally highly reliable, and studies have shown that Wikipedia is often just as accurate as *Encyclopedia Britannica*, the institution that it has, in many ways, replaced. The English Wikipedia now has around 120,000 active editors. What gets people to build a global encyclopedia, and a global brand, for nothing? It's called the 'incentive economy'—prestige, recognition, a desire for fact, an obsession with accuracy. But also—and this is the power of many newer brands—just the feeling of taking part in, of being part of, something worthwhile.

and transforms what is seen as 'normal'. The brands then take on a life of their own, as audiences start to identify themselves as, for instance, 'Yegna girls', and start to feel a much stronger sense of self-confidence.

## Good business

Perhaps the strongest reason for a positive view of branding is the increasing interdependency between commercial and social impact. After a string of corporate scandals and crashes—Enron, BP, Lehman Brothers, Volkswagen—people demand a much higher level of social responsibility. To earn, and keep, the commitment of the people who matter—consumers, employees, regulators, the media—organizations now keenly pursue social as well as commercial impact. Companies like Unilever also see social objectives as a way to inspire innovation, and to become much more efficient in the use of scarce resources. Walmart, the world's largest retailer, sees sustainability as good business, and social responsibility helps it to live up to its brand slogan 'Save Money. Live Better'. Profit, for most of the world's CEOs, now depends partly on purpose. Increasingly, therefore, organizations will have to use their brands not just to achieve commercial aims, but to secure social goals too.

# Chapter 8
# A future for branding?

We've seen that branding, though a very old practice, has recently become a big topic, a board-room priority, and a field of academic research. Its scope has expanded into culture, politics, education, cities, countries, celebrities, and more. But how is the practice of branding changing? Has it reached its peak? Or does it have a long future ahead of it?

It's possible to discern three areas in which change is happening: the scope of branding (what gets branded), the target of branding (who branding is for), and the spirit of branding (how branding works). In each of these, there's no simple transition from the old to the new. Instead, there's a dialectic, a conflict between two forces. It's rather like a soap opera, with three strong storylines. Like all good storylines, they thrive on conflict: in each case, there's not a clear winner, only opposing forces. But if there's one thought that unites these storylines, it's that traditional branding is now challenged by a newer, less corporate alternative.

## What gets branded?

There's a live debate in business about the best way to organize, or the best form of organization—and therefore what kind of organizational entity needs to be branded.

The publicly owned corporation continues to be the dominant form. This kind of organization, answerable to its shareholders, and seeking constant growth in profits, proved itself in the last century to be a highly effective way of making money. Apple is, perhaps, the supreme example: an astonishingly wealthy empire sitting on cash reserves of $200 billion. In a globalized world, scale is more important than ever, so businesses continue to merge together into ever greater units: recently Kraft, for instance, has joined Heinz, and Shell has merged with BG. These corporations aim to be self-sufficient, to do things themselves, to own their intellectual property. In the business landscape, they are corporate citadels.

But at the same time, many alternative organizational forms have grown in strength. Some of the world's biggest companies today are state-owned (like China Mobile) or privately owned (like IKEA). In some markets, employee-owned co-operatives (John Lewis, Mondragon) are very successful. Even China's Huawei is partly employee-owned. There's a new breed of social enterprises, like Cafédirect, or benefit corporations, like Etsy, Patagonia, and the British food company COOK. There are much looser, but clearly branded, movements—more 'organizings' than 'organizations'—like the Black Lives Matter movement. And the last ten years have seen, of course, an unprecedented crop of start-ups. None of these organizations is driven by the short-term demands of the stockmarket; some of them are fuelled by an anti-corporate spirit; almost all of them aim for goals beyond pure profit.

The traditional corporation uses branding as a way to maximize shareholder value, by achieving price premiums and securing long-term revenues. But alternative forms of organization may have other aims too. Social enterprises may want to build support for a particular cause; start-ups in the digital world may be aiming not for immediate revenue but for network effects.

And many organizations—both conventional and alternative in form—are operating in a much more collaborative way. For example, when business depends on complex technologies that are hugely expensive to develop, they choose to work with organizations that have those technologies, rather than developing them for themselves. This means organizations are acting less as self-sufficient citadels, and much more in constellations with others. This can feel very different. Phil Mirvis, an academic expert on organizations, says 'the company is no longer the centre of its universe'. Instead of standing at centre-stage, controlling a web of suppliers and distributors, companies find themselves working as equal partners with collaborators (and, often, competitors) in a kind of organizational ecosystem.

## Citadel or constellation

The storyline here, then, is the clash between two philosophies: the citadel and the constellation. You could see Apple as the model citadel, and Google as a conspicuous constellation. And yet of course the truth is more complex. Apple's App Store depends on a constellation of independent developers, and Google's parent Alphabet is turning into a conventional-looking conglomerate. Organizations that begin as rebellious start-ups grow, and inevitably take on the apparatus of the traditional corporation.

In branding, the consequences are fascinating. Traditional global brands, sometimes called 'powerbrands', continue to grow: Apple, Pepsi, Mercedes-Benz, Vodafone, and many more. Some of them, though, occasionally try to look small and un-corporate, using a trick known as 'debranding'. Starbucks, for instance, has a neighbourhood coffee shop in Seattle called Roy Street Coffee and Tea. Its website says it's 'inspired by Starbucks', but actually it's owned by Starbucks.

At the same time, paradoxically, many of the world's newer brands have tried to look *more* corporate. Many online businesses started life with informal, unsophisticated, almost hand-made, brand identities. The priority for them was a brilliant product and a memorable name, not a slick logo. Some, like Instagram and Airbnb, were handwritten. Others, such as Yahoo and eBay, were bouncy and cartoon-like. Even the mighty Google had a typographically awkward logo. One by one, they have switched to much more carefully designed, much more conventional, much more corporate brand identities, in order to signal to users and regulators that they are proper, grown-up, money-making businesses.

Behind the scenes, ownership is changing—for example, Zipcar has been bought by Avis and Yahoo by Verizon—and it remains to be seen how these version 5 brands will develop under new owners. Some internet brand companies are now partnering with traditional businesses: Alphabet, for instance, has set up a bioelectronics business with GlaxoSmithKline, called Galvani. How will these joint ventures get branded?

At the same time, big brands have emerged that are shared by many companies. Perhaps the biggest brand on the planet is Android, which, though legally owned by Google, is in practice shared among hundreds of phone and tablet makers.

## Brand as affiliation

The new model that's emerging is the purposeful constellation—organizations joining together to pursue more than just commercial goals. With social media, memes and hashtags can become global phenomena in a matter of hours. They are symbols that people adopt, identify with, give meaning to, and share. Though they're owned by no-one, and certainly not by any commercial organization, they are brands. In the wake of the terrorist attack in 2015 on the French satirical newspaper *Charlie Hebdo*, millions of people used the slogan 'Je suis Charlie'. The phrase became a mark of affiliation, a temporary but potent un-corporate brand.

So, though branding is still usually about positioning and ownership, it's increasingly also about purpose and *affiliation*. Its dominant role is still to get people to buy things, but there's an emerging role: to give people, and other organizations, a reason to affiliate. The conference organizer TED—whose purpose is to spread 'ideas worth sharing'—has given up a degree of control over its brand, allowing groups around the world to affiliate to the brand and organize their own TEDx events.

These shifts in the nature of the organization will continue, and we'll see more branding that aims to be un-corporate in one way or another: to signal social purpose, to look small and local, to bring organizations together, and to exert charm rather than just power.

Of course, if a brand is an intrinsically corporate thing and the world is moving towards the un-corporate, there will no longer be a place for it. Perhaps, in an un-corporate world, there will just be shifting, informal 'organizings', none of which is permanent enough to build a brand.

## Who's branding for?

While organizations are morphing in form, another battle is playing out: a power struggle between the producer of goods (the company) and consumer (the people). When it comes to branding, who is in the driving seat?

Over the last ten years or so, producers have grown hugely in power, particularly through the data they have about consumers. Because we now consume so much online, we all leave a trail of data, revealing precisely where we are, what we buy, what we read and watch, and how our preferences are changing over time. This data is, of course, invaluable to producers, and selling the data is now a widespread (though largely invisible) economic activity. Indeed, it's the value of this data that pays for many of those online services that appear to be free. As the chilling phrase goes, 'If it's free, you're the product'.

But at the same time, the internet has given the consumer unprecedented powers. Consumers can now compare products instantly, get impartial products reviews from thousands of their peers, and make very public complaints through social media—all of which was impossible only a few years ago. Alternatively, they can become a 'collaborative consumer', rejecting the old mode of consumption in which each of us owns our own property, in favour of a new mode where goods are shared among many. There's currently, for example, a discernible shift away from car ownership among younger people, towards car clubs like Zipcar—a worrying trend for car manufacturers who could face massively declining sales.

And it's never been easier for consumers to fund, make, or sell things themselves, cutting out the traditional producer entirely. Kickstarter, for instance, makes us all venture capitalists; eBay makes everyone a retailer; Airbnb means anyone can be a mini-hotelier; and with Uber you start your own taxi business. Alongside all this is a massive growth in small-scale production: the 'maker movement' includes the rise of craftspeople using sites like Etsy; and 'hacker culture' is the emerging subculture of clever people finding new ways to solve problems, often using software coding (to be distinguished from the darker kind of hackers who break into computer systems).

## The *consommacteur*

Many of these phenomena are, of course, minority activities, but the underlying shift in mindset is undoubtedly mainstream. Research suggests that, back in 2006, 90 per cent of internet users were passive, simply consuming information. Just six years later, the ratio had switched, and 87 per cent of users were actively contributing content—even if only posting their most recent selfie on Facebook. The internet has activated the consumer, and what the French call the *consommacteur*—half consumer, half actor—is now mainstream.

In some ways, technology has made the consumer more individualistic, more atomized, and everyone has become a one-person brand. In others, it has made it much easier to coalesce into groups, networks, communities, or what are fashionably called 'tribes'.

Academics have taken this thinking further, and proposed an idea called 'service-dominant logic', which questions the traditional sharp distinction between producer and consumer. It proposes that, when consumers buy a service, they almost always play an active role in the production of value. By using the service, they co-create its value. Indeed, they determine what, for them, constitutes value. When I use an airline like Lufthansa, I do some of the work: printing my boarding card, carrying my cabin bag, and so on. When I post a review on Tripadvisor, I'm helping make Tripadvisor a more valuable service.

And the theory goes further and suggests that all exchanges, of products as well as services, are like this—that it's actually better to think of products as a kind of service, which is why the logic is 'service-dominant'. The enterprise, it's argued, cannot actually deliver value. Its power is limited to offering 'value propositions', which the consumer transforms into value. A Hyundai car, a Forever 21 top, even an Oreo biscuit, has no value until someone uses it.

Back in the marketplace, there's an interesting battle, with branding as an important weapon. Producers, with ever greater data in their hands, are getting better at pushing products out, using branding to build loyalty, and deploying a battery of techniques to sell us things at precisely the moment we're most likely to buy. Consumers, at the same time, are becoming cannier, more suspicious, much less loyal, and readier to reject traditional consumption. And both phenomena happen at the same time. Most of us are resistant to branding at one moment, and yet seduced by it at the next.

It's now common practice for companies to recognize a shift in power, and to say that their brands are now 'owned' by or 'co-created' by their customers. At a minimum, this means that organizations recognize that their brands exist outside themselves, in the minds of people out in the world, and can't therefore be directly controlled. All you can do is to nudge your customers towards creating the 'right' kind of meaning. As Marty Neumeier says in his book *The Brand Flip*: 'A brand is not owned by the company, but by the customers who draw meaning from it. Your brand isn't what *you* say it is. It's what *they* say it is.' Pushing this thought to its conclusion, many brand managers now conceive their brands from the outside in, and enlist customers as their most important brand-builders.

## Brand as platform

Out of the battle has emerged the idea of the *platform*. Received wisdom now in Silicon Valley is that companies should make not products to sell to consumers, but platforms on which people can do things: platforms like eBay, or the App Store, or Uber. Marketing people talk less about building emotional 'loyalty', and more about making things that are simply 'useful' to people. The brand expert John Willshire neatly contrasts traditional branding, which he describes as 'making people want things', with the newer mode, 'making things people want'. Out go the advertising people who aim to create desire; in come product and experience designers who just want to make something useful. Branding is more functional, and brand identities more utilitarian. There's a new (and probably often false) modesty in the air.

The question then about these platform brands is: whose are they anyway? Created by a 'producer' company, like eBay, they become the tool of the 'consumer': they become the means by which users achieve their goals. An eBay seller relies on the probity of the eBay brand. The Uber and Airbnb brands are essential badges for Uber drivers and Airbnb hosts. Indeed, Airbnb recognized this

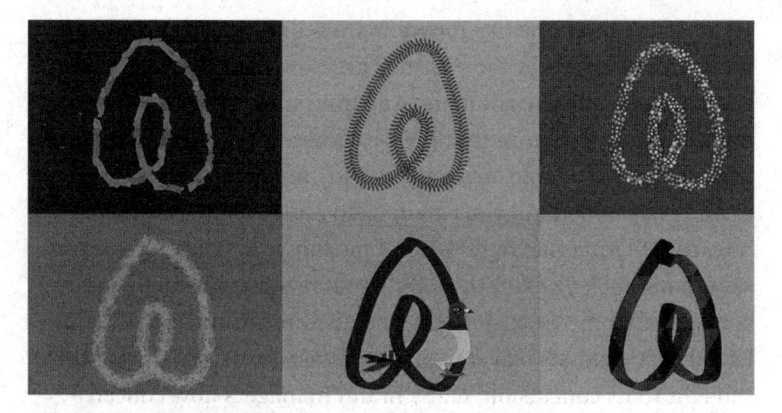

8. A shared brand: the Airbnb logo is called 'bélo', and it's designed for Airbnb hosts to adopt and adapt, making it their own.

in 2014 by redesigning its logo—called 'bélo'—as a kind of template that its hosts can adopt, adapt, and redraw (Figure 8). By 2016, 160,000 people had made their own bélo. In a very literal way, the brand is shared and made by its users, not its original owner.

Already there's a backlash against the 'platform' idea. Businesses like Uber are heavily criticized for taking work away from traditional, regulated taxi drivers. In Germany, for example, the new highly individualized 'Plattform-Kapitalismus' is seen as threatening more traditional, more organized ways of working, where there was solidarity among, rather than competition between, workers.

So branding is still about persuasion, where the producer asserts power, but it is also increasingly about making a useful platform, where the consumer exerts power, and indeed becomes a producer. In this context, the role of the brand, at least for the moment, is to bring more and more users onto the platform, and to keep them there: to produce network effects. This is, as we saw in Chapter 3, branding version 5.

Where will this power struggle go next? One view is that technology will give the consumer more power than the producer. Given enough data, and effective comparison websites, consumers will have complete information about the marketplace, and will base all their buying decisions on a perfect knowledge of all the facts. On this view, brands become much less important. In their book *Absolute Value*, Itamar Simonson and Emanuel Rosen give a clear example: 'You always knew what to expect at Subway or McDonald's. But when you know what to expect at a small restaurant through Yelp or Zagat, brand names are becoming relatively less important.' Of course, you could take the opposite view: as comparison sites force up standards and therefore encourage homogeneity, the non-rational things, the features beyond the facts, will become more important in helping me chose what's right for me.

Another version of the future posits a switch from 'customer relationship management'—the databases the big companies keep about us—to 'vendor relationship management'. In this new world, set out by Doc Searls in *The Intention Economy*, the tables are turned: consumers now keep tabs on producers, we all have databases about them. Instead of companies launching campaigns to sell their products to us, we'll launch campaigns to announce our needs and goals (our 'intentions') to the world, and companies will bid to meet them. If I need a new fridge, I'll declare this intention online, and Bosch, Beko, Candy, Haier, and the rest will fight among themselves to make me the best offer. Again, this could make branding irrelevant. Or it could mean that the brand is part of what the company offers us—the meaning as well as the functionality. Or it could even mean that our own individual personal brands will help us attract the very best deals from the companies.

## How should branding feel?

Alongside the changing shape of the corporation, and the shifting power of the consumer, a third storyline is discernible, to do with the culture of branding: the way that brand managers and brand consultants feel about what they do.

The traditional way of thinking favours single-mindedness. Ever since the advertising guru David Ogilvy started talking about the 'big idea', marketing people—and their advisors—have been unifiers, simplifiers, and rationalizers. The discipline of corporate identity design, now usually called brand consulting, was founded on an impulse to take a mess of different brand names, logos, and messages and turn it into a beautifully organized organization. This transformation would be shaped by an overarching thought. Wally Olins, one of the most influential proponents of this approach, talked about the importance of the 'central idea': one single concept from which every piece of communication and design would flow. The core concept is *identity*. An organization needs to have a single identity, consistent across time and space, in order to flourish, and the logo is the marker of that identity.

This way of thinking meshes well with the traditional approaches of business schools and management consultancies, where organizations are imagined as highly disciplined entities, governed by an overarching strategy. This is the approach of the architect or master-planner: businesses in general, and brands in particular, are best constructed from a blueprint.

The mainstream of organizational thinking is that, in the words of Thomas Friedman, 'the world is flat'. In this view, the victory of capitalism, and the incredibly rapid spread of smartphones and social media, mean that the world is pretty much the same everywhere. A big idea can work universally, and the goal of every start-up is to 'scale' their business, so that the same software that served a hundred customers can serve a billion.

Most big global brands use something like the big idea approach. BMW, for instance, is still the 'ultimate driving machine', a slogan first used in 1975. Microsoft is still very much the same everywhere in the world. And newer brands from India and China tend to emulate this kind of thinking, where a brand is built through a consistent logo, slogan, colours, and communication style. Indeed, recent research suggests that these traditional branding tools are still extremely effective at burning brands into people's minds.

## Against the formula

But the last ten years or so have seen the rise of a contrary view: that plurality, complication, and even messiness might be a good thing. The thinking is that the world moves too fast for blueprints. Five-year strategies and ten-year brand positionings are out-of-date as soon as they're written. In addition, customers don't want imposed ideas. They will shape what a brand is about much more effectively than the brand's owner can control it. And, it's argued, the world *isn't* flat: cultures still differ enormously, and management by formula never quite works. Indeed, the secret to attracting the commitment of customers may be to create variety, localness, and constant novelty.

Finally, many practitioners now feel differently about branding. A mistrust has developed for the formula, a boredom with the sameness of brands, a fatigue with the big idea. Instead of focusing on a single brand *identity*, practitioners talk about designing a multifaceted customer *experience*.

This is the approach not of the architect but what academics call the *bricoleur*—the handyperson, the do-it-yourself-er—making things out of whatever lies to hand, and learning by trial and error.

The explosion of technology start-ups has encouraged this new mood. In these businesses, neat, single-minded strategies and business plans are rejected in favour of rapid, multiple experiments. Success comes not from intellectual neatness but creative messiness. Methods used in software engineering—agility, rapid prototyping, sprints, independent teams—have been transplanted into management philosophy, and the summit of this conceptual mountain is a radically decentralized management approach called 'holacracy', meaning a hierarchy of units that are simultaneously autonomous and interdependent.

In branding, the most obvious symptom is visual—the emergence of variant, generative, and animated logos. In 2000, Tate launched four different versions of its logo, and a decade later, MIT Media Lab announced a new logo with 40,000 self-generating variants—though both have subsequently been simplified. Google frequently runs a special logo-of-the-day, called a Doodle. AOL's logo is white on white, invisible until something else moves behind it: it was designed to be not static but animated.

## Brand as pattern

Branding experts talk about 'liquid brands' or 'moving brands', but they mean more than just liquid logos or moving logos. They mean that the ideas behind the logo are themselves much less fixed. Experience design expert Marc Shillum has argued that branding is about 'creating patterns, not repeating messages'. It's an interplay of many small ideas, not one big idea. Starbucks has moved away from a formulaic approach to its coffee shops, preferring, it says, 'identity to identical'.

Branding from beyond the West may be pointing the way. Mandarin Oriental, from Hong Kong, is a hotel group that has broken out of the Western, formulaic model. Muji has built a retail brand by rejecting the more ostentatious modes of Western branding. China's innovative 'content ecosystem' business LeEco is building a brand that spans Eastern and Western styles. Huawei is not a conventional corporation, and may well therefore develop a different kind of brand. Distinctively African brands are now playing on the world stage, like Jumia or the Ethiopia shoe maker Sole Rebels.

The drama here is that many organizations flip from control to liberation and back again. Coca-Cola is master of the formula, and yet also embraces liberation, printing multiple labels with not one brand name but a wide range of first names—Erin, Kelly, Rebecca, Tim, and so on, in the Coca-Cola typeface. Yet this, of course, is just a more sophisticated kind of formula. The big internet brands are loose and multiple in some ways, and yet still depend on a consistent name, logo, and user interface to create network effects. And most of the new Eastern brands—though oriental in management style—emulate the branding techniques of the West: in the airline industry, Emirates and IndiGo are two very successful examples. We're seeing a constantly shifting interplay between traditional consistency, based on a tight sense of brand identity, and a looser kind of coherence, based on a more plural sense of brand experience.

## Death and life

All three of these storylines question the future of branding. If organizations become looser organisms, will they need or want brands? If customers become more powerful than producers, will brands become irrelevant? If the trend from consistency to pattern grows, will branding, as we know it, gradually disappear?

My view is that branding will continue to be essential, but that it will become less formal, less pompous, less monolithic, less institutional, less purely commercial, less corporate. In scope, branding will reach less formal kinds of organization, and even the biggest will try to look smaller and more informal. Indeed, we're just at the beginning of a shift to the start-up and the social enterprise and the idea of 'open-source' technologies. In role, branding will aim not to persuade people just to buy, but enlist people to take part. And in style, branding will less and less follow the Western model: it will be less tight and controlled and neat and consistent in its form. We're just at the beginning of the rise of Asian and African brands.

Of course, these three storylines are closely interrelated: looser, less controlled organizations suit the needs of powerful, active consumers, and are best expressed through looser, less consistent branding. This dynamic is set to accelerate.

Branding, in other words, will live on. The human practice of creating value by using marks on objects to make meanings will always be with us.

# References

## Chapter 1: The triumph of branding

**Coca-Cola in Africa**
<http://www.coca-colacompany.com/stories/coca-cola-offers-consumers-reasons-to-believe>

**80% of marketing directors believe their products are differentiated**
<https://hbr.org/2012/03/living-differentiation>

**People wouldn't care if 74% of brands disappeared**
<http://www.havasmedia.com/press/press-releases/2015/top-scoring-meaningful-brands-enjoy-a-share-of-wallet-46-per-cent-higher-than-low-performers>

**Brand accounts for more than 30% of the stockmarket value**
<http://www.economist.com/news/business/21614150-brands-are-most-valuable-assets-many-companies-possess-no-one-agrees-how-much-they>

## Chapter 2: What is 'branding'?

**Definitions of 'brand'**
Kornberger, Martin (2010). *Brand Society*. Cambridge: Cambridge University Press.
Barden, Phil (2013). *Decoded*. Chichester: John Wiley.
Aaker, David A. and Joachimsthaler, Erich (2009). *Brand Leadership*. London: Simon & Schuster.

Keller, Kevin Lane (2012). *Strategic Brand Management*. London: Pearson.

Neumeier, Marty (2006). *The Brand Gap*. Berkeley, CA: New Riders.

## Chapter 3: The history of branding

### The Cadbury story
Cadbury, Deborah (2010). *Chocolate Wars*. London: HarperPress.

### A 1955 article
Gardner, B. B. and Levy, Sidney J. (1955). The Product and the Brand. *Harvard Business Review* 33/2 (March–April): 33–9.

### The producer-consumer
Toffler, Alvin (1980). *The Third Wave*. New York: Willam Morrow.

### No visible logo
<http://www.independent.co.uk/life-style/fashion/news/how-anonymous-designers-are-trading-on-their-creators-lack-of-ego-10433788.html>

## Chapter 4: How branding works

### System 1 thinking
Kahneman, Daniel (2011). *Thinking, Fast and Slow*. New York: Farrar, Straus and Giroux.

### A brand is an upstream reservoir
<http://www.britishbrandsgroup.org.uk/upload/File/Lecture-1.pdf>

### Loving the brand
Batra, Rajeev, Ahuvia, Aaron, and Bagozzi, Richard P. (2012). Brand Love. *Journal of Marketing* 76: 1–16.

### A study by management consultants
<http://www.forbes.com/sites/marketshare/2012/03/26/only-one-quarter-of-american-consumers-are-brand-loyal/#13afab486e9a>

### Loyal switchers
Sharp, Byron (2010). *How Brands Grow*. Oxford: Oxford University Press.

**Brand equity**
Keller, Kevin Lane (2012). *Strategic Brand Management*. London: Pearson.

**BrandZ's valuation of the Google brand**
<http://www.millwardbrown.com/brandz/top-global-brands/2016>

## Chapter 5: The branding business

**Deep inside Procter & Gamble**
<http://www.brandingstrategyinsider.com/2009/06/great-moments-in-branding-neil-mcelroy-memo.html>

**Strategic brand leadership**
Aaker, David A. and Joachimsthaler, Erich (2009). *Brand Leadership*. London: Simon & Schuster.

**A 2015 survey**
<http://marketing.hallandpartners.com/acton/attachment/6945/f-0598/1/-/-/-/-/2015%2007%2009%20-%20IPA%20Booklet.pdf>

## Chapter 6: Branding projects

**The Ryanair story**
Interview with Kenny Jacobs, 2015.

**Jeff Bezos on 70% shouting**
<http://www.forbes.com/global/2012/0507/global-2000-12-amazon-jeff-bezos-gets-it.html>

**Tony Hseih on 'your culture is your brand'**
<http://www.huffingtonpost.com/tony-hsieh/zappos-founder-tony-hsieh_1_b_783333.html>

## Chapter 7: The ethics of branding

**Three critics**
Packard, Vance (1957). *The Hidden Persuaders*. New York: David McKay.
Berger, John (1972). *Ways of Seeing*. London: BBC.
Klein, Naomi (1999). *No Logo*. Toronto: Knopf.

## Chapter 8: A future for branding?

**Active consumers**

<http://www.bbc.co.uk/blogs/bbcinternet/2012/05/bbc_online_briefing_spring_201_1.html>

**Your brand is what they say it is**

Neumeier, Marty (2015). *The Brand Flip*. Berkeley, CA: New Riders.

**The mainstream of organizational thinking**

Friedman, Thomas (2005). *The World is Flat*. New York: Farrar, Straus and Giroux.

# Further reading

I hope this book has opened your eyes to some of the ways branding works in today's world. If so, you may want to look more deeply into the subject. There are thousands of books and other resources: this is my short-list of the most rewarding ones.

The two academic giants of branding are Kevin Lane Keller and David Aaker. If you like big and encyclopedic textbooks, then Keller's *Strategic Brand Management* (Pearson, 2012) is exhaustive and up-to-date; and it's also worth reading Aaker's *Building Strong Brands* (Simon & Schuster, 2002).

The other most widely read textbooks are *Creating Powerful Brands* by Leslie de Chernatony, Malcolm McDonald, and Elaine Wallace (Routledge, 2011) and Jean-Noël Kapferer's *The New Strategic Brand Management* (Kogan Page, 2012).

For an overview of academic theories about branding, *Brand Management* by Tilde Heding, Charlotte F. Knudtzen, and Mogens Bjerre (Routledge, 2016) is beautifully organized and invaluable.

If, like me, you're fascinated by the central role brands play in our lives as consumers and workers, then read Martin Kornberger's *Brand Society* (Cambridge University Press, 2010): a masterly overview of how brand drives both production (how it influences management) and consumption (how it influences lifestyles). You may also enjoy Adam Arvidsson's challenging book *Brands: Meaning and Value in Media Culture* (Routledge, 2006).

To drill into the role branding can play in management, look at the fascinating *Taking Brand Initiative* by Mary Jo Hatch and Majken Schultz (Jossey Bass, 2008). It's also worth reading David Aaker and Erich Joachimsthaler's book *Brand Leadership* (Simon & Schuster, 2009), which makes a strong case for treating brand as a central and strategic and long-term organizational asset. For a sceptical counterpoint, try *Simply Better* by Patrick Barwise and Seán Mehan (Harvard Business School Press, 2004), and, even more thought-provoking, John Kay's book *Obliquity* (Profile, 2010).

For an overview of the subject from the point of view of practitioners, I recommend the work of two writers, Marty Neumeier and Wally Olins. Neumeier's latest book, *The Brand Flip* (New Riders, 2015), is energetic and brilliantly designed. And Wally Olins's final book, *Brand New* (Thames & Hudson, 2014) is a worthy summation of an extraordinarily influential career. You'll also enjoy Debbie Millman's interviews with a range of practitioners in *Brand Thinking* (Allworth Press, 2011).

To find out more about how brands actually work, read Byron Sharp's *How Brands Grow* (Oxford University Press, 2010), a wonderfully nonconformist analysis, questioning (rightly, in my view) ideas like brand loyalty, positioning, and differentiation. And *Decoded* by Phil Barden (Wiley, 2013) is a refreshingly clear account of what behavioural economics and neuroscience tell us about how brands make us buy things.

Finally, to explore design in branding, look at Alina Wheeler's *Designing Brand Identity* (Wiley, 2013), which is comprehensive and (as you'd hope) fully illustrated; and Michael Johnson's energetically visual exploration, *Branding in Five and a Half Steps* (Thames & Hudson, 2016).

# "牛津通识读本"已出书目

| | | |
|---|---|---|
| 古典哲学的趣味 | 福柯 | 地球 |
| 人生的意义 | 缤纷的语言学 | 记忆 |
| 文学理论入门 | 达达和超现实主义 | 法律 |
| 大众经济学 | 佛学概论 | 中国文学 |
| 历史之源 | 维特根斯坦与哲学 | 托克维尔 |
| 设计，无处不在 | 科学哲学 | 休谟 |
| 生活中的心理学 | 印度哲学祛魅 | 分子 |
| 政治的历史与边界 | 克尔凯郭尔 | 法国大革命 |
| 哲学的思与惑 | 科学革命 | 民族主义 |
| 资本主义 | 广告 | 科幻作品 |
| 美国总统制 | 数学 | 罗素 |
| 海德格尔 | 叔本华 | 美国政党与选举 |
| 我们时代的伦理学 | 笛卡尔 | 美国最高法院 |
| 卡夫卡是谁 | 基督教神学 | 纪录片 |
| 考古学的过去与未来 | 犹太人与犹太教 | 大萧条与罗斯福新政 |
| 天文学简史 | 现代日本 | 领导力 |
| 社会学的意识 | 罗兰·巴特 | 无神论 |
| 康德 | 马基雅维里 | 罗马共和国 |
| 尼采 | 全球经济史 | 美国国会 |
| 亚里士多德的世界 | 进化 | 民主 |
| 西方艺术新论 | 性存在 | 英格兰文学 |
| 全球化面面观 | 量子理论 | 现代主义 |
| 简明逻辑学 | 牛顿新传 | 网络 |
| 法哲学：价值与事实 | 国际移民 | 自闭症 |
| 政治哲学与幸福根基 | 哈贝马斯 | 德里达 |
| 选择理论 | 医学伦理 | 浪漫主义 |
| 后殖民主义与世界格局 | 黑格尔 | 批判理论 |

| | | |
|---|---|---|
| 德国文学 | 儿童心理学 | 电影 |
| 戏剧 | 时装 | 俄罗斯文学 |
| 腐败 | 现代拉丁美洲文学 | 古典文学 |
| 医事法 | 卢梭 | 大数据 |
| 癌症 | 隐私 | 洛克 |
| 植物 | 电影音乐 | 幸福 |
| 法语文学 | 抑郁症 | 免疫系统 |
| 微观经济学 | 传染病 | 银行学 |
| 湖泊 | 希腊化时代 | 景观设计学 |
| 拜占庭 | 知识 | 神圣罗马帝国 |
| 司法心理学 | 环境伦理学 | 大流行病 |
| 发展 | 美国革命 | 亚历山大大帝 |
| 农业 | 元素周期表 | 气候 |
| 特洛伊战争 | 人口学 | 第二次世界大战 |
| 巴比伦尼亚 | 社会心理学 | 中世纪 |
| 河流 | 动物 | 工业革命 |
| 战争与技术 | 项目管理 | 传记 |
| 品牌学 | 美学 | |